Unpaid Costs of Electrical Energy

This book is a publication of the National Energy Strategies Project of Resources for the Future (RFF). The project was designed to study the technical, economic, institutional, environmental, and human health aspects of alternative energy systems for the future, and was financed through a special grant from the Andrew W. Mellon Foundation and general support to RFF from the Ford Foundation.

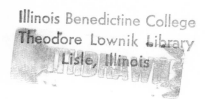
Unpaid Costs of Electrical Energy

Health and Environmental Impacts from Coal and Nuclear Power

WILLIAM RAMSAY

A Study Prepared for
the National Energy Strategies Project

Published for Resources for the Future by The Johns Hopkins University Press

Library of Congress Catalog Card Number 78-15668
ISBN 0–8018–2172–X
ISBN 0–8018–2230–0

Contents

Figures and Tables

ix

Tables

Foreword

This book reports on one part of a study under way at Resources for the Future that deals with U.S. energy options for the future. In the full study, we approach the subject of future energy choices within a comprehensive framework covering the various energy forms and sources. Such a comprehensive treatment offers the possibility, not otherwise attainable, of revealing the full range of flexibilities which exists within energy supply and demand systems.

In the past, we in the United States have been content in the main to let the market make energy choices for us. For various powerful reasons, however, public decisions will be playing an increasingly important role in the future. The purpose of this book, and the comprehensive study of which it is a part, is to help in the public decision-making process by providing data and analyses which illuminate the nature of the energy choices that are open for the future and the tradeoffs among them.

An electricity study, standing alone, may seem to be something of a departure from the rationale which motivates our broad effort. We decided, though, that the research covered in this book—completed ahead of other parts of our broader study—justified separate publication in advance of the total study. It is a safe guess that electricity generation in central stations will continue to be an important energy technology for the future, and that, for an extended period of time, coal and nuclear fuels will continue as major energy sources for such plants. Clearly, therefore, the comparison of coal and nuclear electricity technologies in their various significant dimensions serves an important public purpose. The public health and environmental quality impacts are particularly crucial in evaluating these technologies. And the nature and extent of these impacts are of importance not only in the coal–nuclear context, but also as a standard by which to judge other alternative energy sources.

This book offers a comprehensive examination of the comparative health, safety, and environmental aspects of the two technologies—what the author calls "unpaid costs," to distinguish them from the ordinary cost elements that are covered in conventional accounting—for the entire chain of supply from the mine through the generating station. Although a large number of detailed impacts are identified and, to the extent possible, measured, the focus of the study is not so much on the specific aspects as on the overall comparisons which take into account all such impacts within a total framework. To perform such a synthesis it is necessary to examine the separate components in a thorough and evenhanded fashion; the detailed footnote citations attest to the care with which the underlying data have been assembled, examined, and evaluated.

The analysis makes it plain that many of the underlying scientific data are of questionable validity. Mechanisms linking cause and effect are often poorly understood, and measurement is frequently not firmly established. Scrupulous attention to the uncertainties in the underlying data repeatedly yields wide-ranging estimates of impacts, not the one true value that would simplify the problem of choice. Nevertheless, the book's projection of health and environmental impacts to possible energy mixes in the years 1985 and 2000 make it evident that the impacts considered are far from negligible, even taking uncertainties into account.

Data problems make comparisons of the two technologies difficult, even for specific individual impacts. Add to this difficulty the fact that widely differing impacts need to be taken into account and the truly formidable nature of their comparison becomes apparent. We are dealing here with such matters as human lives lost to air pollution and radiation, illnesses from these same two sources, possible weapons proliferation dangers connected with the use of nuclear fuels, effects on land from the mining of coal and uranium, miners' occupational deaths and illnesses, climatological impacts, damages to property, and esthetic impacts. How can such a set of diverse impacts be homogenized into common units of measurement?

Ramsay's solution to this problem is not to attempt to obtain a single yardstick of measurement, such as reducing all impacts to monetary terms. Instead he develops the concept of "value orientations," for each of which we can assess the comparative impacts of coal and nuclear electricity technologies. Within these value orientations he is often able to establish a case for the superiority of one technology over the other; for example, in protecting human health nuclear technology appears to be more benign than coal, while for avoiding possible—even if improbable—catastrophes coal technology appears to be superior.

Out of the welter of disparate impacts and uncertain underlying data the hopelessness of reaching firm answers that will clearly establish the superiority of one technology compared with the other becomes apparent. Can there be any guidance for public decision making in such inconclusiveness?

Ramsay's thoughts on this subject are important. He suggests a three-pronged strategy for the nation: (1) to continue a coal–nuclear mix in new plant construction nationally on the basis of the economic and other considerations now resulting in such a combination of technologies; (2) to push forward on research in order to advance knowledge of the true magnitude of the impacts that are of major societal concern, thus leading to an improved basis for future choices; and (3) to place a heavy emphasis on introducing control technologies that will mitigate the impacts which are thought to be dangerous, even in the absence of a finely tuned calculation of the comparative costs and benefits of reducing these impacts. Such an approach, he argues, is essential if we are to break the logjam which now impedes decisions on supply expansion and at the same time to satisfy the legitimate concerns about possible (but often poorly documented) negative impacts. Although this strategic concept has much to recommend it, its detailed implementation can still give rise to litigation, delays, and public controversy because there will continue to be the problem of just how much mitigation to buy, even though we abandon the idea of deciding the issue by way of a formal cost–benefit analysis.

It might be argued that the recommended strategy resembles the practices which are already being used in decision making. However, what we have now is a hit-or-miss effort to develop coal or nuclear power while accommodating conflicting objectives and satisfying differing interest groups. This process results in public confusion and impedes forward movement. Ramsay proposes a clear-cut national strategy which would define the objectives being sought; the public would know what was being done and why.

Two major issues bearing on technology choices for central station electricity are essentially missing from this book: (1) the question of how much electricity the United States will require in the future, and (2) the financial costs of coal and nuclear technologies. On the question of electricity demand, in particular, there are alternative future rates of growth which need to be examined within an options framework for their broader economic and social impacts. Many unsubstantiated opinions in respect to future energy consumption are competing in the marketplace of public discourse; a careful research treatment of the subject is critically important. The energy-demand question is included within our full study, along with the broader treatment of energy-supply alternatives, including the financial costs for coal and nuclear technologies.

It is our hope that this book will help to improve public understanding of the coal–nuclear comparison which is a major factor in the current energy debate. The data and analyses which examine the various separate environmental, health, and safety impacts of the two technologies should help to guide the reader through the intricacies of these subjects, while the overall comprehensive comparisons should provide an appropriate framework for considering the broader questions of choosing between the two technologies.

Sam H. Schurr, Director
National Energy Strategies Project
Resources for the Future

Preface

The problem of coal–nuclear electricity is a key part of the total energy picture, and as such is an essential element in analyzing policy alternatives of all kinds. The coal–nuclear alternative is of special interest because its possibilities for supplying energy are so great, yet the drawbacks of each technology also seem formidable in that many involve health and environmental costs. Since these costs are generally not included in marketplace prices, they form a topic of special interest for economic analysis.

Carrying out this section of Energy Strategies Project has been facilitated by the existence of a great deal of information on the various health and environmental impacts associated with both nuclear power and coal. In addition to documentation on individual aspects, various surveys exist. In particular, the Ford–MITRE report of 1977 examines in depth many of the nuclear issues, in line with its special policy interests in the development of the breeder reactor. Therefore, the chief task that remained was not one of identifying types of impacts but of making a critical evaluation of existing impact data. Some earlier data turned out to be of questionable quality; data from other older studies had become obsolete through advances in technology or because of intervening criticisms of a study's methodology. Fortunately, such was not always the case, but more often than not I have had to return to original sources or to consult with experts in order to derive a plausible and consistent set of estimates.

These estimates of "unpaid costs" all tend to have a high degree of uncertainty, sometimes because of basic scientific doubts (as in air pollution) or because of possible future changes in technology (as in coal mining). One novel aspect of my approach is that some effort has been made to compare types of uncertainties. Even more important, the concept of uncertainty itself is treated as a major determinant in policy decisions. The related question of differing social values placed on different health and environmental impacts is not ignored or subsumed into a complex scheme of monetization, but it is explicitly treated through a consideration of different types of value orientations. For example, the public attitude toward reactor accidents can be seen to combine aspects of both concern for expected health impacts and possible elements of risk aversion vis-à-vis improbable events. These "health" and "catastrophe avoidance" value orientations are the basis for my recommendations for mitigation—or abatement—policies. Finally, the estimates of impacts have been applied to electrical energy scenarios for the years 1985 and 2000, in order to display the level of impacts that might occur under the Carter administration's National Energy Plan or similar measures.

The work in this book must be complemented with knowledge of the financial costs of coal and nuclear power if overall cost decisions are to be made on a rational basis. However, the nonfinancial costs that have been treated may also be directly useful in making decisions regarding the use of coal or nuclear electricity, especially when costs of coal and nuclear electricity are similar, as has happened often within the last ten years. The results here could also be relevant to the development of newer sources of energy, since comparing the health and environmental costs of coal and nuclear power with those of cleaner technologies could provide a justification for premium prices or developmental subsidies.

William Ramsay
The Center for Energy Policy Research
Resources for the Future

Acknowledgments

The research supporting this book has been carried on as part of the National Energy Strategies Project, through a special grant from the Andrew W. Mellon Foundation and general support to RFF from the Ford Foundation. I wish to thank these foundations for their support and all my colleagues on this project for their help. In particular, I have had many discussions on the concepts in this book and the manner of their presentation with the director of the project Sam H. Schurr, and my debt to him is very great for his suggestions and detailed comments on the text. I have benefited from the research efforts and useful criticisms of Eliahu J. Salmon and perceptive reviews by Edward J. Burger, Jr., M.D., Harry Perry, and especially from those of Milton Russell.

Many members of the National Energy Strategies Forum, an outside advisory group to RFF, were kind enough to review all or parts of the book. John W. Anderson of the *Washington Post*; Richard E. Balzhiser of the Electric Power Research Institute; Jack F. Bennett, EXXON Corporation; Isaiah Frank of the Johns Hopkins University; J. Herbert Hollomon of the Massachusetts Institute of Technology; Tjalling C. Koopmans of Yale University; James W. McKie of the University of Texas; Norton Nelson of the New York University Medical Center; Howard Raiffa of Harvard University; and Robert Williams of Princeton University have either commented on oral presentations of this material or have reviewed the manuscript. In particular, I would like to thank the following for their detailed criticisms: Lester B. Lave of Carnegie-Mellon University; Amory B. Lovins, consulting physicist; Laurence I. Moss, consultant; Robert H. Socolow of Princeton University; and Alvin M. Weinberg of the Oak Ridge Institute for Energy Analysis.

The material on air pollution has benefited from a review by some members of the Advisory Panel to the project on the Health Implications of Coal Liquefaction and Gasification. I wish to thank the following reviewers: A. Paul Altshuller of the Environmental Protection Agency;

Donald Borg of Brookhaven National Laboratory; N. Robert Frank of the University of Washington; Gerald Rausa of the Environmental Protection Agency; William L. Russell of Oak Ridge National Laboratory; Carl Shy of the University of North Carolina; and Frank E. Speizer of Harvard Medical School. Other reviewers who provided useful criticisms were Cyril L. Comar and Leonard A. Sagan of the Electric Power Research Institute.

I have received valuable comments from my colleague Elizabeth Wilman. Also, I am indebted to Seymour Abrahamson of the University of Wisconsin for perceptive comments on health effects, and I am very grateful to Kenneth E. Boulding of the University of Colorado for his thorough review and excellent suggestions on a variety of topics.

I am grateful to my friends and former colleagues at the U.S. Nuclear Regulatory Commission who have reviewed all or parts of the manuscript, in particular Albert Kenneke, James Beckerley, and Robert Jaske. A special thanks is due to Stephen McGuire for his assistance on occupational health.

I wish to thank Sally Nishiyama for her invaluable help in research. Her efforts made possible the efficient collection and organization of a vast amount of material on many subject areas. I am grateful to Betty Hines, Maybelle Frashure, Adrienne Plater, and Flora Riemer who bore the brunt of the typing.

Notwithstanding advice and criticisms, all conclusions here represent the results of my own analysis and interpretation of the data.

W. R.

Unpaid Costs of Electrical Energy

1 Introduction

The Effects of Coal and Nuclear Power on Human Health and the Environment

The dangers to the public health and environment from using coal and nuclear energy to generate electricity have stimulated great public concern in our energy-conscious age. The perils of nuclear energy—reactor melt-down accidents, nuclear wastes, and the spread of nuclear weapons among nations and even to terrorist groups—have been especially prominent in public debate. But we are all well aware that coal, too, has its drawbacks—polluted air and strip-mined landscapes being the most visible ones. If we include effects that are not so widely publicized, such as fatal coal-transportation accidents or the long-term effects of uranium-milling wastes, we see that the present dangers from either technology could be very great. In addition, there are possible long-term effects as well: the carbon dioxide released into the atmosphere from burning coal may change the average temperature of the world, leading to as yet uncertain but possibly disastrous consequences. We call these health and environmental problems the "unpaid costs of electrical energy" because most of them do not show up in our monthly utility bills. But they are just as costly—in money, lives, or in a degraded environment—as any other kind of expense to society.

Unfortunately, it is going to be difficult, if not impossible, for us to avoid these dangers. The ordinary costs that electric utilities incur in generating electricity from coal and nuclear power appear to be similar in size. This means that to a great extent energy policy decisions about these two technologies are apt to depend on how their health and environmental impacts compare.

1

The second factor—one that makes this problem a crucial one—is that it is not a question of nuclear, or coal, or something else but rather one of *either* coal, *or* nuclear, or *both*. In 1976, almost half the electricity in the United States was generated by either hydropower or oil or natural gas, but in the future these sources will become relatively less important. Most of the best sites for large-scale hydroelectric installations have already been taken, and it should be obvious, with the steep rise in oil prices since October 1973, that in most cases oil is going to be too expensive to fuel electric power plants in future years. Indeed, both oil and natural gas are being treated under the National Energy Plan (NEP) as precious commodities that must be conserved for such special uses as gasoline for automobiles and natural gas for home heating and cooking.[1] Not only do oil and gas have to be replaced as suppliers of electricity, but proportionately more electrical energy may have to be supplied as a fraction of energy requirements,[2] in order to substitute for these scarce fuels in other uses in homes, business, and industry. So additional sources of electricity will probably be needed in larger quantities than ever before.

The most important additional sources of electricity almost surely have to be coal, or nuclear, or both, for the next fifteen to twenty-five years— at least if conventional sources turn out to be the only practical answer. But what about a newer, unconventional, renewable source of electricity or of energy in general?

The Question of Renewable Energy Sources

In the very long term, measured in centuries, we obviously have to look past coal and uranium to other sources of energy. It is likely that these sources could be renewable—or at least very long-lived sources, such as solar energy, geothermal, and fusion power. The possibilities for their use have been perceptively analyzed by Lovins.[3] However, there are several obstacles that stand in the way of utilizing these renewable resources to solve our electricity and other energy problems within the next few decades. The main problem areas are price, quantity, quality, and side effects.

---

[1] Executive Office of the President, Energy Policy and Planning, *The National Energy Plan* (Washington, 29 April 1977).

[2] Electrical energy would increase from 28 percent to 33 percent of gross energy, according to the published NEP (ibid., p. 95) between 1976–85.

[3] Amory B. Lovins, *Soft Energy Paths: Toward a Durable Peace* (Cambridge, Mass., Friends of the Earth/Ballinger, 1977).

Price

The direct use of the sun to heat homes and provide process heat could take some of the pressure off the need for new sources of electricity, or solar energy itself could be used to generate electricity. The unit price of energy from solar home space heating appears to be, however, at least 50 percent greater than prices projected for the other means in the foreseeable future.[4] Other indirect solar energy sources—such as waves and warm ocean currents—could turn out to be economical, but at this time, they are still speculative. Fusion energy is as yet merely a dream and could turn out to be either cheap or expensive.

Naturally, all these generalizations about costs could change if a new technology is developed, or if clever ways of trimming costs, such as neighborhood heating systems, prove practical. But in dealing with present trends, cost and, therefore, price remain a problem.

Quantity

Even if prices are acceptable, the quantities of energy that are available at prices close to a hypothetical acceptable level are limited. Some geothermal energy is competitively priced right now, but the total amount of this cheap energy appears to be rather small. Similarly, biomass conversion in order to produce electricity—such as the burning of wood, agricultural residues, or municipal refuse—is economical now for some types of biomass fuels. But again, the amount currently available at a reasonable cost is limited. Even though direct use of solar energy is probably now economical as a replacement for home hot-water heating by electricity, this application alone would not solve much of the energy problem.

Quality

Many renewable sources are not steady suppliers of energy. Direct solar energy is intermittent, as is wind and wave energy, and tidal energy obviously ebbs and flows. The way to get rid of most of these problems is to develop better storage systems. Using batteries, flywheels, or hydrogen

[4] See, for example, Stanford Research Institute, *Solar Energy in America's Future, A Preliminary Assessment,* DSE-115/2, Energy Research and Development Administration (2nd ed., Washington, GPO, 1977) the "Reference Scenario Solar" in fig. 2-5, p. 20.

gas as storage mechanisms so far seems to be an expensive option, while pumped hydroelectric facilities can be economical in some locations but not practical everywhere. For home or district solar heating, a good storage system is essential. However, existing water and rock storage systems are exceedingly bulky and expensive, at least relative to the amount of energy they provide.

Side Effects

Geothermal and fusion power have some of the same types of side effects as coal and nuclear power—air pollution and radiation. As a matter of fact, so does biomass conversion, while other solar types appear to have many fewer health and environmental impacts. However, impacts exist, whether from the trivial problem of television interference caused by wind generators to the effect on fatality rates that accidental falls from rooftop solar systems will have.

Solutions have been proposed for all of these problems. The price problem disappears, for instance, if it is supposed that competing fossil fuels will become quite expensive in the meantime, and if the use of relatively cheap electricity with heat pumps (a sort of inverted refrigerator) to heat houses does not prove to be economic over the long run. The quantity problem is easily got around if one assumes that little or no more electricity and much less heat energy of other kinds is needed. Some decreases in demand are easy to come by with conservation methods, or by clever substitutions for projected uses of heat and electricity. Reductions in demand are not so simple and apparently imply a reworking of life-styles— a possible but not an obviously desirable goal. Storage costs could be lowered by technical advances or styles in energy use could be modified so that people would be content with a less constant level of comfort.

Most important of all, the side effects of many of these new technologies appear to be very few, at least relative to those from coal and nuclear power. But in a way, that is just what this book is all about. For the one sure way to make, say, direct solar home heating economical over the next few decades is for the public to decide that it is worthwhile paying more in order to avoid the deleterious health and environmental effects of coal and nuclear power.

We certainly do not maintain here that problems with the renewable, so-called softer energy technologies are insoluble. Over the long run, they may solve themselves or may be solved at the expense of some other cost increases to society. But what is obvious is that in order to make an energy option based on renewable sources work in the near future, the public may have to agree to pay a premium price so as to justify the health and environmental effects associated with coal and nuclear energy. We cannot know how great a premium we can afford to pay for a new technology unless we understand the relevant health and environmental problems of the old. Therefore, whether or not we are optimistic about new energy sources, understanding what the unpaid costs of coal and nuclear energy are is a task of the utmost importance if the public is to make well-informed decisions on energy policy.

The Unpaid Costs

This book looks at the unpaid costs of coal and nuclear energy in sufficient detail so that the key distinctions—as seen against a background of unavoidable uncertainties—can be understood in the context of energy policy decisions. These unpaid costs, or impacts, are measured in many different ways. Some are measured in the number of fatalities caused by the use of coal or nuclear power, while others are recorded as cases of illnesses or nonfatal accidents. Impacts on the environment and natural resources may be measured in such disparate units as cubic feet (water) or acres (land use). We will briefly discuss the knotty problem of making sense of all these units together, but first it is useful to look at the general plan of the book.

One obvious impact of energy use is air pollution. Through their smokestacks, coal-fired power plants emit sulfur and other chemicals that contribute to air pollution in cities and in the countryside. In chapter 2 we will see that while the threat to health—to say nothing of the loss of visibility and other side effects—is incontrovertible, it is difficult to determine how severe the impact is. Power plants contribute only a part of the pollutants in the atmosphere, and the likelihood that a certain amount of pollutants emitted from a coal-fired power plant will reach nearby populations is difficult to determine. Indeed, as they spread through the atmosphere, the original polluting compounds may change into other compounds with different characteristics. To cap these difficulties, much too little is known about the probability that the levels of common pollutants usually found in the atmosphere will cause illness and death in human populations. For example, uncertainties in our basic knowledge are such that our estimates of air pollution–health effects fall within a very wide range—between zero and 7,000 fatalities for every 2 trillion kilowatt-hours (kWh) of electricity generated by coal—that is, about the same amount of electricity that was generated by all means in the United States in 1975.[5] Nonfatal respiratory or cardiac illness is also likely to be associated with coal-caused air pollution, but, again, the range of estimates is necessarily very wide.

Nuclear power, being a new technology, involves a great many issues of policy significance. These issues, with some reason, have excited numerous, often passionate protests within the past decade. Chapter 3 examines the routine radiation problem and estimates that nuclear power facilities emit very little radiation into the surrounding air and water during their normal operations. This radiation level is low, both compared with other normal sources of radiation and, more cogently, with other nuclear radiation impacts. But some of the elements that are emitted from nuclear power plants and from the mining and milling of uranium ore last an exceedingly long time. Consequently, they constitute a small but noxious heritage for our descendants—a few fatalities (for each 2 trillion kWh of nuclear generation) occur each year and will continue to do so into the indefinite future.

Potential catastrophic accidents in nuclear reactors (see chapter 4) are another source of public concern. Since there have been no nuclear accidents of any consequence in commercial power plants, we are forced to rely on theoretical calculations to tell us how likely they are. The one detailed calculation that exists estimates that the worst nuclear reactor accident could indeed involve almost 50,000 casualties, but such an accident would be very unlikely indeed. Considering all reactors and all types of accidents occurring year after year, the average fatalities range from one to twenty per 2 trillion kWh. Even if this were somewhat of an underestimate, such a calculation would be reassuring to many. Nevertheless, we might be adverse to allowing the possibility of such catastrophes in our society—if we could avoid them at a small enough cost.

The situation is different for nuclear wastes (see chapter 5), where the risks to society could well be negligible. True, these wastes from spent fuels and other products of nuclear generation are indeed dangerous substances. The time frame for the effects—measured in half-lives of the radioactive elements—is extremely long, sometimes hundreds of thousands of years. And it is difficult to devise any absolutely foolproof scheme

[5] Two trillion kilowatt-hours (kWh) is called 1 USW (U.S. Wattage) in this volume.

to prevent them from escaping into the environment after being disturbed by future water movements or by other natural or human-mediated processes. But it does seem possible to take precautions so that such escapes would be exceedingly unlikely. So if all goes well, long-term safe burial of fuel wastes should be possible with very small risk to future generations.

The most disturbing dimension of the nuclear problem may be political (see chapter 6), since uranium and plutonium from nuclear fuels can be used to build nuclear weapons as well as to produce nuclear power. It is true that making weapons from many ordinary fuels or fuel wastes would be véry difficult or, at least, enormously expensive. But the possible consequences of such an action are so horrendous that there is no alternative but to take great pains to prevent the most sensitive types of nuclear fuel material from falling into the hands of terrorists. Also, nuclear power stations could be a very convenient, if sometimes awkward, source of plutonium and other bomb-grade materials. Therefore, it is conceivable that the use of nuclear power can be associated with an increase in the spread of nuclear weapons capabilities and thus, perhaps, with an increased likelihood of nuclear war.

Both coal and nuclear power have effects on the natural environment as well. Lately, scientists have expressed increased concern about power plant emissions that affect the climate, especially those from coal-fired plants. Even though chapter 7 estimates that the isolated effect from coal-fired power plants in the United States is relatively small (measured in thousandths of a degree, for each 2 trillion kWh), we must recognize that it may contribute to a worldwide problem that is as yet poorly understood.

Other environmental and resource and social effects can be fully as complex as the health issues (see chapter 8). Land use is a relatively straightforward story: strip-mining of coal involves tearing up a good deal of the landscape, for example, hundreds of thousands of acres in our unit of comparison. But even so, these areas are slated for reclamation under current legislation. The amount of land devoted to uranium mill tailings (residues) is miniscule in comparison, but it is part of a growing burden that society is leaving to future generations—land that may be indefinitely unusable for many future purposes. Other environmental problems may be more difficult to analyze: for example, chemical pollution of streams by acidic mine effluents and the effects of waste heat discharged from power plants are problems that vary greatly with locality and with changing patterns of government regulation. Still other problems deal with so many other factors in society and planning for future economic activity that it is difficult to assess them in the framework of coal and nuclear power alone. Consumptive use of water resources is a prime example of this.

Social effects range from alleged general influences on life-styles—for instance, excessive use of modern appliances—caused by the centralized character of power systems, to a not so subtle total of several hundred fatal collisions of motorists with coal trains. In between these extremes is the complex mixture of benefits and costs represented by the energy boomtown problem, a social dilemma going beyond the coal–nuclear question itself.

The coal miner trapped in the cave-in is apt to be the forgotten man in this whole picture: public debates occasionally neglect the connection between electricity derived from coal or nuclear power and patterns of occupational deaths, illnesses, and accidents. Black lung from coal mining and lung cancer from uranium mining are of additional concern to workers. Some argue that such health impacts should be—as some indeed are—compensated for by disability payments, or at least by higher wages for riskier jobs, and that they are therefore not unpaid costs. As will be seen in chapter 9, we do not agree that a mine fatality is any less of an unpaid cost than impacts on the general public, and we believe 100 to 300 fatal mining accidents per 2 trillion kWh should be considered a major problem.

This formidable list of impacts from coal and nuclear power will be summarized in chapter 10—based on the generation of 2 trillion kWh of electricity. The routine fatalities and illnesses associated with coal exceed those from nuclear. That comparison, however, does not include effects of possible terrorist bombs or nuclear wars related to nuclear energy. Furthermore, environmental effects, possible special attitudes toward catastrophes, and implications for future generations complicate the comparison. These issues must be treated separately, as will be done in chapter 12.

In order to present the coal–nuclear electricity comparison in a concrete setting, chapter 11 will look at what the actual and planned amounts of coal and nuclear generation in the United States are, focusing on the example of the NEP proposed by the Carter administration. There, we will calculate what the overall consequences might be for the nation from different choices of coal and nuclear energy. For the year 1985, under the NEP, fatalities from the coal sector would range between 200 and 7,000, while they would range from 20 to 90 for about one-third as much electricity generated by nuclear plants. The plan as written extends only to 1985, but various predictions for the year 2000 can be made, depending on the growth in demand for electricity and the mix of coal and nuclear power. One estimate of electricity demand is made in chapter 11, and two different coal–nuclear mixes are chosen: (1) a "normal" development of nuclear energy (at ten times the 1976 level); and (2) a restricted nuclear development or "nuclear moratorium" scenario. There is a significant difference between the two choices. Some special nuclear safety and waste problems would be abated by the restricted scenario. On the other hand, a nuclear moratorium would increase the expected net number of fatalities and illnesses as well as measurably increasing the amount of strip-mined land. It would also have some measurable effect upon the amount of the carbon dioxide added to the atmosphere.

Comparisons and Complications— Uncertainties and Values

We can readily list fatalities, illnesses, acreage of land disturbed, and so on, without having any sensible way to evaluate the relative health and environmental costs of coal and nuclear power. Obviously, the impacts differ in kind so that they are not readily comparable. The basic difficulty comes down to the question of values. How much is a premature death worth when compared with a number of illnesses or with 2,000 acres of disturbed land? There are also other, more subtle questions, Do we as a society have special attitudes toward catastrophes as opposed to average numbers of deaths, illnesses, and property damage every year? Does society also feel some special responsibility toward future generations, or even to special social groups in the present? These questions are difficult ones to answer. Consequently, we have not tried to add up all the impacts in terms of a common denominator—such as dollars—but have instead identified four important value orientations that should be examined when making policy decisions. These are (1) the preservation of health; (2) the preservation of resources and the environment; (3) the avoidance of catastrophes; and (4) equity values.

However, even within each of these value orientations, weaknesses in data and analysis complicate the assessment. For example, the relative importance of fatalities from coal and nuclear depends greatly on whether the upper or lower end of the range for coal (for example, 200 versus 7,000, in 1985) is closer to the truth. The uncertainty in data and analysis for air pollution, which is the prime cause of this wide range of possible coal fatalities, is also mirrored in smaller ways in all the impacts considered here. Even if we were to make a policy decision on routine fatalities alone—a procedure not recommended here—a decision against coal might be only marginally better if air pollution fatalities were very low, but it might be an overwhelmingly obvious choice if those fatalities turned out to be very high.

Since economics and—as we will see below—mitigation (antipollution) procedures have to be taken into account too, the distinction between degrees of "inferiority" is important. Of course, scientific advances in the future could reduce uncertainty, and help us with these difficult decisions. For example, even such modest steps as more complete measurements of actual air pollution levels could be important. And with sufficient effort, advances can certainly be made in understanding the relevant physical and chemical processes for both coal and nuclear power. In fact, we stress this research element in our discussion of interim strategies (see page 168).

Mitigation and Changing Technologies

Any categorization of unpaid costs must be a gun pointed at a moving target. Health and environmental costs are not fixed, but depend upon technology, just as our knowledge of them depends on the current state of scientific research. New methods of cleaning up coal are being continually developed. So it might turn out that some sizable damage costs of today could be eliminated tomorrow in an economic manner. Indeed, some proposed new methods of cleaning up coal almost amount to new ways of generating power—for example, by turning coal into gas before it is burned. The impacts from nuclear power could be changed, for instance, by requiring that nuclear reactors be sited underground or at great distances from population centers. The possibility of mitigation, or abatement, is an important dimension in the policy process, and some of the most important technologies will be briefly considered in this book.[6] Also,

---

[6] To elaborate on the relative desirability of mitigation in different fields would take us too far afield. However, it must be noted that social planners should, ideally at least, take into account all possibilities—not just those falling within the restricted coal–nuclear framework. For example, one could argue against a power plant being sited in a scenic rural setting, but if the power plant were kept out, within the next year the site might well be subdivided for new suburbs. We can save miners from airborne radioactive particles inside uranium mines, but we cannot stop them from smoking. Indeed, the smoking tends to compound the radioactivity problem, evidently because of synergistic effects of carcinogens in the tobacco, the deposition of radioactivity onto the particulates in the tobacco smoke, or the inhibition of lung-clearance effects.

the adoption of more stringent requirements for emissions from coal-fired power plants will be considered in chapter 11. Incidentally, this possibility for mitigation also means that unpaid costs may not remain unpaid, but may be absorbed into future electricity bills: note that chapter 11 assumes that a reduction in the range of predicted deaths has been "purchased" by the adoption of the Best Available Control Technology (BACT) for coal-fired power plants,[7] as has been mandated in recent legislation.

Technology for generating electricity changes, too. Many experts think that the so-called breeder reactors, those that use uranium many times more efficiently than do present nuclear power plants, should be used to generate power in the United States. Such a change in technology would inevitably bring about its own peculiar health and environmental problems (see chapter 4).

Interim Strategies

With currently available data, no clear case can be made that either coal or nuclear power is associated with a greater impact on the environment and the public health. Thus, it can be concluded that proposing any kind of final choice of coal versus nuclear power on the basis of health and environmental impacts would be unjustifiable *at the present time*. So we maintain that there is no reason to alter the present trend to a mix of coal and nuclear electricity-generating capacity in the near future, but instead that both these economically feasible energy options should be kept alive. It could be that uncertainties about values and data will remain so severe that an intelligent choice between coal and nuclear power—or one in favor of both—will never be possible: however, we believe that such an expectation is too pessimistic. Therefore, given the magnitude of the health and environmental costs on either side, we consider it to be essential that research is carried forward at heightened levels in order to work toward resolving these uncertainties. This research program is one element of the interim strategy that will be discussed in more detail in chapter 12.

The other element of the interim strategy involves mitigation. Given the uncertainties in values and data, it is going to be impossible in our view to make balanced, rational decisions on such abatement or mitiga-

---

[7] Some of the other environmental costs may be paid or partially paid, for example, in payments to workers with black lung. For simplicity of presentation, all health and environmental costs have been considered here: this complication would have to be explicitly treated in a study of both financial and health and environmental costs.

tion procedures as scrubbers to clean carbon dioxide out of the flue gases from coal-fired power plants. In the absence of such a balanced decision, the worst danger is that no decision at all will be made. Therefore, from the point of view of developing energy options, the best choice for society has to be to provide for more, rather than less, in selecting mitigation measures. This seems a necessary premium to pay in order to muster a social consensus—which after all would depend on securing the agreement of individuals with differing value structures—that would enable the timely development of whatever supplies of electricity may be necessary in the United States from now until the year 2000.

2 Air Pollution from Power Plants

Air pollution caused by power plants is a danger to health, but how much of a danger?

What of other effects of air pollution?

Is cleanup feasible?

Coal-fired power plants make significant contributions to air pollution which is hazardous to human health.[1] A large power plant located 40 miles from New York City could increase the total of some air pollutants in the city by a few percentage points.[2]

The most dramatic effects of air pollution on health have been observed during acute episodes, when atmospheric temperature inversions hold down large amounts of pollutants. Such episodes in Donora, Pennsylvania, in 1948, and in London, in 1952, produced symptoms of respiratory illness in many thousands and could be convincingly related to the deaths of many persons in Donora and of several thousand in London.[3] Although some air pollution is produced from natural sources, such as trees or volcanoes, by far the most significant part comes from the burn-

---

[1] See William Ramsay, "Coal and Nuclear: Health and Environmental Costs" (Washington, Resources for the Future, August 1978) chap. 1, for a review of coal air pollution; also see Cyril L. Comar and Leonard A. Sagan, "Health Effects of Energy Production and Conversion," *Annual Review of Energy* vol. 1 (Palo Alto, Calif., Annual Reviews, Inc., 1976) pp. 581–600.

[2] See U.S. Congress, Senate, Committee on Public Works, *Air Quality and Stationary Source Emission Control,* Report prepared by the Commission on Natural Resources of the National Academy of Sciences/National Academy of Engineering/National Research Council, 94 Cong. 1 sess., ser. no. 94–4 (March 1975), p. 631, corrected for present EPA standards.

[3] See W. P. D. Logan, "Mortality in the London Fog Incident," *The Lancet* vol. 1 (14 February 1953) pp. 336–338; H. H. Schrenk, H. Heimann, G. D. Clayton, W. M. Gafafer, and H. Wexler, *Air Pollution in Donora, Pennsylvania: Epidemiology of the Unusual Smog Episode of October 1948,* Bulletin 306 (Washington, U.S. Public Health Service, 1949).

ing of fossil fuels—oil, natural gas, and coal.[4] The combination of hydro-carbons and nitrogen oxides that produces the eye and lung irritations characteristic of Los Angeles-type smog in urban areas can be blamed principally—though not entirely—on automobile exhaust.[5] But fossil fuel-fired power plants are responsible for a major part of the emissions of sulfur compounds and particulates (that is, small particles of various minerals);[6] this sulfur–particulate combination was implicated in the acute air pollution episodes occurring in London and Donora.[7]

If we were trying to examine general air pollution control policy, we would be interested in exactly what percentages of which kinds of pollution are caused by power plants and other sources. While this larger problem deserves—and receives—the attention of the public, that of power plant emissions can and should be examined separately as part of our investigation into the unpaid costs of electricity. So we will examine here the extra contributions made to air pollution as a result of encouraging the use of coal for generating electricity.

Key Pollutants: Sulfur and Particulates

It is no surprise that serious irritation of the lungs can occur during acute episodes of air pollution. It is well known that sulfur dioxide, the compound emitted when sulfur burns—particularly when oil and coal containing sulfur as an impurity are burned in a power plant—can irritate the bronchial tract. Furthermore, it has been found in tests on laboratory animals that related compounds of sulfur, inhaled in the form of droplets or carried on very small solid particles, can cause five to twenty times as much difficulty in breathing (as measured by airflow resistance) as does sulfur dioxide (SO_2) itself.[8] Since the sulfur dioxide emitted from power plant smokestacks tends to change into these other sulfur compounds (sulfates) in the atmosphere, which then often combine with small particles of minerals (fly ash) emitted during combustion, it would not be

---

[4] See U.S. Congress, Senate, *Air Quality,* p. 283.

[5] Coal-fired power plants do emit nitrogen oxides. But photochemical smog seems to require hydrocarbons also, mainly those from petroleum sources. See ibid., pp. 777–780, for a discussion of the chemistry.

[6] Ibid. Power plants contributed over 60 percent of the sulfur in 1972–73.

[7] See Logan, "Mortality," and Schrenk and coauthors, *Air Pollution.*

[8] For comparable weights of sulfur; see Mary O. Amdur, "Aerosols Formed by Oxidation of Sulfur Dioxide: Review of Their Toxicology," *Archives of Environmental Health* vol. 23 (December 1971), pp. 459–468; and Ramsay, "Coal and Nuclear," p. 1–2n.

surprising if coal-fired power plants presented a serious health hazard to the public.

While it is clear that there can be a hazard, the nature and extent of the danger are quite controversial. A typical coal-fired power plant does emit some 70 million lb of sulfur dioxide a year, even under present federal air pollution standards.[9] But the levels of sulfur dioxide, various sulfates, and particulates that are detected at typical air pollution monitoring stations could be considered either high or low, depending on one's point of view. Concentrations detected in industrialized cities (and increasingly in adjacent rural regions) are certainly large when compared with·those measured in the clean air of open spaces. But the amounts *usually* seen in the air are typically some ten to one hundred times less than the concentrations thought proper for use in laboratory tests involving even human volunteers, much less guinea pigs.[10] Acute air pollution episodes can show unmistakable results—the Donora episode had a severe illness rate of 10 percent and a death rate of over 0.1 percent.[11] But such episodes apparently involved quite high doses for relatively short periods, while for most air pollution, the doses are low but often longer-lasting. Therefore, it is very difficult to determine how many deaths and illnesses are caused by the usual levels of air pollution, and doubly difficult to decide what the air pollution-related effects of adding one more coal-fired plant to an electrical generating grid would be. One way of approaching the problem is to examine mortality statistics and reports of illnesses, relating fluctuations in them to fluctuations in air pollution levels. And studies have been done that relate sulfur dioxide or sulfate levels to recorded health statistics. But the results have been exceedingly controversial, since the nature and extent of the air pollutants themselves are poorly known, or only spottily measured, and the timing and causes of death and illness are difficult to correlate.[12] When other factors are included, such as

[9] This figure is based on the emission of 1.2 lb of sulfur dioxide per million Btu (see U.S. Congress, Senate, *Air Quality*, p. xliv), standardized to a hypothetical 1-GW (that is, a 1 million-kW) plant producing 6,570 billion kWh a year (22.4 × 10^{12} Btu electric), as described in the preface to Ramsay, "Coal and Nuclear." Assuming a 38 percent conversion efficiency, 70.8 million lb of sulfur dioxide are produced.

[10] Compare the EPA's 24-hour sulfur dioxide ambient standard (0.365 mg per cubic meter) with some of the experimental maximum human doses, as reviewed in Amdur, "Aerosols" (for example, 5 mg per cubic meter, and 39 mg per cubic meter). To be sure, these last two are short-term doses.

[11] See Schrenk and coauthors, *Air Pollution*, pp. 13 and 163.

[12] See reviews in Ramsay, "Coal and Nuclear," pp. 1-6–1-9; and in U.S. Congress, Senate, *Air Quality*, pp. 138ff. Also see Lester B. Lave and Warren E. Weber, "A Benefit–Cost Analysis of Auto Safety Features," *Applied Economics* vol. 2 (1970) pp. 265–275; Lester B. Lave, and Eugene P. Seskin, "Air Pollution and Human Health," *Science* vol. 169 (21 August 1970) pp. 723–733; Lester B. Lave, "Air

weather, movement of populations, and all the other variations in people, economics, and geography that complicate interpretations of health statistics, the difficulties become apparent. On the other hand, people who are already susceptible to respiratory difficulties will surely suffer from increases in air pollution.[13] The question remains, How many suffer how much from sulfur-related emissions?

An additional difficulty exists: one power plant is generally only a single contributor among a mélange of industries, automobiles, and other power plants that produce the air pollution in any one area. On the other hand, even a power plant located at a remote site will undoubtedly contribute to air pollution in relatively distant cities—indeed, we increasingly believe that pollutants can spread over wide geographical areas—but to what extent? The sulfur is transformed into sulfur dioxide in the plant, then into sulfates in the atmosphere, and then carried by winds to other locations. Model calculations have been carried out to predict these effects,[14] but the possibility for error is great.

So the picture is one of poorly understood chemical processes, lack of medical data, and statistical studies of community health that attempt valiantly to separate out effects of smoking, temperature changes, and other factors from air pollution effects, and often end up as less than totally convincing.[15] It is not impossible, for example, that very few

---

Pollution Damage: Some Difficulties in Estimating the Value of Abatement," in Allen V. Kneese and Blair T. Bower, eds., *Environmental Quality Analysis, Theory and Method in the Social Sciences* (Baltimore, Johns Hopkins University Press for Resources for the Future, 1972) pp. 213–242; L. D. Hamilton, ed., *The Health and Environmental Effects of Electricity Generation: A Preliminary Report,* BNL 20582 (Upton, N.Y., Brookhaven National Laboratory, 30 July 1974); and David P. Rall, *A Review of the Health Effects of Sulfur Oxides* (Bethesda, Md., National Institutes of Health, National Institute of Environmental Health Sciences, 9 October 1973) p. 13.

[13] Bertram Carnow, "Sulfur Oxides and Particles." Paper presented at Conference on Health Effects of Air Pollutants, at the National Academy of Sciences, Washington, D.C., 3–5 October 1973, p. 2.

[14] See U.S. Congress, Senate, *Air Quality;* W. A. Buehring, W. K. Foell, and R. L. Keeney, *Energy/Environment Management: Application of Decision Analysis,* Research Report RR-76-14 (Laxenburg, Austria, International Institute for Applied Systems Analysis, May 1976); Brookhaven National Laboratory, Biomedical and Environmental Assessment Group, "The Effect of Air Pollution from Coal and Oil Power Plants on Public Health," BEAG-HE 11/74 (Upton, N.Y., Brookhaven National Laboratory, 17 May 1974); and L. D. Hamilton, *Health Effects of Air Pollution,* BNL 20743, U.S. Energy Research and Development Administration (Upton, N.Y., Biomedical and Environmental Assessment Group of Brookhaven National Laboratory, July 1974), as reviewed in Ramsay, "Coal and Nuclear," pp. 1-17–1-21.

[15] For a review of data problems, see Greenfield, Attaway, and Tyler, Inc., *Sulfur Oxides: Current Status of Knowledge,* EPRI EA-316, Project 681-1 (Palo Alto, Calif., EPRI, December 1976), sect. 1.

fatalities, if any, can be attributed to air pollution from power plants, at least when the pollution remains below certain levels.[16] But it would still be rash to assume that the emission by a power plant of known lung irritants—like sulfur dioxide and sulfates—do not have some effect on public health, uncertain though the size of the effect may be.

The situation with fatalities is the trickiest, and we suggest here estimates that range widely. These extremely uncertain values are based on several model calculations of sample power plants emitting an extra amount of pollutants into surrounding regions. The highest model result is taken as an upper limit for typical power plants in the United States. The effects at the lower limit are taken as bounded by zero, since solid evidence on mortality at ambient levels is so slim (see appendix A, page 28). As figure 2-1 shows, this means that we estimate deaths—per 2 trillion kilowatt-hours (kWh), a unit we define here as "1 USW," or the amount of electricity generated by *all* means in the United States in 1975[17]—as ranging from values approaching zero on up to 7,000.

The illness estimates are also very rough. We believe the results of existing one-plant model calculations—with allowances for uncertainties—give about as good an idea of the size of the problem as is possible (see appendix A). Again, the limits for error that we suggest are wide. As shown in figure 2-1, the variable shading of the bars in the bar graphs gives an idea of a possible range of uncertainty, based on the models and on estimates of contributions to overall disease rates. For example, figure 2-1 predicts that the number of asthma attacks closely associated with air pollution from 2 trillion kWh of coal-fired electricity generation is somewhere between 100,000 and 10 million. In contrast, the estimated number of attacks in the entire United States in 1970 (normal incidence) is shown as 40 to 50 million. If we realize that coal currently generates half the electricity in the United States, or close to one-half the U.S. wattage,

[16] See Ramsay, "Coal and Nuclear," append. A. Compare with D. Higgins, "Epidemiology of Sulphur Oxides and Particles." Paper presented at Conference on Health Effects of Air Pollutants, at the National Academy of Sciences, Washington, D.C., 3–5 October 1973; and John S. Neuberger and Edward P. Radford, *Review of Human Health Criteria for Ambient Air Standards in Maryland,* a report to the Bureau of Air Quality Control, Department of Mental Hygiene, State of Maryland (Annapolis, State of Maryland, August 1974).

[17] This unit is then 228.3 GW-years, or 304.4 750-MW (1,000 kW) plant-years. The pollution models consulted applied only to incremental additions to coal-fired capacity (that is, one plant of a given size). A large number of additional plants could change background levels. Therefore, the results of these models can, strictly speaking, only be applied to additions measured in fractions of a USW. In view of the gross uncertainties involved, however, such difficulties may not be unduly restrictive. In a national context (see chap. 11, fn. 11), the scaling error involved could go either way.

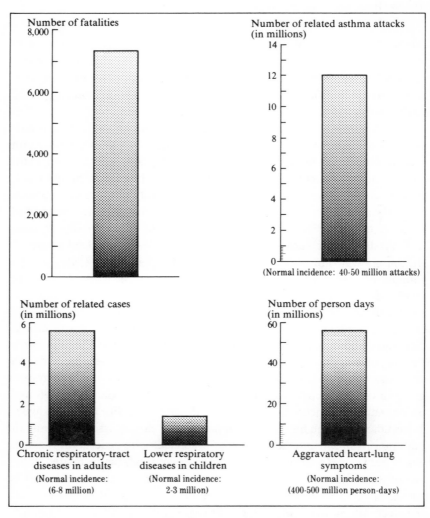

Figure 2-1. Estimates of the number of cases of fatal and nonfatal illnesses associated with (sulfur–particulate) air pollution from power plants (per 2 trillion kWh = 1 USW). Approximately 2 trillion kWh were generated in the United States in 1975; only half of that was from coal. We call this unit a USW (U.S. Wattage). Data is taken from appendix A, and Ramsay, "Coal and Nuclear: Health and Environmental Costs" (Washington, Resources for the Future, August 1978) chap. 1. (The variable shading of the bars, here and elsewhere, suggests the uncertainties involved.)

some of the disease-rate upper limits predict millions or tens of millions of additional cases per year of the diseases shown, caused by (or aggravated by) air pollution from power plants. Some may consider these estimates incredibly large. However, the tens or hundreds of thousands of cases predicted at the lower limit may be impressive enough.

Real world uncertainties for both deaths and illnesses could be larger—both ways. Recent reviews of the data supporting the estimates given have been exceedingly critical, raising the question as to whether even the lower limits for diseases are too high.[18] Some have even argued that a certain level of sulfur compounds in the air is desirable![19] On the other hand, it is conceivable that figure 2-1 may not show the worst: two kinds of bad surprises might be in store for us, making the air pollution danger from coal-fired power plants greater than we think. For one thing, the U.S. Environmental Protection Agency (EPA) has set certain limits on the amount of sulfur dioxide and particulates permitted in the air (termed *ambient concentrations*). But it is not uncommon for ambient concentration standards to be exceeded. For one year the EPA has reported that over half of all air quality regions showed excessive annual levels of particulates. For example, in southwestern Pennsylvania in 1974, most monitoring stations showed that particulate (and sulfur dioxide) standards were exceeded.[20] The situation is especially complex because many particles are formed *after* emissions have interacted in the atmosphere. For example, it has been estimated that high particulate levels in Los Angeles persist in part because more than 40 percent of the particulates are of this secondary type. Since the effects of high concentrations are rather definite, but the effects at low levels are more questionable, some students of the

[18] See the comprehensive review of the EPA Community Health and Environmental Surveillance System (CHESS) studies in U.S. Congress, House, Subcommittee on Special Studies, Investigations and Oversight, and Subcommittee on the Environment and the Atmosphere of the Committee on Science and Technology, *The Environmental Protection Agency's Research Program, with Primary Emphasis on the Community Health and Environmental Surveillance System (CHESS): An Investigative Report*, 94 Cong. 2 sess., Serial SS (November 1976). Note also the critical discussion in Greenfield, Attaway, and Tyler, Inc., *Sulfur Oxides*, concerning the studies on which the dose-response models used in the results of fig. 2-1 are based.

[19] According to F. Fraser Ross ["A 1977 Approach to Sulfur Oxide Emissions." Paper presented at the American Society of Mechanical Engineers/Institute of Electrical and Electronics Engineers meeting, Los Angeles (September 1977)], they are desirable for agriculture.

[20] For primary annual standards, see U.S. Environmental Protection Agency (EPA), *Monitoring and Air Quality Trends Report, 1974*, EPA-450/1-76-001 (Washington, EPA, February 1976), pp. 20 and 54. Oxidation of metals can cause their release into the atmosphere as secondary pollutants.

problem believe that the certainty of adverse consequences would grow disproportionately if actual pollution levels were to climb well above the EPA standards.[21]

The second bad surprise is that new acute episodes of the Donora type could produce locally catastrophic numbers of deaths and illnesses. We are at the mercy of the vagaries of weather as to when and where such episodes might happen. However, these episodes should be less likely to occur under the EPA's present air quality standards.[22]

Nitrogen Oxides, Trace Elements, and Other Pollutants

Sulfur compounds are by no means the only pollutants coming from the smokestacks of coal-fired plants. As a matter of fact, the estimates just made of fatalities and illnesses attributed to sulfur emissions could also be due in part to the other elements usually present in the polluted air.

In the process of burning, the nitrogen in the air—as well as any nitrogen in the fuel—can be combined with oxygen to form nitrogen oxides. Sixteen percent of all U.S. nitrogen oxide emissions in 1972 were estimated to come from coal-fired power plants.[23] In tests on laboratory animals some of these oxides have been shown to be harmful at high concentrations. They also can combine with other compounds—mainly those emitted from automobile exhaust and other petroleum uses—to form photochemical (Los Angeles-type) smog. And one of the compounds, nitrogen dioxide, is a brown gas that is both an irritant and a contributor to the obscuration of the atmosphere.

The EPA has set standards for the allowable concentration of nitrogen dioxide in the atmosphere. But since there are so few data from experiments or statistical studies relating nitrogen oxides to deaths or illnesses, it is difficult to estimate how serious the problem is. The number could conceivably be as much as three hundred fatalities for every 2 trillion kWh (1 USW).[24] Existing evidence is exceedingly thin,[25] but as for other

[21] U.S. Congress, Senate, *Air Quality*, p. 147.

[22] Carl Shy and Frank Speizer, private communications.

[23] U.S. Congress, Senate, *Air Quality*, p. 147.

[24] Ramsay, "Coal and Nuclear," p. 1-5; and Stephen M. Barrager, Bruce R. Judd, and D. Warner North, "The Economic and Social Costs of Coal and Nuclear Electrical Generation: A Framework for Assessment and Illustrative Calculations for the Coal and Nuclear Fuel Cycles," SRI Project MSU-4133 (Palo Alto, Calif., Stanford Research Institute, 1975) p. 29.

[25] See Neuberger and Radford, *Review of Human Health Criteria,* for a brief but

pollutants, health effects might appear only later, as a result of induced chronic diseases. Evaluating this problem will become of increasing concern, because it is so difficult to avoid creating nitrogen oxides in any combustion process and to control their emissions.

All coal contains minerals in the form of ash. Often these minerals include potentially dangerous toxic trace elements and compounds, such as mercury, lead, cadmium, selenium, nickel, asbestos, and arsenic. Arsenic is apparently also a carcinogen, as is asbestos. The organic compound benzo(a)pyrene, found in many coal effluents, is highly carcinogenic.[26] Once again, the problem of establishing a definite relationship between small amounts of harmful materials spread over a large area, in a mixture with other harmful elements, makes it difficult to draw conclusions about the size of the risks.[27] But often cancer occurs only years after exposure, and after long latency periods, and we could be in for unpleasant surprises in future years if potential problems are neglected now. The possibilities are worrisome, and a great deal of the current study of coal-induced health effects now centers on the movement of trace elements, their persistence in the human environment, and their effect on human health. This concern could reasonably extend to possible genetic effects from all kinds of air pollutants that could produce congenital diseases and other problems in future generations. However, genetic impacts are likely to be small when compared with the ordinary disease effects.[28]

Finally, hundreds of tons of carbon monoxide and millions of tons of carbon dioxide are emitted by each typical coal-fired power plant every year. The poisonous compound carbon monoxide, even at low doses, undoubtedly contributes to cardiac disease, but we do not have sufficient data to determine how serious the problem is from current power plant emissions:[29] automobiles are the principal culprit in creating high levels

---

incisive critique. A speculation on the eventual induction of emphysema related to chronic vascular congestion is cited there.

[26] M. R. Kornreich, *Coal Conversion Processes: Potential Carcinogenic Risk,* MTR-7155 (McLean, Va., MITRE Corporation, METREK Division, March 1976) pp. A-2–A-4.

[27] Neuberger and Radford, *Review of Human Health Criteria.*

[28] William Russell, private communication. However, "small" is a relative concept: even a 1 percent increase in genetic disorders due to coal mutagens would be 1,000 cases per million live births, as pointed out by Seymour Abrahamson (private communication). And, he continues, "The cost of a lifetime of genetic disease may well outweigh many transitory somatic disorders."

[29] John R. Goldsmith, "Environmental Epidemiology and Metamorphosis of the Human Habitat," *American Journal of Public Health* vol. 57, no. 9 (September 1967) pp. 1532–1549, and personal communication.

in heavily traveled city streets. Carbon dioxide, an unavoidable product from the combustion of coal and other fossil fuels, is not poisonous but may contribute to climatic changes, which will be discussed later.

Other Air Pollution Damages

Property Damage

The chemicals contained in polluted air can also damage materials; specifically, they cause deterioration of paint and damage zinc and other metals, to say nothing of such exotic problems as the defacing of the inscription on Cleopatra's Needle in New York's Central Park.[30] It has been estimated that for every new coal-fired power plant (standardized to a "1-gigawatt" (GW), or 1-million kW, size),[31] such damages run between $700,000 and $7 million per year. If this total cost were prorated and included in the "monthly bill" of an average American family whose electricity is supplied by the coal-fired plant, the extra cost would range from 20 cents to $2, or about $200 million to $2 billion per USW (see appendix B, page 31).

Crop Damage

We should not be surprised that the same emissions that can eat stone can also attack plant life. Agricultural damage from air pollution has been observed near large cities. The part due to each new coal-fired power plant (including imputed acid rain damage to crops) has been estimated at the equivalent of a hypothetical monthly surcharge on the average family "monthly electric bill" of from 7 cents to 70 cents.[32]

---

[30] William Ramsay and Claude Anderson, *Managing the Environment: An Economic Primer* (New York, Basic Books, 1972) p. 195.

[31] See U.S. Congress, *Air Quality,* pp. 631, and 695–699; the Research Corporation of New England, *Effects of Power Plant Emissions on Materials,* EPRI EC-139, TPS 75-616, Summary Report (Palo Alto, Calif., EPRI, July 1976) p. 2-2; and Ramsay, "Coal and Nuclear," p. 5-25.

[32] See Ramsay, "Coal and Nuclear," p. 5-25; and U.S. Congress, Senate, *Air Quality,* pp. 631 and 695–699.

Acid Rain

Perhaps even more worrying is the general acid rain problem.[33] Marked increases in the amounts of acid rainfall have been found in the north-eastern United States, even in locations well-removed from concentrations of fossil fuel-combustion sources. The exact source of the acids is not clear, but we naturally suspect that sulfuric and nitric acids may be produced from the sulfur dioxide and the nitrogen oxides present in polluted air. The consequences of the increased acidity are difficult to judge. But even fairly low levels of acid could be expected to leach nutrients out of the soil, injure leaf surfaces, and otherwise endanger the health of plant and animal communities. Effects on fish and other aquatic life in rivers and lakes are especially important: newly hatched salmon are unable to survive very long when acidity rises above moderate levels.[34] It is difficult to say just what the future overall impact of such chemical tinkering with the environment would be: perhaps acid rain would, on the average, add only a relatively small increment to normal acids in the soil and in surface waters, producing problems only in special cases.[35] On the other hand, future ecological catastrophes involving a widespread killing-off of plants and, therefore, animals, are not out of the question. At any rate, no such widespread danger to communities of plants and lower animals and, therefore, to the world food chain—which, in turn, would affect the world energy exchange balance—can be taken lightly.

Visual Degradation

Most of the impacts and other types of damages caused by air pollution are the result of invisible molecules or of extremely small droplets or particles. But both these smaller particles and the somewhat larger particles that are less dangerous to health and, at times, the brown gas nitrogen dioxide help to obscure the atmosphere and degrade the visual landscape. Unfortunately, this esthetic value is difficult to measure. But if we can one

[33] This has been reviewed in Ramsay, "Coal and Nuclear," p. 5-17. See G. E. Likens and F. H. Bormann, "Acid Rain: A Serious Regional Environmental Problem," *Science* vol. 184 (14 June 1974) pp. 1176–1179; and James N. Galloway, Gene E. Likens, and Eric S. Edgerton, "Acid Precipitation in the Northeastern United States: pH and Acidity," *Science* vol. 194 (12 November 1976) pp. 722–723; as opposed to John O. Frohlinger and Robert Kane, "Precipitation: Its Acidic Nature," *Science* vol. 189 (8 August 1975) pp. 455–457. Also see Ross, "A 1977 Approach," for an optimistic view.
[34] Ross, "A 1977 Approach," p. 14.
[35] Ibid., pp. 12–13.

day measure at least *minimum* values by indirect means—for example, by looking at effects on property values—we might expect it to make significant contributions to the hidden unpaid costs of fossil fuel-generated power. In fact, one study estimated that reducing sulfate levels in Saint Louis by about one-third would increase property values of single-family units by some $40 million to $100 million.[36] However, these values should include some health and other environmental costs also.

Figure 2-2 summarizes some of these nonhealth dangers. The property damage estimates are uncertain, and the shading of the bars gives some indication of this uncertainty.

The Clean-up Problem: Costs and Effectiveness

Some of the pollution from coal burning can be cleaned up—but at a price. Of course, we have already assumed that new coal-fired power plants would be cleaner than existing ones. Specifically, we have assumed that the EPA emissions standards for sulfur dioxide and nitrogen dioxide in new power plants will be met by one means or another. But any other existing Clean Air Act regulations in effect will also have to be satisfied, specifically, the controversial new legislation and recent EPA regulations designed to prevent the "significant deterioration" of many airsheds.[37] To satisfy such new rules, power plants might have to emit a lesser amount of pollutants, or other sources of pollution would have to be reduced to prevent an overall rise in the prevailing (ambient) pollution level.

It is impossible to foresee exactly how much all this would cost. But we accept here that costs will be met for enforcing the existing EPA emissions standards for new plants and will, therefore, not be unpaid costs. If emissions were to be reduced still more because of the Clean Air Act requirements, the paid costs of generating power in a clean way will go up even more, while unpaid health and environmental costs should be correspondingly less. Naturally, users of electricity will find the extra antipollution equipment costs added into their monthly electricity bill. Leaving it until later to examine whether these additional billed costs would be worthwhile, we can look here at the possibilities for pollution control.

---

[36] Ronald G. Ridker, *Economic Costs of Air Pollution: Studies in Measurement,* Praeger Special Studies in U.S. Economic and Social Development (New York, Praeger, 1967), adjusted from 1967 to 1975 dollars.

[37] See, for example, *Energy User News* vol. 2, no. 19 (16 May 1977), p. 16; and *Clean Air Act Amendments of 1977*), Conference Report to Accompany H. R. 6161 (*Clean Air Act Amendments of 1977*), H. Rept. 95-564, 95 Cong. 1 sess. (3 August 1977).

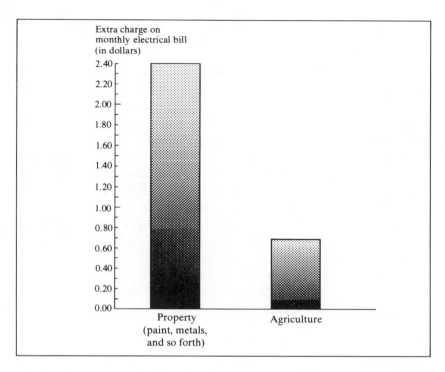

Figure 2-2. Estimates of nonhealth damages from air pollution caused by coal-fired power plants, in terms of the amount hypothetically prorated and added to the average residential "monthly electric bill" [$1.00 per bill equals about $0.9 billion per USW (2 trillion kWh)]. These are the total costs to society, apportioned among all users of residential electricity, as a monthly charge to each customer; compare an average 1975 residential bill of $21.97 to an "equivalent bill" of $54.46. One dollar is about one-half mill per kilowatt hour (for all electricity). See also text and appendix B; and Ramsay, "Coal and Nuclear: Health and Environmental Costs" (Washington, Resources for the Future, August 1978) pp. 5-24 and 5-25.

A straightforward way to meet, or to improve on, emission standards is to burn coal containing reduced amounts of sulfur. Such low-sulfur coal is available, but often it is located in Montana, Wyoming, and other Western states far from Eastern markets, and many potential low-sulfur reserves have not yet been developed. So low-sulfur coal often is available only at a relatively high price and in relatively modest quantities. Ordinary high-sulfur coal can also be physically cleaned or treated chemically to dissolve sulfur and other undesirable minerals. But these cleaning processes are not yet commercially available at levels of efficiency that will clean up high-sulfur coal to the level of EPA standards.[38]

Ultimately, the coal can be turned into a low-quality (low-Btu) gas before burning. Indeed, one basic coal-gasification process is that long used in New York City and other U.S. cities before cheap natural gas became available. The sulfur can then be cleaned out of this gas, and the clean gas burned. Modern gasification processes are under fairly extensive development but are still very expensive. If sulfur compounds were to be reduced in this manner, the total annual costs, according to some estimates, would range from $60 million to $120 million extra for each new power plant, resulting in a $20 to $40 addition to the "monthly electric bill."[39] For this relatively huge expenditure—greater than the 1975 average residential electric bill—one might be able to buy a reduction in sulfur levels that is 60 percent below the EPA standards. As emphasized before, it is uncertain what that reduction would mean in reduced health costs. But if everything were proportional,[40] such percentage decreases in sulfur would imply corresponding percentage decreases in the deaths and illnesses shown in figure 2-1.

Another way to solve the dirty-coal problem is to remove the sulfur during the combustion process, by forcing air up through a bed of coal and limestone (fluidized-bed combustion), or by burning coal in special (cyclone) furnaces. Such methods are now under development, but are not yet commercially established for large central power stations. But some—like fluidized-bed combustion—could have one big advantage: its advocates claim that the total cost for power generation might be less than that for present coal-burning methods. And it has been estimated that by this process sulfur emissions would be reduced by 90 percent.[41]

Finally, the sulfur can be removed from the smoke or flue gases themselves. In most conventional forms of coal combustion, particulates in the flue gas will have to be removed at the stack anyway, by means of a vacuum cleaner-type arrangement (bag house) or by a device using electric fields to collect the particles (electrostatic precipitator). The sulfur

[38] But progress is being made. For example, one recent technique claims to be able to make 30 to 40 percent of U.S. coal environmentally acceptable at a cost of $2.50 to $5.00 per ton, or $2.00 to $4.00 per monthly bill [*Energy Resources Report* (1 April 1977) p. 129].

[39] University of Texas, "Alternative Technologies for the Central-Station Generation of Electricity," draft report, Resources for the Future, National Energy Strategies Project (18 March 1977) tab. 5.4-2.

[40] For a discussion of this problem, see U.S. Congress, Senate, *Air Quality*, 1975, p. 147; and Ramsay, "Coal and Nuclear," append. A.

[41] See University of Texas, "Alternative Technologies," tab. 5.8-2.

can also be removed at this point by means of a "scrubber" that absorbs the sulfur in a solution of compounds of calcium or some other suitable chemical. Such lime or limestone scrubbers are now being put into use. Opinions differ on whether they are reliable pieces of equipment, and their cost can be fairly high, an additional $7 to $10 on the "monthly electric bill." In return for this nonnegligible expenditure, one can eliminate over 90 percent of the sulfur.[42]

Recent legislation and currently proposed regulations may prevent our making a free choice between these clean-up technologies. A Best Available Control Technology (BACT) has been proposed in these measures as a requirement for all fossil fuel-power plants.[43] Such a technology has not yet been officially designated, but it seems evident that scrubbers, at least, would qualify; it is also a possibility that some of the other processes would also be certified as acceptable controls if they proved to be reliable and commercially practicable. But just the use of low-sulfur coal alone would no longer be acceptable as a pollution control measure.

Such varied possibilities for cleanup suggest that there will likely be ample opportunity for the public—or its representatives—to make decisions on further reducing the unpaid health and environmental costs from coal-fired power plants provided that the public is willing to pay the extra clean-up costs in terms of higher electricity costs. We will look into this price increase and its justifications later, after examining some of the other unpaid costs of electricity.

Conclusion

It seems obvious from laboratory experiments and severe air pollution episodes that air pollution from power plants is bad for one's health. This is especially true for those who suffer from lung or cardiac disorders. But

---

[42] Ibid., tab. 5.8-2, gives the equivalent of $7 to $10. A recent survey of existing systems, U.S. Federal Power Commission, *The Status of Flue Gas Desulfurization Applications in the United States: A Technological Assessment* (Washington, Federal Power Commission, July 1977) p. 24, gives an average capital cost of $90 per kilowatt and operating costs of 3.1 mills per kilowatt, or a minimum of $10 added to the "monthly electric bill."

[43] U.S. Congress, Senate, Subcommittee on Environmental Pollution, Committee on Environment and Public Works, *Clean Air Act Amendments of 1977: Hearings on S. 251, S. 252, and S. 253,* bills to amend the Clean Air Act, as amended, 95 Cong. 1 sess., ser. no. 95-H7, pt. 1 (Washington, 1977); and the Executive Office of the President, Energy Policy and Planning, *The National Energy Plan* (Washington, GPO, 29 April 1977).

evidence of *how* deleterious it is at ordinary polluted air levels is very thin indeed. We estimate fatalities per 2 trillion kWh (or USW, that is, total U.S. electrical usage in 1975) to range from as high as 7,000 deaths to very low rates. Various pollution-related diseases, however, are likely to occur at rates of tens of thousands, or even millions, per USW. Approximate estimates of damage to materials and agricultural products predict respectable levels of unpaid costs. And pollution-related acids in rain could conceivably cause serious ecological effects.

National policies have been proposed to force cleaning up the sulfur emissions from power plants. But promising measures are under intensive development to provide both cleaner air and coal-fired electricity—at a price.

Appendix A: Fatality and Illness Calculations

A very few model estimates have calculated sulfur dioxide emissions from power plants, transport and diffusion, conversion to sulfates, and consequent dosage to a specified population and response of that population to the dose. The models do not take into account the average national conditions, but in view of the uncertainties in the structure of the atmospheric models, and more particularly in view of the overwhelming uncertainty in dose-response relationships (see the references in footnote 18), such problems may be lost in the noise—even though such interesting phenomena as the long-range transport and extended lifetimes of sulfates are then ignored.

At any rate, normalized to an emission of 35.4 million lb of sulfur for our standard plant (emitting 1.2 million lb of sulfur dioxide for each million Btu out of a total of 5.89×10^{13} Btu), the following values are obtained from three different models: Brookhaven, 24;[44] the North model, 15 for an urban location and 5 for a rural one;[45] and Buehring, 1.5×10^{-3} for an urban location and zero for a rural one.[46]

We take the Hamilton results as the upper bound. Hamilton's are also about twice the average of the results of the North model, which we use in

---

[44] Hamilton, *Health Effects;* the original referenced annual sulfur emissions, 150 million lb.

[45] U.S. Congress, Senate, *Air Quality,* pp. 6–25ff.; original sulfur emissions, 96.5 million lb.

[46] Buehring, Foell, and Keeney, *Energy/Environment Management,* 1976; original sulfur, 35 million lb.

estimating illnesses (see below). We take zero as the lower bound: this choice is based not only on the Buehring results but also on critiques of epidemiological studies made by Greenfield, Attaway, and Tyler, Inc., and Tabershaw/Cooper Associates, Inc.[47]

These results, for the 304.4 standard 1-GW plant-years (1 GW = 1 million kW) in a USW (see footnote 17) give a range of zero to 7,000 fatalities per USW.

It must be noted that some multicorrelation analysis studies give considerably higher figures. In particular, Lave and Seskin suggest that a 50 percent reduction in air pollution would correspond to an approximate 5 percent decrease in general mortality.[48] Coal-fired power plants contributed about 45 percent of total sulfur dioxide in the early 1970s.[49] As used here, 1 USW unit of new coal plants probably produce about 60 percent as much sulfur dioxide (at a 0.72 percent sulfur effective average) as the approximately 0.4 USW of coal-fired generating capacity in 1972, using coal with a 3 percent sulfur content. Therefore, these higher estimates would say that about 3 percent of the overall mortality rate could be attributed to each additional USW—neglecting the differences between decreases and increases in ambient levels and unknown scaling effects. Three percent of a total U.S. annual mortality rate of 2 million would, of course, be some 60,000 persons, an order of magnitude above the estimate taken here. The not-negligible problems in such correlation models are reviewed by the authors and discussants in a paper by Lave and Seskin.[50]

The results of the North and Buehring models for nonfatal illness give divergent values, probably even taking different population distributions into account. The model results for the diseases, adapted to the standard plant with sulfur emissions (as defined above and averaged over rural and

[47] Greenfield, Attaway, and Tyler, Inc., *Sulfur Oxides;* and Tabershaw/Cooper Associates, Inc., *A Critical Evaluation of Current Research Regarding Health Criteria for Sulfur Oxides,* PB-245 651, U.S. Federal Energy Administration (Springfield, Va., National Technical Information Service, April 1975).
[48] Lester B. Lave and Eugene P. Seskin, "Does Air Pollution Cause Mortality?" in *Statistics and the Environment,* Proceedings of the Fourth Symposium of the American Statistical Association, 3–5 March 1976 (Resources for the Future Reprint 141).
[49] U.S. Congress, Senate, *Air Quality,* p. 237; U.S. Atomic Energy Commission (AEC), and the Institute of Nuclear Science and Engineering, *Electric Power Generation: Comparative Risks and Benefits,* combined proceedings of workshops at Oregon State University, 21–25 August, 1972 and 20–24 August, 1973 (Corvallis, Oregon State University, 1973) p. 173; and U.S. Department of Commerce, Bureau of the Census, *Statistical Abstract of the United States, 1975* (Washington, GPO, 1975) p. 553.
[50] Lave and Seskin, "Does Air Pollution."

urban plant locations), are chronic respiratory disease in adults (North, 18,600, and Buehring, 2,800); lower respiratory-tract disease in children (North, 4,500, and Buehring, zero); aggravation of heart–lung symptoms in the elderly, given in person-days (North, 186,000, and Buehring, 1,200); excess asthma attacks (North, 38,000, and Buehring, 300). These figures are for particular choices of ambient pollutant concentrations.

One verson of a normal incidence of these cases is taken from those used in the North model:[51] these incidences are shown in figure 2-1. The North model results in the averaged form are consistent with normal incidence—though perhaps implausibly high in some cases (smoking and other factors must also be important agents)—and are adopted here as maximum values. In terms of 1 USW, these values for chronic respiratory disease are 6 million; for children's lower respiratory-tract disease, 1 million; for heart–lung symptoms, 60 million; and for asthma, 10 million.

In getting a lower limit, we take into consideration Bernard Goldstein's estimates that perhaps 10 percent of chronic respiratory disease cases and 5 percent of excess asthma attacks can be attributed to air pollution.[52] Since 1 million USW of coal-fired generation corresponds to perhaps 30 percent of all sulfur dioxide emissions—neglecting mechanisms of sulfate formation, as well as other totally unrelated pollutants—then we would infer from these estimated percentages some 200,000 associated cases of chronic respiratory disease and some 700,000 extra attacks of asthma. (Even these estimates might be high; compare the Buehring model results.) In view of the great uncertainties present, we select a lower bound that is low enough to include the Goldstein estimates by choosing it two orders of magnitude below the maximum derived from the North model. The results are shown in figure 2-1.

Appendix B: The "Monthly Electric Bill" Calculation

Impacts that can be expressed in dollars are expressed in terms of the monthly amounts that would be added to the bill of each residential customer in order to cover the costs, if such costs were covered. This extra cost would correspond not only to added direct increases in electricity, but also to increases in prices of other goods made more expensive by more ex-

51 U.S. Congress, Senate, *Air Quality,* p. 608.
52 Ibid., pp. 145–147.

pensive electricity used in their manufacture or sale. According to the Edison Electric Institute (EEI),[53] the ratio of total revenues to residential customer revenues is 2.49, so from EEI table 41-S, we get the monthly residential bill of $21.87 for electricity, which would correspond to an "equivalent monthly bill" of $54.46 of total national electricity value.

EEI table 44-S also shows 8,176 kWh yearly or 681 kWh per month used per residential customer. Every dollar increase in the "monthly electric bill" would therefore correspond to a 1.47 mill surcharge on residential electricity. Based on EEI tables 10-S and 19-S, the total residential sales constitute 30.6 percent of total electricity generated. So every dollar increase on the "monthly electric bill" corresponds to a surcharge of 0.450 mills per kilowatt for *all* electricity generated (not just residential). In terms of the 6.57×10^9 kWh plant-years used in Ramsay,[54] this is equivalent to a $2.96 million increase per plant-year. In terms of 1 USW (2 trillion kWh) generated, $1 on the monthly bill equals $900 million yearly. Uncertainties in values surely overwhelm inflationary discrepancies, but the dollars here may be thought of as 1975 dollars.

[53] See Edison Electric Institute, *Statistical Yearbook of the Electric Utility Industry for 1975*, no. 43, EEI Publication No. 76-51 (New York, EEI, October 1976) tab. 10-S, 19-S, 36-S, 41-S, and 44-S.
[54] Ramsay, "Coal and Nuclear," Preface.

3 Routine Radiation from Nuclear Plants

Is normal radiation an insignificant threat to health?

Are long-lasting radioactive gases a problem?

What about plutonium and the breeder?

There are not many good sides to the existence of the Bomb, but one of them may be that we know now, thirty-odd years after its advent, a good deal about radiation and its effects on health. What we know about radiation is vastly more than we know about the effects of emitting toxic trace elements in the smokestack gases of coal-fired power plants. To be sure, we know much less than we would like to, but we can be relatively confident that reasonable upper limits can be set on the damage from normal operations of nuclear power plants.

We must be reconciled, of course, to the fact that operating a nuclear power plant inevitably leads to the release of radioactive atoms into the environment. We know that rays from the decay of these atoms can impinge on the human body from a distance and can enter the body through ingestion of food or water or by breathing contaminated air. They can cause a wide variety of damage to the cells of human beings and other organisms. We are all familiar—from descriptions of Hiroshima and Nagasaki—with what happens when large doses of radiation damage the bone marrow or intestinal lining, leading to acute radiation sickness and death. Cell changes caused by radiation can also lead to cancer of various kinds, often long after the initial exposure. It is also evident that changes in the cell's genetic material could lead to undesirable mutations in future generations.[1]

---

[1] For a further discussion, see William Ramsay, "Coal and Nuclear: Health and Environmental Costs" (Washington, Resources for the Future, August 1978) chap. 2 and append. C.

Radiation escaping during the normal operation of nuclear power plants occurs at too low a level to cause radiation sickness. Indeed, most types of radiation emanating from reactors present much less risk to the public than natural radiation—that is, radiation from outer space or from naturally occurring radioactive elements in rocks and earth. As a matter of fact, it is impossible to tell by measurements whether such small amounts of radiation actually do cause cancer or genetic defects. The tumors and mutations involved would be indistinguishable from any others and would be just a small addition to those already observed. But there are cogent reasons for believing that even extremely low levels of radiation may cause cancer: since carcinogenesis is not well understood, it is possible that if a ray or fast-moving particle destroys even a single site in one cell, that cell could mutate and become malignant. So it is usually assumed that the low-level doses of radiation from nuclear reactors do cause some cancers. These cancers would occur with small probabilities per person, but low doses to large populations could well cause cancers in numbers proportional to those that are induced by high doses to small populations—such as those from nuclear bombs or from special extensive radiation treatments for acute medical problems.[2] However, on the basis of present experimental evidence, it must be remembered that such cancers—from low doses and low-dose rates—have not been shown to occur.[3]

Health Dangers and the Costs of Control

Most critics consider the level of radioactivity from normal operations of nuclear power plants to be very low. Admittedly, one can quarrel about

[2] See National Research Council, National Academy of Sciences, Advisory Committee on the Biological Effects of Ionizing Radiation, "The Effects on Populations of Exposure to Low Levels of Ionizing Radiation" (Washington, November 1972), for a general discussion. For example, patients with the spinal disease ankylosing spondylitis who received radiation to the spine in a dose perhaps fifty times that which most persons receive in a lifetime developed bone cancers in excess of those normally reported (ibid., pp. 125–127). If the radiation dose impact is "linear," the same number of cancers will be produced in a larger population receiving the same product of the dose times the number of persons receiving the dose.

This linearity assumption is in wide use. See the U.S. Nuclear Regulatory Commission, *Reactor Safety Study: An Assessment of Accident Risks in U.S. Commercial Nuclear Power Plants,* WASH-1400, NUREG-74/014 (Washington, October 1975) vol. IV, which argues that it is often an overestimate. On the other hand, for evidence that some low-dose effects could be disproportionately large, see Karl Z. Morgan, Letter to the Editor, *Science* vol. 195, no. 4276 (28 January 1977) pp. 348–349; and Martin Brown, Letter to the Editor, *Science* vol. 195, no. 4276 (28 January 1977) pp. 348–349.

[3] This point is discussed again in appendix B.

the meaning of the word *low*. Over the course of the past few years, the emissions of radioactive elements into the air and water near nuclear power plants have been reduced—at some cost in extra filtering and other treatment of air and water exhausted from the plant—to levels that produce maximum doses ten times lower than those from natural radiation or from routine medical X rays. And at that, very few persons would actually receive such a maximum dose from reactors. The maximum annual dose at the site boundary, located six-tenths of a mile from the reactor at the James A. FitzPatrick Plant near Oswego, New York, was estimated at 2 percent of background radiation, but only three persons lived within one mile of the reactor.[4] Radiation doses to the public are also very low for other parts of the nuclear fuel cycle (mining, milling, fuel conversion and fabrication, and enrichment; see "A Note on Nuclear Proliferation and Technologies," page 70)—except for certain special cases related to long-lived isotopes (see below). This does *not* imply that naturally occurring radiation or medical radiation is safe—indeed, it probably is harmful—or that incremental additions to these levels are satisfactory (see appendix A).

But we may be able to justify the use of the word *low* in another way. Look, for example, at the radiation impacts shown in figure 3-1.[5] It is predicted that the risk of cancer for the general public from these sources amounts to between 0.3 and 1 fatality per year produced by a large nu-

---

[4] U.S. Atomic Energy Commission (AEC), "Final Environmental Statement Related to Operation of James A. FitzPatrick Nuclear Plant," Docket No. 50-333 (Washington, March 1973) tab. 5.5. Actually, the dose of most consequence usually involves radioiodine in milk and, therefore, dairy farms. The largest individual risk for the FitzPatrick plant was 0.013 rem (see Ramsay, "Coal and Nuclear," chap. 2), or perhaps an extra individual risk of death from thyroid cancer amounting to a few chances in 10 million. A rem is the dose equivalent to 100 ergs of energy deposited by X rays in 1 gm of body tissue.

[5] For sources of estimates, see Ramsay, "Coal and Nuclear," pp. 2-7 and 2-18. Estimates are based on recent environmental statements for nuclear power plants; see, for example, U.S. Nuclear Regulatory Commission (NRC), "Final Environmental Statement Related to the Construction of Davis-Besse Nuclear Power Station Units 2 and 3," Docket Nos. 50-500 and 50-501, NUREG 75/083 (Washington, NRC, October 1975), and "Final Environmental Statement Related to Construction of Wolf Creek Generating Station Unit 1," Docket No. STN 50-482, NUREG 75/096 (Washington, NRC, October 1975). The dose taken here is 7 man-rem to the "whole body" and 57 man-rem to the thyroid gland (for short-lived isotopes only, for a 1-GW, 75 percent capacity factor plant-year). Cancer deaths are calculated at $(50 \times 165) \times 10^{-6}$ per whole body man-rem, and include the proportion of thyroid nodules that are malignant, at $(20 - 40) \times 10^{-6}$ per thyroid man-rem. Uncertainties are dose-response only, not dose-measurement. The short-lived fuel-cycle dose is taken as 10 man-rem (see U.S. Nuclear Regulatory Commission (NRC), *Final Generic Environmental Statement on the Use of Recycle Plutonium in Light Water Cooled Reactors: Health, Safety and Environment*, NUREG-0002 (Washington, NRC, August 1976) tab. IV J(E)-8, IV J(E)-9, IV J(E)-10, and IV J(E)-11.

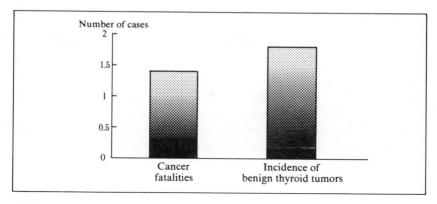

Figure 3-1. Estimates of deaths and illnesses associated with the normal release of short-lived radiation from nuclear power facilities (per 2 trillion kWh = 1 USW). For source of data, see Ramsay, "Coal and Nuclear"; NRC, "Final Environmental Statement Related to the Construction of Davis-Besse Nuclear Power Stations 2 and 3"; and NRC, "Final Generic Environmental Statement Related to Construction of Wolf Creek Generating Station Unit 1."

clear industry generating 2 trillion kWh—which, however, in 1975 provided only about 9 percent of that amount.[6] Benign nodules also appear on the thyroid gland, caused by a radioactive form of iodine that is emitted as a product of the nuclear fission process. But even if all U.S. electricity were produced by nuclear power, the occurrence rate would be only two cases or less. Genetic illnesses (that is, serious diseases caused by genes mutated by radiation) are expected to occur but are very difficult to estimate.[7]

We will see that when compared with the possible coal impacts or with other nuclear impacts, the rates of fatalities and illnesses shown here appear low. In addition, many of these fatalities would show up only after a long latency period, and could be considered conceivably by some as somewhat less tragic than are immediate fatalities.[8]

Additional cleanup of this normal radiation could probably be carried out, but the cost would be great. The U.S. Nuclear Regulatory Commis-

[6] Edison Electric Institute, *Statistical Year Book of the Electric Utility Industry, for 1975,* no. 43, EEI Publication No. 76-51 (New York, EEI, October 1976) tab. 10-S.

[7] National Research Council, "Effects on Populations of Exposure," p. 57.

[8] See William Ramsay and Milton Russell, "Age- and Time-Related Comparisons in Energy Strategies." Paper presented at the Annual Meeting of the Southwest Economics Association, Dallas, Texas, 30 March–2 April, 1977; and Richard Zeckhauser, "Procedures for Valuing Lives," *Public Policy* vol. 23, no. 4 (Fall 1975) pp. 419–464. Note, however, that the same latency effect conceivably could arise with fatalities from low levels of air pollution.

sion (NRC) has directed that additional equipment for treatment of gaseous and liquid wastes from reactors—for example, charcoal adsorbers, pressurized tanks for temporary storage of waste gases, and so on— should be installed if it is calculated that one extra cancer death can be avoided at a cost of less than $10 million.[9] Public agencies usually spend money on safety only if a life can be saved for less than $1 million.[10] So, assuming that the health risks are correctly estimated, it is unlikely that society—in cold-blooded terms—would want to spend more money than it does at present in order to tighten up on these normal emissions of nuclear radiation.

Long-lived Radioactive Elements

One exception to this generally optimistic outlook on radiation originating from normal nuclear operations is the problem of long-lived radioactive elements. As part of the issue of disposal of "high-level wastes" (residues of spent nuclear fuel), the public is well aware of one aspect of this problem: how to store long-lived elements, of which the carcinogenic element plutonium is the most familiar example. But the problem of safe burial of solid and liquid fuel wastes is not the only nuclear disposal problem with which we and future generations should be concerned. A radioactive form of water (containing a form of hydrogen called tritium[11]) and a radioactive form of carbon (carbon 14) are emitted routinely from reactors into local airsheds or watersheds.[12] These radioactive elements, or *radioisotopes,* are emitted in quantities corresponding to

[9] Office of the Federal Register, "Application of Cost–Benefit Analysis Requirements of Appendix I to Certain Nuclear Power Plants," *Federal Register,* 40 FR 40816 (4 September 1975); and U.S. Atomic Energy Commission (AEC), "Concluding Statement of Position of Regulatory Staff: Numerical Guides for Design Objectives and Limiting Conditions for Operation to Meet the Criterion 'As Low as Practicable' for Radioactive Material in Light Water-Cooled Nuclear Power Reactors," Docket No. RM-50-2 (Washington, AEC, 20 February 1974).

[10] For this controversial area, see Joanne Linnerooth, *A Critique of Recent Modelling Efforts to Determine the Value of Human Life,* Research Memorandum RM-75-67 (Laxenburg, Austria, International Institute for Applied Systems Analysis, December 1975).

[11] The water molecule contains an unstable tritium or hydrogen-3 atom instead of ordinary hydrogen 1.

[12] For the following discussion, see Ramsay, "Coal and Nuclear," p. 2-7 and append. B and J; and U.S. Nuclear Regulatory Commission (NRC), *Final Generic Environmental Statement,* tab. IV C-30 and IV C-31: the carbon-14 dose, taken from the latter reference, is 76 man-rem per plant-year. Other long-lived isotopes exist, but the ones mentioned are peculiarly persistent in the human environment and difficult to control.

rather small health risks. Here again, we should understand the word *small* in comparison with other types of illnesses and deaths associated with the generation of electrical power. But, as with plutonium, the effects from tritium and carbon 14 do not occur within a short space of time, but go on for years afterward. The half-life of tritium is less than thirteen years,[13] so that the radiation, while persistent, diminishes to relatively low levels within the same time frame as the operational years of the reactor. The half-life of carbon 14 is 5,470 years, but the carbon 14 (in the form of the ordinary gas carbon dioxide containing a "heavy" carbon-14 nucleus) tends to be absorbed over time into the depths of the ocean. Therefore, the effective half-life may be much less. In fact, calculations predict that it is less than forty years. Since the costs and effectiveness of possible control measures for both elements are rather uncertain, it is important to find out how long term the threat is.

Then there is the problem of radon.[14] Radon is a radioactive gas that is emitted from the tailings piles at uranium mills and from uranium mining operations. It has a short half-life (less than four days), and it decays into radon *daughters,* elements that are dangerously radioactive if breathed into the lungs or ingested on contaminated food. Radon is chemically inert and therefore very difficult to control by filtration, and it is produced by other elements having a half-life of almost 80,000 years. Therefore, its radiation, while still minor as compared with normal background radiation, can be expected to last tens of millennia, long after all uranium-based civilizations have disappeared. The radon-producing elements can probably be cleaned up by covering mine tailings and mining areas. The cost depends on how much reduction is necessary in order to obtain the effect we insist upon: costs are modest if the danger is to be reduced by about 90 percent, because burial under a thick layer of earth will work. For a greater reduction, or for a more permanent and nonerodible covering, more money would be needed. Despite numerous studies, little is being done about the problem at present.

[13] That is, 1 g of tritium decays to one-half of its amount in thirteen years, leaving only 0.5 g, and then to one-quarter of the original amount in twenty-six years, and so on.
[14] See William Ramśay, "Radon from Uranium Mill Tailings: A Source of Significant Radiation Hazard?" *Environmental Management* vol. 1, no. 2 (1976) pp. 139–145, where the corrected dose from mill tailings is taken as 25 man-rem per plant-year. The uncertainty shown is in dose-response and in the ratio of contributions from mines to those from mills. A ratio of five, given in NRC, *Final Generic Environmental Statement,* vol. IV, append. J(E), has been used as an upper bound here. A much smaller contribution from uranium hexafluoride (UF_6) conversion plants has been neglected.

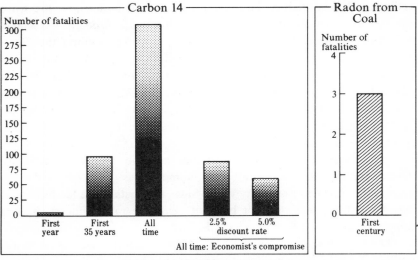

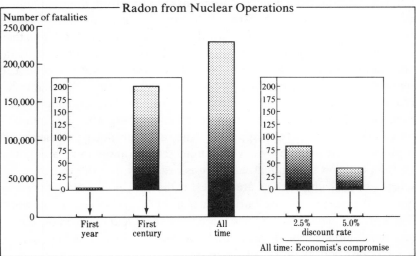

Figure 3-2. Estimates of fatalities from normal operations caused by two long-lived radioactive elements, carbon 14 and radon (per 2 trillion kWh = 1 USW). For source of data, see Ramsay, "Coal and Nuclear," appendixes B and J.

Trying to judge the importance of such long-term effects is difficult.[15] Figure 3-2 shows the impacts for radon and carbon 14 over various lengths of time. Note that figure 3-2 shows only the isotopes emitted from

[15] Ramsay, "Coal and Nuclear," append. B and J.

the wastes which would be produced in order to supply the United States (at 1975 levels) with nuclear-generated power. As shown in figure 3-2, the number of deaths attributed to radon from a nuclearized United States in the first year after its emission ranges between 0.8 and 2, while the carbon-14 fatalities range from 2 to 4. But the number of predicted fatalities over all time from the same sources is large for carbon 14 (100 to 300), while the prediction for radon (as many as 200,000) is huge. After all, we are adding up a virtually constant rate of fatalities (assuming that populations stay about the same) over many thousands of years.

True, if we counted all pollution damages in this manner, we would quickly become involved in apparent absurdities because there are many activities causing a few deaths every few years that would, therefore, cause many hundreds or thousands over centuries and millennia.[16] On the other hand, it seems intuitively wrong to neglect such future effects entirely, especially since radon and carbon-14 wastes will seem superfluous pollutants to future generations.[17] Perhaps some sort of compromise, as that shown in figure 3-2, could represent the usual attitudes we have when we talk about the ways in which we affect the future. At least, such "discounting of the future" is the way economists usually compromise on the value of future ledger items.[18] Doing it this way, the numbers of deaths per USW (2 trillion kWh) would be measured for both gases in tens, instead of hundreds (for carbon 14) and hundreds of thousands (for radon)—at least at the two discount rates shown. But there is some question as to whether discounting these predicted fatalities is appropriate.[19] There is also the problem that it is difficult to determine whether discount

[16] A beach at which one person drowns every fifty years will see 1,000 people drown in 50,000 years; we do not close the beaches to the public.

[17] What especially rubs the wrong way is that in the years A.D. 10,000 to A.D. 10,100, 30 to 200 people might die prematurely to provide 1 USW of electricity in one year, 2000. Radiation health physicists might say such numbers as 30, or even 200, are miniscule when compared with other fatal effects. Economists might say that the other 100 billion people living in that millennium will directly benefit by the money (resources) saved by using nuclear energy in 2000. Others may remain puzzled by the paradox. [See Talbot Page, *Conservation and Economic Efficiency: An Approach to Materials Policy* (Baltimore, Johns Hopkins University Press for Resources for the Future, 1977, chap. 8 and 9).]

[18] The idea behind discounting is that people are impatient. Something valuable now is usually worth more to a person than the same thing would be if one had to wait ten years for it. This is why banks charge interest on loans. The interest measures the "rate of discount." Roughly, 2.5 percent and 5 percent discount rates mean that $1.00 to be received next year is worth only $0.975 and $0.95, respectively, right now. One can verify such evaluations for cash holdings by putting his money in a savings bank (assuming that interest rates look favorable when compared with the rate of inflation).

[19] Richard Zeckhauser, *Processes for Valuing Lives,* Discussion Paper No. 29D (2nd version, Cambridge, Mass., Harvard University, June 1975), and Zeckhauser and Donald Shepard, *Where Now for Saving Lives?* Paper presented at Conference

rates such as those shown (2.5 percent and 5 percent, respectively) are of an appropriate magnitude.[20] Besides making the overall number of fatalities different, relatively high rates of discount would tend to make carbon 14 more of a problem than radon: in figure 3-2 it is shown that at 5 percent, carbon 14 is credited with 60 fatalities at a maximum, compared with only about 40 for radon. Therefore, the discount rate choice would affect our decisions about how to spend funds for cleaning up gaseous wastes.

But there is one disturbing footnote—the fact that coal often contains uranium as a constituent of its ash, so that the ash from a coal-fired power plant could also emit radon over a period far into the future. The relative size of the effect is difficult to determine, because coal ash is far from uniform, and it is difficult to know exactly where ordinary ash and fly ash will end up. This effect (see figure 3-2) for the typical uranium content of coal may be a few hundredths of the radon value from nuclear electricity.[21] The ultimate logic in this problem would be to mine coal ash for uranium, and this has indeed been proposed![22]

The Breeder

Recent energy proposals from the Carter administration strongly advocate an indefinite delay in the use of plutonium as fuel. Plutonium is

---

on Valuing Lives at Duke University, 11 March 1976, Discussion Paper No. 42D (Cambridge, Mass., Harvard University, May 1976). One way of looking at it is that money used to *save* lives can be discounted. If it costs $1 million to save one life in any year, we can spend the $1 million today to save one life this year. Or we can save it for twenty-eight years and get, at 2.5 percent (deflated) interest, $(1.025)^{28} = \$2$ million, with which we can save two lives. In this restricted sense, one life now is "worth" two later.

Naturally, this formulation ignores the differences between individuals. For the present generation, the best justification for doing so is that the identities of the victims are unknowable beforehand—and often even afterward. For future generations, the problem is even worse. But see William Ramsay and Milton Russell, "Time-Adjusted Impacts from Energy Generation," *Public Policy* vol. 26, no. 3 (Summer 1978) pp. 387–403.

[20] See, for example, Ramsay, "Coal and Nuclear," append. I. As explained there, a discount rate of 5 percent is used below, as corresponding approximately to an observed long-term (deflated) utility return on assets. See Edison Electric Institute, *Statistical Year Book*.

[21] See Ramsay, "Coal and Nuclear," pp. 1-22–1-23; and D. G. Jacobs, Oak Ridge National Laboratory, memo dated 10 October 1975, to C. R. Richmond of Oak Ridge National Laboratory, on the subject; and David D. Comey, "The Legacy of Uranium Tailings," *Bulletin of the Atomic Scientists* (September 1975) pp. 43–45. The ash also contains radium, which could contaminate water supplies.

[22] Kirk R. Smith, "The Coal-Uranium Breeder: Uranium from Coal," *Energy— The International Journal* vol. 2, no. 2 (June 1977) pp. 171–177. Note that coal ash concentrates the uranium in coal.

a radioisotope normally produced in ordinary reactors that can be used either as fuel for electricity or for nuclear weapons (see "A Note on Reactor Types"). This means that the breeder reactor—which would breed new fuel from nonfissile material as it generated electricity and would therefore extend uranium supplies for many decades, or even centuries— would also be indefinitely delayed. From the point of view of radiation hazards alone, the breeder reactor, if ever adopted in the United States, would probably make contributions to the radioactivity in the environment, but only at levels similar to those from LWRs. But since the plutonium must be recovered (reprocessed) from the uranium fuel in which it is made, the use of plutonium would also require that we have reprocessing plants to chemically separate plutonium from uranium. It is expected that the average reprocessing plant would contribute only very small amounts of plutonium and similar elements to the human environment.[23] But these plants would release trapped gases in the uranium fuel and therefore significantly increase carbon 14 and tritium emissions. On the other hand, since less uranium per year would be mined, radon emissions would be somewhat reduced. Another chemically inactive gas, krypton 85, would be released in significant amounts from these plants. Its half-life is somewhat less than eleven years, so it would not have an extremely long-term effect. But it would be widespread, since it is an inert gas and therefore a wanderer, and would be among the larger contributors to the health risks from normal operations. Clean-up measures could probably be carried out,[24] but it is not clear—given the minor health risks involved as compared with other risks—whether cleanup would be necessary. Possible changes in the world's climate that could be caused by krypton might also influence a clean-up decision (see chapter 7).

The additional impacts expected from one form of plutonium economy[25]—reusing plutonium in ordinary LWRs—are shown in figure 3-3.[26] They would amount to a doubling of carbon 14 and the creation of a

[23] NRC, *Final Generic Environmental Statement,* tab. IV E-9, shows only 25 man-rem from "uranium and transuranics" from a model plant reprocessing 2,000 metric tons a year—that is, about 125 man-rem or perhaps 0.01 fatality per USW. Mixed-oxide (plutonium-containing) fuel-fabrication plants are assigned only 4.8 man-rem.

[24] U.S. Atomic Energy Commission (AEC), "Final Environmental Statement Related to Construction and Operation of Barnwell Nuclear Fuel Plant," Docket No. 50-332 (Washington, AEC, January 1974).

[25] See Ramsay, "Coal and Nuclear," p. 2-18, and append. B and J; also NRC, *Final Generic Environmental Statement,* 1976, tab. IV C-30 and IV C-31. This example is for the recycle of plutonium in LWRs, but has a relevance to a breeder economy.

[26] "Plutonium economy" means the use of plutonium as a source of commercial nuclear fuel, involving new types of fuel cycles and reactor facilities and, perhaps, political institutions.

A NOTE ON REACTOR TYPES

Light Water Reactors.   The light water reactor (LWR) is the one commonly used for power in the United States. It uses ordinary or "light" water to transfer the heat from the nuclear fission reactions to make steam. Uranium 235 (U-235) atoms in the fuel split up, releasing particles called neutrons and creating heat. The neutrons also from time to time hit the "filler" uranium-238 atoms in the fuel and turn them into atoms of the element plutonium. Plutonium, like U-235, can also fission and produce heat—and can be used in place of U-235 in a nuclear weapon.

Breeder Reactors.   The water in the LWR has the effect of slowing down the neutrons after they are emitted in the fission. This is good for the heat-producing reaction, but it is relatively ineffective for turning uranium 238 (U-238) into plutonium. If some other substance—a liquid metal such as sodium or a molten salt of some kind—is used instead of the water, the neutrons can be slowed down much less, and so much plutonium can be produced that we end up with more fissile fuel than we started out with. This means that a great part of the 99 percent filler U-238 can be turned into fuel. It also means that a great deal of plutonium usually has to be shuffled back and forth and is therefore—theoretically at least—open to possible misuse in nuclear weapons by terrorists or by national governments.

Other Reactors.   There are as many other reactors as there are different media for carrying the heat away and for slowing or not slowing down the neutrons. Reactors with "heavy" water (made with another heavy form or isotope of hydrogen, hydrogen-2) are used in Canada and in India. Gas reactors of various kinds are used in some countries. A special type of high-temperature gas reactor, of which one commercial model exists in the United States, can turn another type of mineral, thorium, into uranium 233 (U-233)—yet a third kind of uranium which can be used for fissile fuel or weapons.

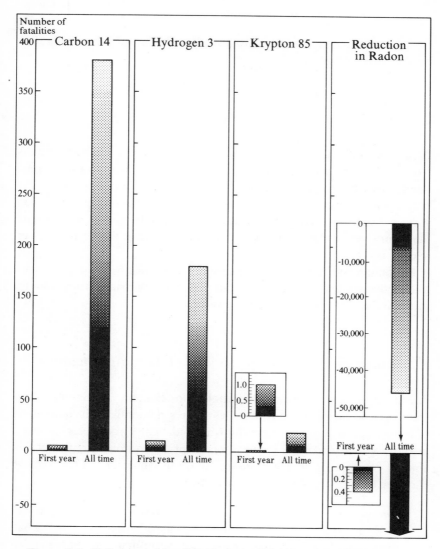

Figure 3-3. Estimates of fatalities from additional radioactive elements released routinely in one form of plutonium economy (plutonium burning in
ordinary reactors) for each USW. For source of data, see Ramsay, "Coal and
Nuclear"; and NRC, *Final Generic Statement.*

significant tritium problem, but would reduce the rate of radon generation by about 20 percent.

Conclusion

Predictions of cancer fatalities based on normal releases of radioactivity from nuclear reactors and related nuclear fuel facilities appear small relative to other health problems caused by the generation of electricity. The only apparent exception is for small effects from long-lived isotopes in gaseous wastes that add up year after year. Therefore, how we evaluate the future versus the present is important in judging the desirability of nuclear power.

Plutonium economies would release more of some forms of long-lived radioactive matter. On the other hand, the radon emissions from uranium mines and mill tailings would be alleviated.

Appendix A: Small Impacts and Their Significance

Are small impacts sometimes negligible? For example, routine radiation from the nuclear plant contributes less than a millionth of the amount of radiation that is received normally from radioactive rocks, cosmic rays, medical X rays, and other medical treatment. Some would argue that this amount of radiation is, therefore, relatively insignificant.[27] This point of view can be supported, but not proved, by two alternate assertions:

1. *Impacts far below a normal natural background are harmless.* It has been noted that we are uncertain about the effects of low-level radiation. Since it is a fact that the human race continues to survive under this constant natural bombardment, the implication could be that there is no real (that is, physical) damage from additional very small increments of radiation. This argument might be even more applicable to the effects of small increments in temperature on global climate. Unfortunately, in neither of these cases do we know this supposition to be so.

[27] See Ramsay, "Coal and Nuclear," append. H, for further discussion and references.

2. *Impacts below natural background are relatively "acceptable."*
Even if all radiation *is* harmful, people usually do not make efforts
to avoid living in brick houses as opposed to wooden ones—even
though radiation levels are noticeably higher in the former. This
observed indifference to a small impact might be taken as evidence
that small differences in radiation risks are acceptable.[28] Therefore,
by this reasoning the routine emissions from the nuclear power
plant, which are even less, could be taken to be acceptable to the
public in comparison to other common risks.

It is not, however, obvious that such risks are *negligible,* even if
it should turn out they are acceptable in some sense. An individual
may well choose not to avoid a risk because the act of avoidance is
itself inconvenient or costly, but policy planners may on the con-
trary be able to help the general public avoid such risks at a decreased total cost to society.

Small risks in and of themselves have not been taken to be negligible
in this book.

Appendix B: The Linear Extrapolation Problem

Even if low linear energy-transfer (LET) radiation (from electrons and
X rays) is taken to induce linear responses, some believe high linear
energy-transfer radiation (neutrons, alpha particles) could induce responses at rates in excess of the linear extrapolation.[29] Furthermore,
Seymour Abrahamson, among others, has contended that some biological
systems are extremely sensitive to low doses but are killed by doses commonly used in experiments from which extrapolations are made. This possibility is allied to the suggestion that extrapolations from the Hiroshima
and Nagasaki bombings underestimate the effects of latent cancers, because the survivors of the initial effects constitute a selected population:
some fragmentary evidence suggests, for example, that people entering
the Japanese cities after the explosions have a higher leukemia rate—from

---

[28] See Chauncey Starr, "Social Benefit Versus Technological Risk—What Is Our
Science Willing to Pay for Safety?" *Science* vol. 165 (19 September 1969) pp.
1232–1238.
[29] Karl Z. Morgan, *Science,* pp. 344–348; and Martin Brown, *Science,* pp. 348–
349.

residual radiation—in subsequent years than the bomb survivors themselves.[30]

Recently, it has been contended that a study of radiation workers in the United States shows a much higher instance of cancer than that expected in other populations.[31] However, others have contended that this new study contains serious statistical errors[32] and fails to control properly for other variables:[33] for example, it is conceivable that the radiation workers show a lower overall death rate than the general population, thus giving a *relatively* high cancer rate.

Some believe, moreover, that the linear approximation could be an overestimate. Repair mechanisms could be important, and low-dose rates could be less effective than high-dose rates.[34]

Also, routine doses are traditionally calculated "conservatively" (assuming ingestion that might not take place, and so on). On the other hand, the radon calculations used here have been roughly corrected for at least some of this effect.

According to William Russell, genetic effects—whatever their consequence—are likely to be linear.

[30] Joseph Rotblat, "The Puzzle of Absent Effects," *New Scientist* (25 August 1977) pp. 475–476.

[31] Thomas F. Mancuso, Alice Stewart, and George Kneale, "Radiation Exposures of Hanford Workers Dying from Cancer and Other Causes," *Health Physics* vol. 33, no. 5 (November 1977) pp. 369–385.

[32] Allen Brodsky, U.S. Nuclear Regulatory Commission, memorandum on "Comments on Published Version of Paper by Mancuso, Stewart, and Kneale" (12 January 1978).

[33] Leonard A. Sagan, "Low Level Radiation Effects: The Mancuso Study" (Palo Alto, Calif., Electric Power Research Institute, mimeo, 1978).

[34] U.S. Nuclear Regulatory Commission, *Reactor Safety Study*, append. IV, sect. 9.

4 Nuclear Reactor Accidents

How likely is a serious nuclear reactor accident?
Will future reactors be acceptably safe?
Are breeder reactors unsafe?

Nuclear energy in general is controversial, but one of the most passionately felt controversies of all has revolved around the question of accidents in nuclear reactors. Are reactors safe? The central issue stems from the awkward technical fact that the heating process generating power in nuclear plants is difficult to turn off. In case of operating problems, the main nuclear reaction in the uranium fuel can be stopped quickly, but the heat from waste products remains at a high level for long periods of time. This means that the nuclear fuel must be kept cooled, or else the metal-encased fuel rod will melt (a meltdown), releasing radioactive gases and clouds of particulates.

Naturally, precautions are taken against such an event. These are backup water supply systems to supply cooling in case of failure in the regular cooling systems that transport the heat used to generate steam. Nuclear power stations also have a large variety of other safety systems, designed to prevent a meltdown or to keep the radioactive gases from escaping into the atmosphere should a meltdown occur. Nevertheless, should the gases and particulates escape, the amount of radioactivity that would be spread about could be quite large, depending on how well the safety systems work.

Fortunately, such an accident has never happened. Unfortunately, this makes it difficult to analyze whether nuclear power plants are sufficiently safe. We must estimate the likelihood that such an accident would happen, guess at its consequences, and decide whether the risk is too great for the advantages of using nuclear power in the first place. Naturally, no such theoretical answer to the problem will ever satisfy the most demanding critics of nuclear energy. And one cannot pretend that theory is preferable to experiment. But even so, theory may be better than nothing.

Accidents and Predictions of Accidents

Nuclear power is unusual among modern technologies in that such a theoretical analysis does exist. Trying to clear up the doubts about safety that have clouded the future of nuclear electricity, the U.S. Atomic Energy Commission (AEC) and its successor, the Nuclear Regulatory Commission (NRC), issued in 1975 a complex mathematical study of the probabilities of nuclear reactor accidents.[1] Since no large accidents, and relatively few minor ones, have ever occurred, the study relied on estimates of the probability that each of the different pieces of equipment and various safety procedures in the plant might fail. All these individual probabilities were combined, as they might enter into the chances of nuclear meltdowns and other serious accidents, and numerical predictions of reactor safety were made.

The Reactor Safety Study, often called the Rasmussen report for Norman C. Rasmussen, the director of the study (see "A Note on the Rasmussen Report"), predicted that *on the average* the damages to health and property by radioactive contamination, as a result of nuclear reactor accidents on a year-in–year-out basis, would be small. Here, the word *small* means as compared with effects from naturally occurring radiation or with risks from coal-fired power plants. A range of estimates adapted from the Rasmussen results is shown in figure 4-1.[2] The predicted fatalities (ranging from 1 to 20) and illnesses (ranging from 20 to 200) are significantly larger than those predicted for normal operations (at least for short-lived isotopes). Still, the incidence of fatalities from nuclear reactor accidents is less than that for many other coal- and nuclear-related ones, such as

[1] See U.S. Nuclear Regulatory Commission, *Reactor Safety Study: An Assessment of Accident Risks in U.S. Commercial Nuclear Power Plants*, WASH-1400, NUREG-74/014 (Washington, October 1975). Nuclear safety is reviewed in William Ramsay, "Coal and Nuclear: Health and Environmental Costs" (Washington, Resources for the Future, August 1978) pp. 2-9–2-16.

[2] The derivation of the values—based on the U.S. Nuclear Regulatory Commission's *Reactor Safety Study* calculations—is discussed in Ramsay "Coal and Nuclear," and summarized there on p. 2-15. The uncertainties cited in the report represent radiation dose-response uncertainties only. Note that the final version of the report made some assumptions—a lesser relative effect for low-dose rates—that make it less conservative than the usual radiation dose calculation.

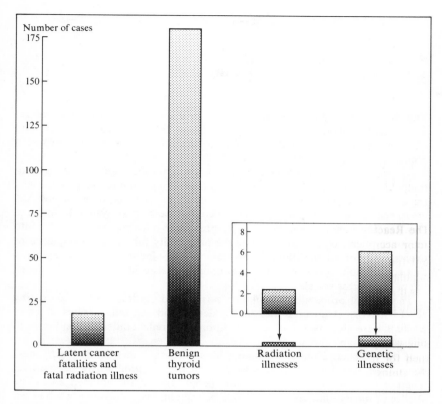

Figure 4-1. Estimates of fatalities and some illnesses that can be expected to occur as a result of nuclear power plant accidents, prorated per USW.

the fatal occupational diseases and accidents to coal workers (see chapter 9). The predicted incidence of nonfatal illnesses is also small as compared with coal-related illnesses.

What the average numbers shown in figure 4-1 fail to show is that most of the predicted effects do not stem from a series of small accidents happening all the time, but are a result of a number of medium-sized accidents that have a chance of happening with relative frequency, and a very few serious accidents that should happen very rarely indeed. The worst-case accident, for example, was predicted to kill some 3,000 people by acute radiation sickness and some 45,000 others by radiation-induced cancers over a period of years. The yearly probability of such an accident occurring in any one reactor was predicted, at the outside, as being only five chances in one billion. This turns out to be a very small risk when com-

A NOTE ON THE RASMUSSEN REPORT—
A THEORY OF NUCLEAR ACCIDENTS

The Reactor Safety Study calculated the probability that (1) a nuclear reactor accident would occur with a significant release of radioactivity, and
(2) the radioactivity would be carried to locations where it could expose a
population to possible health risks.

All possible components in the plant that might break down so as to eventually lead to such an accident were examined. For example, one possible way
for an accident to occur would be for a large pipe to break, then for both the
emergency core cooling system and the containment spray system to fail, and
then for the containment itself to be breached, releasing radioactivity into
the atmosphere. One must calculate the probability for this total sequence of
events, and for all the different possible events—including human errors—
that could lead to a core meltdown or other serious accident, such as the burst-
ing of the reactor vessel.

This type of probability calculation was carried out for two typical existing
reactors. Normal uncertainties in the design and the failure rates of components were also taken into account in order to reflect differing conditions in
one hundred typical reactors.

If the radioactive material gets outside the reactor, then its destructiveness
depends on whether the wind is blowing in the direction where people live,
whether there is rain, and how many people live in the affected area. The
chance of ninety different kinds of weather conditions occurring at each of six
representative sites was then calculated, taking into account local populations.

For example, the probabilities for a worst-case accident could be calculated
as follows:[3] (1) The probability of an accident occurring in each reactor in
which a substantial amount of radioactivity would be released was 5 in 1
million;[4] (2) the probability of the weather being unfavorable and exposing a
large population to the radioactivity was 1 in 1,000; (3) the chance of a
worst-case accident happening was then 5 out of 1 billion for each reactor-
year; and (4) the number of latent cancers inflicted on such a large population from such an amount of radiation would be 48,000; (5) this can be inter-
preted to mean that we "expect" only 0.0002 fatalities per reactor-year from
this worst-case accident.[5]

---

[3] Ford Foundation, *Nuclear Power Issues and Choices,* report of the Nuclear
Energy Policy Study Group, administered by MITRE Corporation (Cambridge,
Mass., Ballinger, 1977) p. 226.

[4] This figure (taken from ibid., p. 226) represents an upper bound, as estimated
in the U.S. Regulatory Commission's *Reactor Safety Study,* p. 90. The mean value
is 1 in 1 million.

[5] Ibid., p. 229.

pared with each citizen's chances of being struck by lightning, for example. But some people might think that the risks of a catastrophic accident happening only rarely are a somewhat different proposition—maybe worse, maybe better—than, for example, the few random deaths yearly caused by constant small leaks of radioactive material into the air near a power reactor. After all, normal radiation from reactors is uncertain in its effects because there is no answer to the question, *who* will be affected? Radiation from reactor accidents is doubly uncertain, because the answers are unknown to the questions, *When* might an accident happen? *How much* radiation might be emitted?

Other unknowns are troublesome as well. The effect of an accident would depend on the nature of the winds and rains that would carry the radioactive material from the plant and deposit it where it could do damage to the surrounding population. The Rasmussen report averaged out weather and population over a great number of sites. It is perfectly proper to average these factors out. But, as was pointed out in the recent Ford-MITRE study,[6] our future projections of accident hazards might be slightly more pessimistic if additional nuclear plants tended to be located closer to densely populated centers or, more likely, if rural areas around existing plants become more urbanized.

Critics and Catastrophes

Does the Rasmussen report solve all our questions regarding safety? Hardly. In the first place, even though the report has received approval in some quarters,[7] it has not gone without criticism elsewhere.[8] Various critics, who have maintained that the risks are underestimated, have disagreed as to whether they are underestimated by a factor of 10 or 100, or more.[9] Obviously, as we shall see in comparing these risks with the total risks for coal, the degree of understatement could be important. Perhaps these disagreements will be resolved by a comprehensive review of the

[6] Ford Foundation, *Nuclear Power Issues and Choices,* p. 231.

[7] As just one example, note the seal of approval given by the Australian AEC, as cited in *Nucleonics Week* (6 January 1977) p. 4.

[8] *Science* vol. 192 (25 June 1976) pp. 1312–1313.

[9] See Henry W. Kendall, "Nuclear Power Risks," a Review of the Report of the American Physical Society's Study Group on Light Water Reactor Safety (Cambridge, Mass., Union of Concerned Scientists, 18 June 1975); American Physical Society, "Report to the APS by the Study Group on Light-Water Reactor Safety," *Reviews of Modern Physics* vol. 47 (Summer 1975) suppl. 1; Ford Foundation, *Nuclear Power Issues;* H.-P. Balfanz, and P. Kafka, *Kritischer Bericht zur Reaktorsicherheitsstudie,* WASH-1400 (Critical Report on the Reactor Safety Study) IRS-

whole report that is presently planned.[10] In the meantime, it should be noted that a recent review of the subject, while exceedingly critical of many parts of the Rasmussen report, has calculated on actuarial grounds that the dangers of a nuclear reactor accident were, at most, equal to 500 times Rasmussen's value.[11] Five hundred times a minor impact turns out to be a larger but not overwhelming effect.

Naturally, any study is only as good as its data. And data problems exist. Critics have pointed out the great difficulty of estimating the probability that an event initiating an accident will occur.[12] Some possibilities are especially difficult to treat, such as a string of accident-causing events that occur together (see "A Note on The Rasmussen Report") and it could be that the study makes mistakes in this area.[13] The behavior of the Emergency Core Cooling Systems (ECCS) cannot really be tested until there is an actual accident. Some have thought that the cooling water would not actually penetrate into the overheated reactor core at the time of the accident; however, recent tests on this issue are encouraging if not conclusive.[14] We have also been witnesses to the drama of former employees of nuclear plant manufacturers or of the NRC publicly questioning the accepted reliability figures for components of subsystems.[15] And what about the effects that might have been omitted altogether, such as fires, similar to the serious one that occurred at a nuclear plant in 1975? True, the final Rasmussen report calculated that the inclusion of fires would not have changed the results very much.[16] But where there is one omission, could there not be more?

In view of such difficulties there is no reason to place overwhelming confidence in the Rasmussen report. On the other hand, no other detailed

---

I-87, MRR-I-65 (Cologne, Institut für Reaktorsicherheit der TÜV E.V., Laboratorium für Reaktorregelung und Anlagensicherung, April 1976); Christoph Hohennemser, Roger Kasperson, and Robert Kates, "The Distrust of Nuclear Power," *Science* vol. 196, no. 4285 (1 April 1977) pp. 25–34.

[10] See *Energy Daily* (19 August 1977) p. 4.

[11] See Ford Foundation, *Nuclear Power Issues,* p. 230. To be sure, this would be 3,000 fatalities per USW. Others might suggest considering the ten times greater experience we have with naval reactors, implying <300 per USW. For example, see Alvin M. Weinberg, "To Breed, or Not to Breed?" *Across the Board* (The Conference Board Magazine) vol. 14, no. 9 (September 1977) p. 18.

[12] American Physical Society, "Report," p. S-5.

[13] See Ford Foundation, *Nuclear Power Issues,* p. 228, for the contention that mistakes were made.

[14] *Nucleonics Week* (29 July 1976) p. 4.

[15] Hearings on the *Investigation of Charges Relating to Nuclear Reactor Safety,* before the Joint Committee on Atomic Energy, 94 Cong. 2 sess. (1976).

[16] U.S. Nuclear Regulatory Commission, *Reactor Safety Study,* pp. XI 2-4 and 3-53ff.

calculation exists, and critics have not convincingly established that Rasmussen has seriously underestimated the risks.[17] Therefore we accept here the Rasmussen estimates, as modified by modest error limits.[18] But if we give the Reactor Safety Study tentative credence, we should again emphasize that "the risk of a risk"—that is, a small risk that an accident will occur that would in turn cause a health risk—differs from an ordinary risk. A small risk of a catastrophe could look different—either worse to the apprehensive or better to the happy-go-lucky—than the more certain deaths of a given number of coal or uranium miners every year. Catastrophes are qualitatively different from routine small risks, and it is not irrational to view them as being so. Some possible catastrophes will never happen, but improbable events do occur. What was the chance, for instance, that two commercial aircraft would collide over the Grand Canyon? But that crash is now a part of the past, and therefore is recorded as a fact instead of as a very unlikely future happening. In other words, we do not *expect* a very improbable event, but we cannot be entirely surprised if it occurs: hence special human concerns about disasters.

A Psychological Note

One odd risk is that of public reaction to nuclear catastrophes. It is widely thought that if there were a large accident, resulting in deaths and injuries, public reaction would force a shutdown of all reactors.[19] If so, the resulting waste of resources would be an expensive unpaid cost of nuclear power.

The most interesting aspect of such a shutdown is that a nationwide reaction of this kind would be more surprising if the catastrophe were to involve hydroelectric power (a dam break) or an air pollution catastrophe related to coal-fired power. Naturally, there are generally differences in the nature of the health risks concerned for catastrophes involving the different technologies. Nevertheless, there may well be special aspects to the way the public perceives nuclear risks, even when those risks appear

[17] Even the Ford Foundation's *Nuclear Power Issues,* p. 229, suggests that some factors could vary in any direction, despite several faults that would produce underestimates. The criticisms in Balfanz and Kafka, *Kritischer Bericht,* are of uncertain consequence for overall probabilities.
[18] Error limits suggested in the U.S. Nuclear Power Commission's *Reactor Safety Study,* fig. VI 13-30–fig. 13-34.
[19] See Amory B. Lovins, *Soft Energy Paths: Toward a Durable Peace* (Cambridge, Friends of the Earth/Ballinger, 1977) p. 55. Although a critic, Lovins reflects common industry scuttlebutt. See also Weinberg, "To Breed," p. 19.

to be equivalent to other nonnuclear risks in type and magnitude. The reasons for such a special status are not clear, but anxieties related to nuclear war and to fears of radiation and radiation-related death have been suggested as possible motivations.[20] On the other hand, the unfamiliarity and newness of the nuclear power industry may play an important role, in that the public must learn to judge a whole array of potential consequences of a new technology.[21] Fragmentary evidence that unfamiliarity may be important has been observed in studies showing that people have more anxiety about a local nuclear plant if they live moderately close to the reactor site (several kilometers away) than in the immediate neighborhood (less than a kilometer away).[22] Unfortunately, it is not possible to tell whether such phenomena are indeed psychological, that is, irrational in nature, whether they represent a strong distaste for catastrophic risks, or whether they merely reflect a public skepticism as to the opinions (or capabilities) of nuclear experts. Furthermore, is such an attitude consistent with recent polls showing strong public support for developing nuclear technology?[23] If such special attitudes toward nuclear risks are important, they are fully as legitimate—though perhaps not as immutable—an unpaid cost of nuclear power as any other.[24] And such costs would become tangible in monetary terms if the occurrence of a catastrophic accident led to a lengthy or even permanent shutdown of all reactors in the United States.

Safer Reactors?

What could be done to improve reactor safety? A significant amount of money already goes into research and regulation to improve safety by preventing and mitigating the results of accidents in nuclear power plants.

[20] See Philip D. Pahner, *A Psychological Perspective of the Nuclear Energy Controversy,* RM-76-67 (Laxenburg, Austria, International Institute for Applied Systems Analysis, August 1976) p. 7.

[21] See Helga Nowotny, *Social Aspects of the Nuclear Power Controversy,* RM-76-33 (Laxenburg, Austria, International Institute for Applied Systems Analysis, April 1976) p. 10.

[22] See R. Maderthaner, P. Pahner, G. Guttman, and H. J. Otway, *Perception of Technological Risks: The Effect of Confrontation,* Research Memorandum RM-76-53 (Laxenburg, Austria, International Institute for Applied Systems Analysis, June 1976) p. 11.

[23] See, for example, Atomic Industrial Forum, Inc., "Report on Public Understanding of Nuclear Energy," *INFO* no. 110 (September 1977).

[24] See Maderthaner and coauthors, *Perception.*

Expenses for extra standby safety systems are already large. For example, the ECCS required within the last few years for all plants have inevitably added to the cost of nuclear electricity. Every new problem that arises, from cracking of the stainless steel pipes that carry the essential cooling water,[25] to fires in so-called flame-resistant materials that can paralyze control circuits, leads to new and improved safety regulations and therefore to new costs. But there is a question of how much safety can be improved in any pressurized system in a cost-effective manner. Not to mention the problem of the "reliability" of the human beings that run the system; automation can help to alleviate this latter problem but cannot do away with it entirely.

It would help if we were sure that the safety level of new reactors was the same or better than that of the Rasmussen calculation. The Rasmussen results depend on the actual finished engineering of the two reactors studied in detail. Almost every individual reactor—at least up to now—has been a new and different engineering creation, even if the differences have sometimes been minor. Each reactor receives an exceedingly thorough safety review, but even so, the lack of homogeneity means that the Rasmussen results do not necessarily apply to all reactors at all sites. If each plant were to be analyzed separately in the Rasmussen style, the expense would be enormous, since it is unlikely that the detailed calculation can be carried out from blueprints alone.

If a point of sharply diminishing marginal returns has been reached in safety systems, it still should be possible to increase safety levels by siting nuclear power plants farther away from population centers. It has been suggested that plants be sited underground. Unfortunately, there are drawbacks to these solutions. If a small cloud of radioactivity were released just west of Fort Worth and blown eastward by the wind, the individual dose would fall off with distance, but the widening cloud would include more people; therefore, the impacts in both Fort Worth *and* Dallas would be important,[26] even though the site would be relatively "remote" from Dallas. Underground siting promises to be costly and is good only

[25] See, for example, U.S. Congress, Joint Committee on Atomic Energy, *Investigation of Charges*.

[26] According to the way in which radiation calculations are usually done, remote siting does not help solve the primary problem (latent cancers) if populations in the far neighborhood of the site are still large, because the product of dose times persons remains relatively large. [See chap. 3 of this volume; and R. Niehaus, J. J. Cohen, and H. J. Otway, *The Cost-Effectiveness of Remote Nuclear Reactor Siting*, RM-76-34 (Laxenburg, Austria, International Institute for Applied Systems Analysis, April 1976)].

to the extent that the radioactivity released cannot penetrate to the sur-face—a question of some uncertainty.[27] But it would be difficult to achieve levels of safety high enough to satisfy some conceivable standards without moving nuclear power plants to the North Pole, or at least to isolated islands in the Pacific—as indeed has been proposed in recent futuristic studies.[28]

All this legitimately raises the question of how safe is safe enough. As we have seen with coal, it is notoriously difficult to pursue any human ac-tivity without risks. Usually we have to balance risks against benefits, and on this basis the Rasmussen results seem reassuring. But the catastrophic possibilities involved suggest that improving the estimates of nuclear acci-dent risks be given high research priority.

Subsidies and Risks

Is the electricity-using public paying for the possible costs of nuclear catastrophes? This question comes up because if an electric utility has a serious accident in one of its nuclear power plants, its liability is restricted by law—currently to $560 million—under the Price-Anderson Act.[29] Comparing this liability restriction to the probable losses from an accident could give an indirect indication of the value of the unpaid costs of nuclear accidents.

There is also the related implied question that has excited public in-terest in this law: that is, if nuclear reactors are so safe, why does the nuclear industry need a special dispensation against liability? This is a good question, and the Rasmussen study was designed to answer it. The answer seems to have an Alice in Wonderland quality in that the report concluded that the limitation was justifiable because the accidents were so

[27] For an optimistic view, see American Physical Society, "Report," pp. S-110 and S-111.

[28] Wolf Haefele, ed., *Second Status Report of the IIASA Project on Energy Systems, 1975,* Research Report RR-76-1 (Laxenburg, Austria, International Institute for Applied Systems Analysis, 1976); and Cesare Marchetti, "Geoengineering and the Energy Island," in *Second Status Report of the IIASA Project on Energy Systems 1975,* RR 76-1 (Laxenburg, Austria, International Institute for Applied Systems Analysis, 1976), pp. 219–244.

[29] See Ramsay, "Coal and Nuclear," append. D, for a review. Also see U.S. Congress, House, Subcommittee on Energy and the Environment of the Committee on Interior and Insular Affairs, *Oversight Hearings on Nuclear Energy—The Price-Anderson Nuclear Indemnity Act,* 94 Cong. 1 sess. (December 1975) Ser. 94-16, pt. V.

unlikely that no limitation was needed! Therefore, if we accept the Rasmussen results as reliable for an estimate of reactor accident dangers, clearly we have to accept the implication that Price-Anderson liability limitation is not a serious problem. Prorated costs would be less than $40,000 per reactor every year,[30] or about 1 cent on the "monthly electric bill." We would infer higher estimates of risk from the premiums now actually being charged to utilities (for the $125 million for which they *are* liable). But even on the basis of such risk estimates, the effective subsidy for higher liabilities would still be small, representing an unpaid cost of, say, 6 cents on the "monthly electric bill."[31] But again, the billed cost of an *actual* catastrophic accident in any given year would be more like $28, or $25 billion for 1 USW.[32]

The Breeder and Plutonium

Is there a breeder reactor economy in the U.S. for the future? It is difficult to tell. But it may be mildly reassuring to realize that safety problems are likely no worse for the breeder than for ordinary LWRs.[33] Some new instability problems do arise that could conceivably lead to large releases of energy and radiation, because each gram of fuel contains a relatively large number of active (fissionable) atoms. The liquid metal breeder (LMFBR) that has been under development in the United States would also have problems involving the corrosive, extremely chemically active metal sodium that is used to transfer heat from the reactor to the steam generator. On the other hand, the sodium is not under pressure, so that it is easier to avoid the sudden losses of the cooling liquid that can occur in

[30] See the U.S. Nuclear Regulatory Commission's *Reactor Safety Study,* p. XI 4-1, and fig. VI 13-36.

[31] Taking the "real" premium for large accidents as $200,000 per 1-GW plant [see Ramsay, "Coal and Nuclear," append. D; and Hearings on *H. R. 8631: To Amend and Extend the Price–Anderson Act,* before the Joint Committee on Atomic Energy, 94 Cong. 1 sess. (1975) p. 31] and $1 million per plant-year = 34 cents on the "monthly bill" (see chap. 2 of this volume, append. B).

[32] The equivalent of about $25 billion in damages and health liability attributed to one worst-case accident in one year would be $28 on every monthly bill of *all* residential electricity users in the United States all year (U.S. Regulatory Commission's *Reactor Safety Study,* tab. 5-4, p. 89). For the costing basis, see chap. 2 of this volume, append. B.

[33] See Ramsay, "Coal and Nuclear," pp. 2–25ff.; Ford Foundation, *Nuclear Power Issues,* p. 242; and U.S. Congress, Joint Economic Committee, *The Fast Breeder Reactor Decision: An Analysis of Limits and the Limits of Analysis.* Study prepared by Mark Sharefkin. 94 Cong. 2 sess. (Washington, GPO, April 19, 1976).

ordinary pressurized LWRs. Safety concerns for the LMFBR could turn out to be similar in degree, if not in kind, to those for LWRs.

Other new types of accidents might occur within the other parts of the plutonium economy, however. The reprocessing plants that separate the plutonium from the spent uranium fuel could be hazardous. Sudden, large accidental releases of the radioactive wastes in the fuel are not likely to occur during reprocessing; in fact, official predictions of possible accidents show that the probability is small that even one death in such an accident would occur[34]—which would have little impact if the occurrence of the accident is improbable also. There has been some public concern about the handling and shipment of plutonium in general, because— judging from large doses given in animal experiments—even small quantities of plutonium are carcinogenic if inhaled into the lungs. But it has been estimated that only a small amount of plutonium and related elements would be released during normal operations from a large breeder reactor fuel cycle.[35] And it has been argued that in practice much more plutonium than the microgram quantities sometimes quoted would have to be initially dispersed in order to be ultimately inhaled by human lungs and cause cancer.[36] Even if such estimates were correct, some claim that plutonium is still a critical safety hazard when it is deposited nonuniformly in the lung. Such a *hot particle* theory is possible, but there is little convincing evidence to back it up.[37] This is not to say that all these plutonium problems might not turn out to be more severe than we think. We would be dealing with a new kind of technology, one we do not fully understand. But based on what we know at present, and assuming prudent design, only the level of concern appropriate for any technology having certain obvious risks seems called for.[38] And it is fair to also take into account that the use of a breeder would reduce the expected number of yearly fatalities from uranium mining and milling operations.

[34] See U.S. Atomic Energy Commission, *Draft Environmental Statement: Liquid Metal Fast Breeder Reactor Program*, WASH-1535 (Washington, GPO, March 1974) p. 4.1-5.

[35] *Ibid.*, table 4.4.9.1.2.

[36] See Bernard L. Cohen, "The Hazards in Plutonium Dispersal" (Oak Ridge, Tenn., Institute for Energy Analysis, March 1975).

[37] See U.S. Energy Research and Development Administration, *Liquid Metal Fast Breeder Reactor Program*, ERDA-1535, Final Environmental Statement (Washington, GPO, December 1975) 3 vols.

[38] The shipment of plutonium by airplane has been restricted over the past two years. The dangers probably are not great. On the other hand, what were the benefits of shipping the material by air instead of by surface transport? Any extra risk would have been excessive if the benefits gained were trivial.

Conclusion

Even though no catastrophic accidents have taken place, there is an inherent danger of serious, accidental radioactive emissions from nuclear power plants. A large theoretical study has calculated that risks from this problem are small—*on the average*—as compared with other electricity-related risks. Although the Rasmussen study is not above criticism,[39] pending further investigation the results constitute a reassuring best estimate of the risk of nuclear accidents. We must also recognize that there is always the chance that a fairly large catastrophe will occur; it is a legitimate value choice to view such a risk as worse than a noncatastrophic risk.

There is no compelling reason to expect dramatic improvements in the safety of reactors. Breeders and plutonium economies introduce some new safety problems—such as dangers of cancer from inhalation of plutonium and of a more dangerous type of reactor accident—but they may eliminate or reduce other problems, such as other specific types of reactor accidents and part of the impacts connected with the uranium mining and milling industry.

[39] U.S. Nuclear Regulatory Commission, *Reactor Safety Study*.

5   *The Nuclear Waste Problem*

Is radioactive waste disposal the ultimate nuclear problem?

Is the job of protecting future generations an impossible one?

For more than a decade, the U.S. Department of Energy, and the former U.S. Energy Research and Development Administration (ERDA) and the U.S. Atomic Energy Commission (AEC) have been trying to find an acceptable way to dispose of the waste products from nuclear power technology. In chapter 3, we have considered some of the lesser-known waste problems associated with gases emitted during normal nuclear operations, but there are, of course, many other kinds of wastes associated with nuclear power. The most politically troublesome waste problems have been concerned either with the spent reactor fuel itself or the liquid or solid residues from fuel reprocessing. The key difficulty with the fuel is that it contains plutonium and related elements that have very long half-lives, typically some tens or hundreds of thousands of years. This means that the method of disposal has to be relatively fail-safe, unless we intend to oblige future generations to act as custodians for our nuclear trash. One complication stems from the fact that the radioactive decay still going on in the spent fuel makes the wastes literally hot and, therefore, places heat-dissipation demands on any kind of permanent storage system.

Until 1971, the AEC's plan had been to solidify the liquid wastes from the fuel reprocessing and to place them underground in the middle of salt formations.[1] As it turned out, geologists and engineers were somewhat uncertain about the long-term prospects for isolation of wastes in the Lyons, Kansas, location chosen for a trial waste-disposal site, and some Kansans were even more uncertain about whether they wanted a waste-

---

[1] The waste disposal problem is briefly reviewed in William Ramsay, "Coal and Nuclear: Health and Environmental Costs," (Washington, Resources for the Future, August 1978) chap. 2.

disposal site in their state. In the light of such difficulties with geologic storage, emphasis then shifted to storing the waste temporarily—that is, for fifty to one hundred years—in concrete bunkers in the desert, presumably to await the later development of better techniques for permanent disposal. Subsequently, interest in the salt-bed disposal scheme picked up again. Now all that may change once more. The Carter administration has worked actively to prevent the reprocessing of nuclear fuel, so that plutonium will not be recovered and made potentially available for theft or other diversion into nuclear weapons. However, it could turn out that the nation will eventually need the plutonium for extra energy production, especially if the plutonium-fueled breeder reactor becomes essential. Consequently, policymakers now look more favorably on the idea of storing the fuel in some location above or below ground so that it can be retrieved later to reprocess fuel, thus salvaging plutonium and uranium.[2]

One consequence of all this backing and filling is that the public may now have an impression that the waste problem is impossible to solve. Indeed, this problem of waste disposal has recently shown signs, both in the United States and in Europe, of becoming *the* nuclear issue. This current notoriety is probably fed by the fact that these wastes are exceedingly noxious and must be kept isolated for very long periods of time. Consequently, at least one facet of the public's concern with safe, long-term storage is apparently justified.

The Hazards of Storage

If spent fuel wastes are stored at the surface, they must be cooled by water or air for many decades until the heat from decaying elements has abated. As long as the cooling system works and the wastes are isolated from the surrounding environment, there is no reason to feel that they are a health hazard to the public. After all, spent fuel is presently being stored temporarily at each reactor site, with the fuel rods immersed in pools of water. This present system is perhaps inelegant, but it would be surprising if this kind of local storage could not be continued safely over the next decades,[3] or at least until such time as a permanent solution has been found for the waste problem.

[2] Hearings on *Storage and Disposal of Radioactive Waste,* before the Joint Committee on Atomic Energy, 94 Cong. 1 sess. (1975) pp. 16ff.

[3] One must assume that the metal rods encasing the uranium fuel retain their integrity.

Eventually, of course, there should probably be some kind of permanent storage. In fact, it is conceivable that a geologic storage system could also be retrievable over some time period, so that we as a society could change our mind about the use of spent fuel in future years. Storage in salt beds is not the only possibility; rock formations, ice caps, and the ocean floor have all been proposed as storage areas. Even shooting off the wastes somewhere into outer space has had its proponents. All these systems have their advantages and disadvantages, but they all can take advntage of one common fact—the total volume of fuel wastes is really not that large. This fact is not well understood in the public debate on the waste issue. If all the uranium thought to be available in the United States (say, 1.7 million tons) were to be used up as fuel, the total amount of spent fuel would probably be less than 95,000 cubic meters (m³).[4] Such a volume could easily be contained, for example, in the extensive, but not gargantuan space occupied by the offices of the Department of Energy at Germantown, Maryland.[5] Size is relevant to the problem, because it means that it is possible to use fairly expensive means—that is, expensive per unit volume or weight—to secrete the wastes in locations far removed from possible contact with human beings. Calculations show that the possibility is very slight for wastes leaking into local water tables or for contaminating future prospectors drilling for some mineral or other in the year A.D. 20,000.[6] Nuclear planners also have been heartened by the discovery of a former naturally occurring nuclear reactor at Oklo, Gabon, that was created some millions of years ago by accidental leakage of water into a uranium deposit.[7] One worry with nuclear waste is whether it will move or be carried from its disposal location. But at this West African

[4] If reprocessing took place, this would be 11,000 m³. For data on resources, see Ford Foundation, *Nuclear Power Issues and Choices,* report of the Nuclear Energy Policy Study Group, administered by MITRE Corporation (Cambridge, Mass., Ballinger, 1977) p. 81. For data on amounts of fuel and waste, see U.S. Atomic Energy Commission (AEC), *Generic Environmental Statement on the Use of Recycle Plutonium in Mixed Oxide Fuel in LWRs (GESMO)* WASH-1327 (Washington, AEC, August 1974) p. S-25; and U.S. Nuclear Regulatory Commission (NRC), *Final Generic Environmental Statement on the Use of Recycle Plutonium in Mixed Oxide Fuel in Light Water Cooled Reactors: Health, Safety and Environment* [NUREG-0002 (Washington, NRC, August 1976) pp. IV H-18 and IV H-19].

[5] We assume that 360,000 ft² of offices, halls, auditoriums, and so forth, is about 100,000 m³.

[6] See Bernard L. Cohen, *Environmental Hazards in High-Level Radioactive Waste Disposal,* preprint (Pittsburgh, Pa., University of Pittsburgh, 1975); and "The Disposal of Radioactive Wastes from Fission Reactors," *Scientific American* vol. 236, no. 6 (June 1977) pp. 21–31.

[7] See Cyril L. Comar and Leonard A. Sagan, "Plutonium: Facts and Inferences," *EPRI Journal* no. 9 (November 1976) pp. 20–24.

site, the plutonium produced in the reaction appears to have moved less than a fraction of an inch in all that time.

Critics of nuclear power have stressed that such calculations could be seriously wrong.[8] They say that if the strontium 90 produced in one year of spent fuel were to be dispersed into river basins all over the country, it would be enough to contaminate the annual freshwater runoff of the United States to several times the acceptable limits.[9] But this fact only reinforces the requirement that we should not disperse the wastes in a careless manner. More to the point, there seems to be no absolute guarantee that future societies would not drill down to waste depositories by accident or that future, unanticipated geological events would not release the wastes into the environment. All that can be done is to examine whether such risks are reasonably small. Also, it is true that until the detailed design of final waste-storage plans has been carried out, some unknowns will remain. If no reprocessing ever takes place, existing schemes for permanently storing the waste portions of the fuel might have to be adapted to an increased loading of plutonium, much larger proportions of uranium, and, eventually, the decay products of uranium.[10] It seems plausible that such schemes as disposal of wastes into salt beds that are isolated and have been in place for long geologic periods will still turn out to be low-risk solutions.[11] Indeed, one recent model calculation predicts, under fairly general assumptions, that the most critical radioisotopes in spent fuel or wastes could be contained in geologic storage so that, even if some water intruded and the waste-containment package failed, radiation standards for drinking water on the surface could be effectively satisfied.[12]

We should also be aware that not all disposal possibilities have been explored. If all else fails, it might be possible to store the wastes temporarily until their relatively high levels of short-lived radiation die down,

[8] Critics of Cohen's, *Environmental Hazards* have been numerous. See, for example, Frank Von Hippel, Letter, *Physics Today* vol. 29, no. 8 (August 1976) pp. 66–68; Robert O. Pohl, "Radioactive Pollution from the Nuclear Power Industry," *ASHRAE Journal* (September 1976), and Letter, *Physics Today* vol. 29, no. 11 (November 1976) pp. 13–14; see also Bernard L. Cohen, Letter, *Physics Today* vol. 29, no. 11 (November 1976) pp. 87–90.

[9] See Natural Resources Defense Council, as quoted in *Wall Street Journal* (26 July 1976).

[10] Volumes will also be somewhat larger (see fn. 4).

[11] See testimony of Dr. John C. Frey in *Radioactive Waste Management,* Hearings before the Subcommittee on Environment and Safety of the Joint Committee on Atomic Energy, 94 Cong. 2 sess. (May 1976) p. 163.

[12] G. De Marsily, E. Ledoux, A. Barbreau, and J. Margat, "Nuclear Waste Disposal: Can the Geologist Guarantee Isolation?" *Science* vol. 197, no. 4303 (5 August 1977) pp. 519–527. If the glass matrix containing the waste held, the expected levels would be even lower.

and then to dilute them by a factor of 1 part in 10,000 of earth or concrete. This mixture would then have less than the normal amount of radioactivity that occurs in many ordinary rock formations.[13]

As with the problem of gaseous wastes, the extent of our obligation to future generations cannot be sidestepped. It may be that we should ask for a much lower than usual level of risk in waste hazards and should reduce the chance for error—if necessary, by extraordinary and relatively expensive means.[14] Even so, lower risk levels could probably be achieved more easily for spent fuel than for the gaseous wastes radon and carbon 14, which seem to suffer from relative neglect (see chapter 3).[15] The gaseous wastes are present realities, while the impacts from fuel wastes are hypothetical future possibilities.

Other Waste Problems

Besides the high-level wastes just considered, and the gaseous wastes described in chapter 3, there is a large body of so-called low-level wastes—miscellaneous materials from the nuclear industry that are contaminated with radioisotopes. These wastes have included in the past very long-lived elements, but they will no longer be included under present plans.[16] Past methods of burying these wastes have not always been adequate. It was hoped that the burial sites would prevent the migration of radiation outside the site for hundreds of years; instead, at the storage area at Maxey Flats, Kentucky, radioactivity has been detected outside the burial site within ten years or less after burial.[17] Even though radiation levels at some monitoring stations were orders of magnitude above background radiation

[13] See Karl H. Puechl, "The Nuclear Waste Problem in Perspective," *Nuclear Engineering International* vol. 20, no. 236 (November 1975) pp. 950–954.

[14] See Gene I. Rochlin, "Nuclear Waste Disposal: Two Social Criteria," *Science* vol. 195 (7 January 1977) pp. 23–31.

[15] Compare this with the testimony of Charles Hebel in *Nuclear Waste Management,* Oversight Hearings, before the Subcommittee on Energy and the Environment of the House Committee on Interior and Insular Affairs, 95 Cong. 1 sess., Ser. No. 95-15 (1977) p. 9.

[16] See U.S. Nuclear Regulatory Commission, Task Force on Review of the Federal/State Program for Regulation of the Commercial Low-Level Radioactive Waste Burial Grounds, "Low Level Waste Disposal," *Federal Register* 42 (10 March 1977) 13366. Another possible waste problem involves the metal sheath (cladding) that forms the rod holding the fuel, which must also be disposed of separately—but only if reprocessing takes place.

[17] See testimony of Roger Strelow in *Storage and Disposal of Radioactive Waste,* Hearings before the Joint Committee on Atomic Energy, 94 Cong. 1 sess. (1975) p. 70.

levels, there was said to be no measurable danger to the public health.[18] However, the burial ground will be shut down for two years for safety evaluation studies.[19] Since such problems have come up, some general changes in current burial practices, such as reducing the volume of the wastes by compaction, might be worth considering.[20]

One troubling problem is still over the horizon but approaching fairly fast as these things go. We can expect an appreciable number of nuclear facilities to be retired before the end of the century, but what is to be done with obsolete plants? Certainly, they cannot be turned into community centers, since the levels of radiation would be much too high from the left-over reactor vessels and equipment alone. Various possibilities for dealing with the problem exist: the old facilities could merely be guarded, they could be mothballed, completely or totally dismantled, or entombed in concrete. The rub here is that the wastes cannot be conveniently placed thousands of feet below impermeable rock strata in the deserts of New Mexico, but will typically have to be dealt with in place, sometimes in the exurbs of our cities. Costs of this are small but not insignificant: one utility has recently proposed that $1 million per year be collected in order to build up a multimillion-dollar fund for eventually burying or entombing the reactor.[21] Estimated average costs per reactor range from several million dollars (for mothballing) to tens of millions (for complete dismantling).[22] Land use would also be affected since the site would presumably be closed permanently to other uses. On a plant-by-plant basis, perhaps only 100 acres or so would be required; but the eventual cumulative result might be less negligible.

Predicted waste-disposal *costs* are not high, as compared with other costs of electricity. And we should realize that the projection of low costs

---

[18] See U.S. Congress, Subcommittee on Environment and Safety of the Joint Committee on Atomic Energy, *Radioactive Waste Management,* pp. 263 and 267.

[19] See *Nucleonics Week* (29 September 1977) p. 4.

[20] See National Research Council, National Academy of Sciences, *The Shallow Land Burial of Low-Level Radioactively Contaminated Solid Waste* (Washington, National Academy of Sciences, 1976) p. XV.

[21] See *Coal News* (19 November 1976).

[22] See U.S. General Accounting Office (GAO), Comptroller General of the United States, *Cleaning Up the Remains of Nuclear Facilities—A Multibillion Dollar Problem,* B-164052, EMD-77-46 (Washington, GAO, 16 June 1977), p. 14, which gives, for example, a $2.8 million capital charge for mothballing, plus $210,-000 yearly for security surveillance; and $39 million is quoted as a maximum total cost for complete dismantling. Discounting the surveillance charged from thirty years into the indefinite future at 5 percent, one has a total of $7 million for the minimum case. Assuming a thirty-year lifetime, the yearly sinking fund charge at 5 percent is $110,000 and $590,000, respectively, per plant, or 4 cents and 20 cents on the "monthly electric bill" (see chap. 2 of this volume).

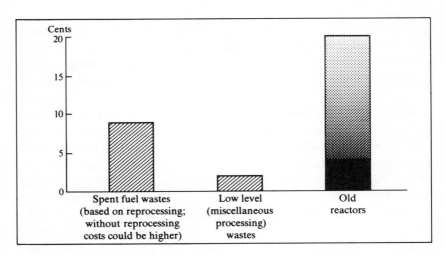

Figure 5-1. Estimated costs of fuel and low-level nuclear waste and old reactor disposal, in terms of extra charges hypothetically added to the average "monthly electric bill" (1 cent added to each bill totals approximately $9 million per USW). Data are taken from footnotes 22 and 23; and also Ramsay, "Coal and Nuclear," chap. 2.

could imply that much more money could be spent, if necessary, on refining methods of disposal. Figure 5-1 shows the proportion between waste costs and other costs for schemes developed at the time that it was still an accepted policy to reprocess nuclear fuels to reclaim the uranium and plutonium.[23] New costs for spent-fuel disposal without reprocessing could be higher, but probably not much so. In fact, decommissioning costs probably will be higher than fuel disposal costs. Presumably all these costs—approximately $100 million to $300 million per USW—will be added to individual electric bills.

Conclusion

Nuclear fuel wastes could conceivably present a difficult problem for society. But the wastes, although they are relatively hard to handle and

[23] See U.S. Congress, Joint Committee on Atomic Energy, *Storage and Disposal,* p. 52, which quotes 0.03 plus 0.01 mills per kilowatt-hour for high-level or transuranic, and 0.01 mills for low-level wastes. At 0.450 mills per dollar on the "monthly electric bill," these costs would then amount to 9 cents and 2 cents, respectively, on the "monthly electric bill."

remain radioactive for millennia, are still not very extensive in volume. It seems very plausible, if not provable, that the problem can be solved at reasonable cost to electricity users and with reasonable safety to future generations. The decommissioning of old reactors may eventually become a more serious undertaking, in that it involves both relatively substantial clean-up costs and a permanent use of land.

6 Nuclear Weapons and Energy Use

Does nuclear power contribute to the likelihood of nuclear war?

Are we putting ourselves at the mercy of nuclear terrorists?

National Nuclear Arsenals

Proliferation—the spread of nuclear weapons capabilities to other nations—is a complex problem, mixing elements of nuclear power with international politics and the arms race. After World War II, the United States proposed international controls on nuclear energy, but on terms that were unacceptable to the USSR. In the 1950s, after the achievement of the H-bomb by both the United States and the USSR, the United States tried to encourage international regulation—as opposed to control—of nuclear energy as part of an Atoms for Peace program of international nuclear development. Out of this effort arose a multinational organization, the International Atomic Energy Agency (IAEA), which now regulates a great deal of international nuclear activity from its headquarters in Vienna. When France and China got the bomb in the early 1960s, many saw this as a sign that shortly many other nations would have nuclear weapons. This feeling provided a major part of the impetus for the nuclear Nonproliferation Treaty (NPT) that was signed in 1970. This binds treaty nations not to acquire nuclear weapons, and it also allows the IAEA to carry out fairly detailed inspections in order to check on a nation's use of uranium fuel.

Two things have lately reawakened alarm about nuclear proliferation. One was India's explosion of a "peaceful nuclear device" in 1974. The other is the worldwide upsurge of nuclear power use and the realization that all power plants produce plutonium at the same time that they produce electricity—plutonium that can be used to make weapons. It is true that the spent fuel must be chemically reprocessed in order to separate out the plutonium. But reprocessing technology is also spreading. Both technologies facilitate the making of bombs (see "A Note on Nuclear Proliferation and Technologies").[1] Many see this trend toward an expanded use of nuclear power as a serious threat to world peace and, indeed, to the preservation of civilization.

International Impasse and U.S. Policy

What can be done to discourage nuclear proliferation? Almost everyone agrees that the IAEA programs auditing the flow of nuclear fuel should be strengthened. It may also be a good idea to encourage as many nations as possible to ratify the Nonproliferation Treaty.[2] But since the treaty does not provide effective penalties should a nation break or merely resign from it—as is allowed—these measures are probably not adequate by any standards. Western nations that supply nuclear fuel and produce nuclear power plants and other systems have been negotiating together informally for several years on setting possible restrictions on exports of power plants and fuel to other countries. The United States itself has always been opposed to the export of enrichment or reprocessing plants.

The latest U.S. policy endorses more radical cures. President Carter has proposed that the use of plutonium in the United States be postponed indefinitely. If plutonium is to be used at all in the rest of the world, the United States will apparently favor internationalization of its use.[3] But the U.S. government would evidently prefer to supply low-enriched uranium for fuel to other countries, thus removing entirely the need for a plutonium economy.[4]

[1] The nuclear proliferation issue is reviewed in William Ramsay, "Coal and Nuclear: Health and Environmental Costs," (Washington, Resources for the Future, August 1978) chap. 3.

[2] Some would argue that the treaty binds the nuclear weapons states to effect technology transfers to other NPT parties; therefore, perhaps it would be better in a legalistic sense to avoid that obligation by discouraging those states that insist on reprocessing from ratifying the NPT.

[3] See Executive Office of the President, Office of the White House Press Secretary, "Statement by the President on Nuclear Power Policy," press release (Washington, 7 April 1977).

[4] Executive Office of the President, Energy Policy and Planning, *The National Energy Plan* (Washington, GPO, 29 April 1977) pp. 70–71.

A NOTE ON NUCLEAR PROLIFERATION AND TECHNOLOGIES

Some of the technical areas related to proliferation are described below.

Reprocessing. Reprocessing is the act of separating out the uranium and plutonium from spent fuels by chemical processes that are relatively simple in principle. Reprocessing is optional, and little has been carried out for light water reactors (LWRs), but it is a necessity for breeders.

Enrichment. Enrichment is a process of sifting out the "filler" U-238 atoms from the fissile U-235 atoms in normal uranium so that the mixture is rich enough to start a nuclear reaction. Enrichment can produce fuels solely for reactors, or fuel for reactors and for weapons. Up until now most enrichment has been done by a very elaborate (and traditionally secret) process called gaseous diffusion. A simpler, but still formidable process, utilizing a centrifuge, will probably become more popular in the future. Even easier processes, using nozzles that spray uranium against a circular wall instead of using a centrifuge and lasers (which are sensitive to the miniscule chemical difference between U-238 and U-235), have not yet been proved, but they could make enrichment (regrettably?) easy to carry out.

Fuels. Ordinary LWRs use a low-enriched fuel (about 3 percent U-235 and 97 percent U-238) which is useless for bombs, at least without further enrichment.

Breeder fuel uses about 20 percent plutonium (instead of U-235) in 80 percent U-238. The use of this fuel for a bomb is marginal, but still conceivable. But the plutonium could be reprocessed out of the mixture for better weapons-building. Shipments of the plutonium portion by itself would be much more worrisome, both for proliferation and for terrorist diversion.

Reactors, Plutonium, and Weapons

Will these actions by the United States make any difference? First, can the United States alone discourage the growth of a world plutonium economy? Perhaps so. The United States is a leading supplier of nuclear facilities and technology and the dominant supplier of enriched uranium fuel to the non-Communist world. Therefore, it can exert pressure directly on potential nuclear states and also indirectly influence other Western countries that are suppliers of nuclear know-how. It can, of course, exert in its foreign policy other types of pressure on the rest of the world. Naturally, because many other nations face more severe long-term energy problems than we do, they may be willing to resist American influence on this question. Nevertheless, it would be surprising if U.S. initiatives were to have no effect at all. The question is, How much influence will the United States have?

Even if the United States and other nuclear supplier nations were to refuse to supply technology, facilities, and fuel, could not new nations build their own enrichment or reprocessing facilities without help? The difficulties are not negligible in starting an independent national nuclear program—perhaps one including weapons—in a lesser-developed country. Brazil and Pakistan have strongly protested U.S. pressures on European suppliers to cancel contracts that supply them with nuclear reprocessing or enrichment facilities. Even a more economically developed nation, South Africa, expressed public concern about the U.S. refusal to provide equipment for their commercial enrichment plant and about possible U.S. pressure on European manufacturers.[5] Even so, a completely independent national nuclear effort is by no means inconceivable, even for lesser-developed nations.

At any rate, is the mere existence of a commercial nuclear power "plutonium economy" in the world a significant factor in proliferation? Nations that have developed weapons in the past have done so through special nuclear production reactors or by reprocessing fuel from research reactors in a clandestine way. Uranium can even be enriched with laboratory-style equipment. Material can also be bought or stolen from the weapons programs of other countries; for example, it was reported that Libya was at one time in the market for a nuclear weapon.[6] Some have argued that those methods of procurement are much easier and

---

[5] See *The New York Times* (30 April 1977) p. 1.
[6] See the *Los Angeles Times* (5 May 1975) p. 2.

cheaper than obtaining plutonium from power reactors.[7] That may be so. It may even be true that fabricating weapons and getting aircraft or missiles to carry the bombs would be much harder to achieve than the gathering of plutonium or uranium. Nevertheless, it might be significant that the governments of the world are not typically directed by impersonal analysts able to plan ahead over considerable periods of time. The politics and emotions of the moment tend to be important in decisions, and timing and availability can be all-important. Indeed, some have suggested that one of the key principles of preventing the national diversion of nuclear materials is that the activities intrinsic to civilian nuclear programs should be as distinct as possible from activities that the country would have to undertake to produce nuclear weapons.[8] If plutonium is readily available without special forethought, it is ipso facto much easier for a nation to carry out any quick decision to develop nuclear weapons. It is also a fact that commercial power reactors in a plutonium economy are the only means of having large amounts of plutonium available without any previous planning. It is this casual buildup in supplies of nuclear bomb material that forms the basis for the concern that many have about proliferation. In this sense, a civilian plutonium economy can affect a national determination to produce weapons by decreasing the time, and the technical and political costs required.[9] Therefore, it seems plausible that avoiding a plutonium economy can make a difference.

It must be conceded, of course, that there is no sure way to stop proliferation. It may be that nuclear warfare, or at least widespread nuclear arsenals, are inevitable. But even so, assuming the worst, anything that can be done to slow down proliferation may be thought by some to be useful. Delay is not only good in itself, it could also provide time to develop new technical or institutional approaches to the problem. Therefore, we would expect that discouraging the plutonium economy and, therefore, the breeder could result in tangible benefits to the nations of the world by delaying weapons proliferation.

[7] See Chauncey Starr, "Social Benefit Versus Technological Risk—What Is Our Science Willing to Pay for Safety?" *Science* vol. 165 (19 September 1969) pp. 1232–1238.

[8] See Harold A. Feiveson and Theodore B. Taylor, "Alternative Strategies for International Control of Nuclear Power," in Ted Greenwood, Harold A. Feiveson, and Theodore B. Taylor, eds., *Nuclear Proliferation: Motivations, Capabilities and Strategies for Control* (New York, McGraw-Hill for 1980s Project/Council on Foreign Relations, 1977) pp. 123–190, especially p. 157.

[9] Ibid., pp. 147–148; see also Ford Foundation, *Nuclear Power Issues and Choices*, report of the Nuclear Energy Policy Study Group, administered by MITRE Corporation (Cambridge, Mass., Ballinger, 1977) p. 286.

Would the stopping of the breeder be enough? Without the breeder and reprocessing, plutonium would not be handled or shipped in compounds readily suitable for weapons use. But in ordinary LWRs the plutonium is still available in the form of spent fuel rods. In place of open reprocessing, a nation having a LWR economy could reprocess uranium secretly in order to obtain material for bombs. A recent study at Oak Ridge, Tennessee, has shown how to design a primitive reprocessing plant that could produce within a week enough plutonium for a bomb by using ordinary spent fuel.[10] Consequently, some might suggest doing away with nuclear power entirely—either by an immediate shutdown or by a phaseout strategy. As noted above, proliferation may proceed by other means as well. But this hypothetical dismantling of the nuclear power industry would probably also tend to delay additional nations from obtaining bombs, and, therefore, possibly it would delay the advent of future nuclear wars. Indeed, one study has estimated that nations without an existing civilian nuclear power industry would require four times as long and expenditures of fifty to one hundred times as much to build and test a nuclear device as would nations with nuclear power.[11]

What difference does this make for American LWRs? Can the status or even existence of a U.S. nuclear economy affect the status of foreign nuclear industries and, therefore, the world proliferation question? Perhaps not. On the other hand, there are two possible indirect ways that there could be a connection:

1. *By inhibiting the U.S. firms supplying nuclear technology and fuel.* U.S. nuclear supplier firms—especially reactor vendors like General Electric and Westinghouse—constitute a very important part of the world market. Their reactor business in turn depends heavily on sales to domestic utilities. At least in the short run, any phaseout of the U.S. nuclear industry would quite likely have a severe effect on the U.S. firms, as well as on world nuclear trade and on the effectiveness of securing nuclear technology and fuels. Presumably, this effect would weaken in the longer run, as foreign suppliers would take over. The possible role of the Communist world would also have to be taken into account in estimating this effect.

---

[10] See *Nucleonics Week* (27 October 1977) p. 1. The construction of the plant would take four to six months, however.

[11] See PanHeuristics, *Moving Toward Life in a Nuclear Armed Crowd?* U.S. Arms Control and Disarmament Agency ACDA/PAB-263, PH76-04-389-14 (Los Angeles, Science Applications, Inc., April 1976).

2. *By the demonstration effect.*   A hypothetical U.S. rejection of the nuclear option would encourage nuclear opposition in the rest of the world—particularly in areas of Western Europe where nuclear power is a political issue. Such a stance would be taken to indicate that the United States thought the proliferation (and perhaps safety) dangers of the nuclear industry were too great to be tolerated domestically. An example of this kind set by the predominant nuclear power in the world—both in the civilian and military sense—would possibly have an important influence. This influence can be called "moral" or "political," or whatever, but it is evident that it is not necessarily negligible in character. Furthermore, such a rejection of nuclear power would be a necessary step in ensuring consistency between foreign and domestic policy, if the U.S. government then chose to use its foreign policy to actively encourage the denuclearization of the rest of the world. The Carter administration has adopted an analogous type of comprehensive policy initiative in its campaign to discourage a plutonium economy.

These effects would operate ineffectively, if at all, in a foreign policy vacuum. Progress toward deterring or delaying worldwide proliferation would probably depend crucially on U.S. foreign policy initiatives, perhaps on nuclear disarmament, and quite possibly on modifications to U.S. security guarantees and alliances, and on new economic and military aid agreements.[12] The foreign policy regarding both political and energy matters will inevitably determine domestic fuel policy, because a partial or total denuclearization of all the world *except* the United States is implausible.[13] Therefore, a passive policy of a nuclear moratorium or phaseout in the United States might be a necessary concomitant to an active U.S. foreign policy designed to discourage the proliferation of both nuclear materials and weapons.[14]

Naturally, such complexities of action must take into account foreign policy goals and the possibility that even radical nonproliferation policies may not be effective. And policies that reflect a radically different point of view on global politics—such as ensuring peace by a maximization of

[12] See Richard K. Betts, "How to Keep the Nuclear Club Exclusive," *Across the Board* (The Conference Board Magazine) vol. 14, no. 9 (September 1977) pp. 25–34.

[13] See, for example, the discussion in chap. 11 of Amory B. Lovins, *Soft Energy Paths: Toward a Durable Peace* (Cambridge, Mass., Friends of the Earth/Ballinger, 1977).

[14] See Ford Foundation, *Nuclear Power Issues,* pp. 297–299, for a summary of concerted moves against proliferation.

weapons inventories, rather than by disarmament—must be considered. Indeed, one could view proliferation as a useful incentive toward disarmament and therefore toward the prevention of a war that would otherwise be inevitable, or aver that a small war sooner is better than a big war later. But the possibility must still be faced that U.S. nuclear power, even in its present form, may contribute indirectly to unpaid health costs resulting from nuclear wars that are associated with the worldwide proliferation problem.

Proliferation Risks

What risks are associated with both the breeder and the LWR industry in the United States, in terms of possibly adding members to the nuclear weapons states? We can examine at least the structure of some of the risks, even though it is difficult to estimate their probabilities and consequences. Appendix A discusses some of the logic of the problem and emphasizes two points: (1) that the number of possible casualties in a major nuclear war is very large; and (2) the fact that civilian nuclear power may be only one factor affecting the likelihood of nuclear warfare could be relatively unimportant, given these large casualties. In other words, a small piece of a large problem could still be a large problem. If this is indeed so, Appendix A illustrates how intuitive concerns about proliferation could be justified in terms of a conventionally phrased risk analysis. It is quite believable that the mere existence of the U.S. nuclear industry—making reasonable assumptions about U.S. foreign policy—could imply concomitant health effects that would be as large or larger than the others we have been considering. Furthermore, even if the proliferation connection should be exceedingly tenuous, the particular catastrophic nature of the risk could well justify special concern about this problem (see chapter 12).

Mitigation: Technical and Institutional Solutions

Given the possible consequences, a search for ways to mitigate the dangers is worthwhile. The simplest and surest way to solve the problem would be through a change in technology. Such a technical approach to mitigation would come about—at least so far as the plutonium economy is concerned—either through changes in the nature or availability of reprocessing or of enrichment. Reports from France about enrichment processes that were touted as relatively secure against usage for proliferation may have been premature, but new proliferation-resistant enrichment schemes remain a theoretical possibility.[15] There is an existing test reactor in Idaho, the molten-salt reactor, which reprocesses continuously by extracting the waste (fission products) from a liquid fuel, while the plutonium remains inside,[16] making plutonium diversion exceedingly difficult. Another possibility could be to use reactors having a thorium cycle which involves a "denaturing" of fissile uranium in ordinary uranium that makes extraction of the fissile material very difficult.[17] None of these schemes has yet been proved reliable and economic.

Institutional changes have been widely recommended as a solution to the plutonium problem. One of the standard ideas has been the tightening up of IAEA safeguarding of nuclear materials. The difficulty there is that the IAEA safeguards under the nuclear NPT have been restricted to an auditing of national nuclear procedures. How can such a system really be effective against countries that have some determination, however slight, to manufacture nuclear weapons? The principle is that of deterrence through early warning, and the inherent problem with this is that if discovery does not take place early enough to allow significant actions to be taken, then the deterrent is not useful.[18] Perhaps the NPT approach could be supplemented by some more stringent set of uniform sanctions—both nuclear and nonnuclear, such as credit stoppage and trade embargoes— to be applied against a new bomb-building nation.[19]

Another institutional answer is that developed by conferences of suppliers, restricting imports and exports in an informal framework, not under the IAEA. Such restrictions would only be as strong, of course, as the strength of the common interests holding such a group together. Naturally, we must also assume that the policies of any one nation could also constitute an "institution" acting in such a way as to discourage proliferation. The U.S. decision against the breeder is one example of this. It

[15] See *Energy Daily* (6 May 1977) p. 1. Such methods may, however, depend on special geometrical tricks of less than general utility.

[16] The molten-salt breeder reactor uses liquid fuel that is reprocessed (purified of fission products) continuously, without the plutonium leaving the plant. See *Energy Daily* (10 May 1977) p. 2.

[17] See Feiveson and Taylor, "Alternative Strategies," pp. 130–131.

[18] See Victor Gilinsky, "Plutonium, Proliferation, and Policy," *Technology Review* (February 1977) pp. 58–65.

[19] See *Nucleonics Week* (27 October 1977) p. 7, reporting on a paper by Joseph W. Harned.

has also been proposed that the United States try to destroy the market for enrichment facilities by dumping enriched fuel on the market at very low prices.[20] Undercutting other suppliers, of course, gets into rather sensitive areas of international economics and politics.

A newer approach is the idea of multinational reprocessing of spent fuel. If these multinational regional fuel centers included also enrichment facilities,[21] it is possible that the internationalization of the whole industry could prevent many nations from gaining easy access to plutonium or other materials through a civilian nuclear power program, where again the definition of *easy* is, of course, subject to debate. Unfortunately, with the breeder technology such multinational fuel facilities would probably involve increases in typical transportation distances for fresh fuel—which would contain weapons-grade material—and could, therefore, increase the risk of theft of weapons materials in transit by some national groups or even by other nations.[22] It is, therefore, difficult to be sanguine about the possibilities for institutional solutions to the plutonium problem in any context in which all reactors are still owned by individual nation-states. Indeed, some have worried about the training in scientific and technical aspects of nuclear energy that the multinational fuel centers could give to engineers and technicians from a variety of countries.[23]

The multinational approach, while new in its present form, echoes the by now ancient proposals made by a special U.S. State Department committee in 1946.[24] Their scheme was more far-reaching, suggesting that dangerous activities—including not only enrichment and reprocessing, but also mining and special production reactors—be internationalized. National nuclear power activities would have been restricted to operating reactors using "denatured" plutonium. Since denaturing of plutonium no longer appears a reliable safeguard,[25] any modern version of this would probably involve the complete internationalization of power production. Although such an idea may be radical, especially in the context of usual

[20] See Richard Wilson, *Nuclear Power and the Proliferation of Nuclear Weapons* (preprint, Cambridge, Mass., Harvard University, 1976).

[21] See Vinay Meckoni, "Regional Nuclear Fuel Centers," *International Atomic Energy Agency Bulletin* vol. 18, no. 1 (11 February 1976).

[22] See Feiveson and Taylor, "Alternative Strategies," p. 164.

[23] Ford Foundation, *Nuclear Power Issues*, p. 296.

[24] Chester I. Barnard, J. R. Oppenheimer, Charles A. Thomas, Harry A. Winne, and David E. Lilienthal, *A Report on the International Control of Atomic Energy*, Secretary of State's Committee on Atomic Energy, U.S. Department of State Publication 2498 (Washington, GPO, 16 March 1946).

[25] Mason Willrich and Theodore B. Taylor, *Nuclear Theft: Risks and Safeguards* (Cambridge, Mass., Ballinger, 1974) p. 12.

power grids, it does fit in with "energy island" proposals recently made for the future geographic concentration of power production.[26]

Even if difficulties in devising institutional schemes to stop proliferation were to prove too formidable, institutional answers could have some relevance for the subnational diversion or terrorist problem, which will be discussed below.

The Terrorist Menace

In the late 1960s and early 1970s, the number of bombings or attempted bombings of various kinds in the United States was running at a rate of about 2,000 a year, with a yearly average of 20 to 25 deaths and 170 to 180 injuries involved. Fortunately, none of these incidents involved nuclear weapons.[27] Hijacking of airplanes continues to occur internationally, while truck hijacking has become increasingly common in the United States within recent years. None of these hijackings has involved uranium or plutonium that could be used for nuclear weapons, but we must consider the possibility that future terrorists, criminals, or revolutionaries may try to gain possession of highly enriched uranium or plutonium in order to make nuclear weapons. The chances of this happening depend, in the first place, on the future outlook for terrorism and related activities. Has the peak of terrorist activity, arising out of the special conflicts of the 1960s, begun to taper off? Possibly, but experts on the subject point out that society has become permanently more vulnerable to terrorism as a result of the development of vulnerable means of transportation—such as aircraft—and the direct encouragement that a ubiquitous television gives to such newsworthy activities as the holding of hostages. Advances in small-weapons technology may also be important, if the Soviet ground-to-air missile discovered in the possession of some terrorists in a recent incident in the Rome airport is any indication. It is probably, therefore, safe to assume—at least from the point of view of energy policy—that terrorist threats are something that we have to anticipate living with during the next quarter-century or so.

[26] Cesare Marchetti, "Geoengineering and the Energy Island," in *Second Status Report of the IIASA Project on Energy Systems 1975*, RR 76-1 (Laxenburg, Austria, International Institute for Applied Systems Analysis, 1976) pp. 220–244.

[27] The diversion problem is reviewed in Ramsay, "Coal and Nuclear," chap. 4 and append. G.

Nuclear Terrorism—Fact or Fiction?

From the point of view of a terrorist, there are many disadvantages to using nuclear weapons. True, it seems to be possible for a small group of persons to make a nuclear weapon by using the plutonium obtained directly from reactors—even though the U.S. military nuclear weapons program subjects "reactor plutonium," which contains nonfissile plutonium isotopes, to costly purification before use. But the danger of radioactive contamination and the technical problems involved in getting the material together—by setting up one's own small enrichment or reprocessing plant, or by stealing guarded shipments of material—are formidable. The difficulties are formidable especially when compared with making a conventional bomb that could be of similar effectiveness for demonstrations, threats, or extortions—at least in terms of energy released.

Terrorists could utilize other kinds of nuclear threats. Plutonium, while relatively harmless as a source of direct radiation through the air, could cause cancer if inhaled, and it is theoretically possible to spread plutonium in the air in a public place like Times Square as part of a terrorist incident. Unfortunately for terrorists, plutonium may not be as carcinogenic as it is sometimes thought, and even at that, the cancers would not be likely to appear for ten to thirty years. Naturally, the delayed-action aspect could be thought of as peculiarly terrorizing in itself; however, terrorists would have to take into account basic scientific doubts about plutonium toxicity at small doses. Therefore, such a toxic bomb could be considered an inferior or, at least, a quite tentative threat.[28]

Terrorists or revolutionaries, as well as antinuclear demonstrators, might also threaten to sabotage nuclear facilities. It would indeed be possible to spread radioactivity by blowing up a nuclear reactor, but in practice such a power plant "bomb" might be difficult to arrange, due to the complexity of the nuclear power plant and its many extra safety systems, to say nothing of probable time delays in the release of radioactivity that might allow evacuation of the surrounding population. But such a possibility cannot be excluded.

If the only threat from stolen nuclear material were from ordinary criminals, we could probably look on the danger as minimal, just because of these practical difficulties; but terrorism is not always rational, in the sense of being cut and dried. Terrorism is theater, and the television set is an

[28] See Bernard L. Cohen, "The Hazards in Plutonium Dispersal" (Oak Ridge, Tenn., Institute for Energy Analysis, March 1975).

important part of the problem.[29] Popular fears of nuclear energy may provide an important temptation toward nuclear terrorism. But a saving grace could be that terrorists typically want to gain the sympathy of at least some segments of the public, and the results of nuclear terrorism might be too horrifying and too indiscriminate to use, in a public relations sense. It is not clear, though, whether the threat of nuclear terrorism or, at least, nuclear hoaxes might still appear promising to some Gavrilo Princip of the future.[30]

Protection of Nuclear Facilities

Nuclear facilities are protected like banks, using guards to discourage robbery by outside persons, and auditors to discourage embezzlement. The auditing programs in U.S. plants that produce plutonium for experimental purposes—such as the Kerr–McGee plant in Oklahoma[31]—have sometimes been crude and unreliable in the past, but it seems clear that newer plants could easily keep track of the plutonium as a part of the automated process-control techniques that are so much used in modern industry. The only real trouble is that a nuclear embezzler needs only a baseball-sized amount of plutonium to make a nuclear explosive, and no process-control system can be perfect; there must be a practical limit to the quantities that can be accounted for. The problem is greatly lessened if the plutonium economy is deferred. For if there is no reprocessing, the accountability problem becomes much less. Such large amounts of materials would have to be embezzled—either from uranium mills, from enrichment plants, or from the pools of water that hold the spent fuel from nuclear reactors—that successful embezzlement would be extremely difficult.

Theft and sabotage are another problem. Preventing terrorists, revolutionaries, or criminals from entering a nuclear facility and stealing material for a bomb or sabotaging the plant is a question of guards, fences, and tamper-proof safes. It should be possible, by spending a large amount of money, to make nuclear plants and fuel material unattractive targets.

[29] Brian M. Jenkins, *Will Terrorists Go Nuclear?* Report P-5541 (Santa Monica, Calif., Rand Corporation, November 1975).

[30] The assassin of Archduke Franz Ferdinand in Sarajevo, in 1914, favored pistols and bombs, perhaps the latest technology for portable weapons at that time.

[31] This is the site of the still mysterious plutonium-contamination incident and fatal automobile accident involving Karen Silkwood, as reported in *The New York Times* (2 May 1975).

Guards could be quadrupled, and sophisticated communications equipment could be installed. Vehicles could be sent in convoys, and if there is no plutonium economy, thefts typically might have to deal with radioactive spent fuel inside shipping casks weighing many thousands of pounds. Sabotage, while still possible,[32] can become a major undertaking because most facilities deal with highly radioactive materials that must be heavily shielded and handled with care.

A special problem that arises is that difficult or expensive thefts could still be carried out if terrorists or revolutionaries had strong support in money and other resources. Therefore, terrorists belonging to groups supported by militant national governments could well carry out complex diversions of nuclear material. Such governments could in fact be seeking nuclear weapons for themselves by indirect means, or could be acting for some general political advantage.

Can internationalization of the nuclear fuel cycle stop the terrorist problem? Probably only if all sensitive processes were contained in the multinational center, and the highly fissile fuels were then denatured or spiked with radioactivity before outside shipment, in order to make them difficult to steal. Even then, it would seem possible that terrorists or revolutionaries could sometimes secure help from friendly governments to gain access to materials inside the regional center. Again, there is, unfortunately, no hard and fast line between proliferation and the nuclear terrorism problem.

Costs and Risks

Naturally, it is very difficult to determine what the risks are. Some bomb threats and hoaxes have occurred, and an occasional rifle shot has been heard in the vicinity of reactors in the United States. Europe has seen more action. The bombing of the Fessenheim reactor construction site in France in 1975 may have been only the first of a series of incidents that, although associated with general antinuclear movements, are also often connected with terrorist group activities—France and Germany have recently been shaken by violent antinuclear demonstrations.[33] If there is no use of plutonium as a fuel, the dangers of theft from the LWR fuel cycle

---

[32] See *Safeguards in the Domestic Nuclear Industry,* Committee Print 17, House Subcommittee on Energy and the Environment, of the Committee on Interior and Insular Affairs, 94 Cong. 1 sess. (August 1976) p. 11.

[33] See *Energy Daily* (3 October 1977).

seem rather small, unless cheap enrichment methods prove to be effective. Serious sabotage may occur, depending on the tastes of terrorists or other interested parties. Although admittedly we have little experience to go on, some have argued that the dangers from nuclear terrorism in a LWR economy should be at least smaller than those from nuclear proliferation.[34]

If a plutonium economy is adopted—as it evidently will soon be in France, Germany, and other countries, and, perhaps eventually, in the United States—the situation may be different. New regulations that have lately come into effect for increasing guards and other protection measures at U.S. nuclear facilities would then dictate a sizable increase in the nature, extent, and cost of protective measures.[35] Still, the costs of such measures are typically low at reasonable levels of effectiveness; huge guard forces are probably neither socially feasible nor technically efficient. It is probable that protective measures could come to no more and probably much less than an extra tenth of a cent per kilowatt-hour at the very most, or less than an additional $2 on the "monthly electric bill."[36]

One latent danger in taking protective measures—especially for the plutonium economy—is that excessive security could conceivably impinge on the civil liberties of citizens. For example, it has been proposed that nuclear facilities be protected under classification and clearance rules similar to those used by the U.S. Department of Defense.[37] What would the consequences of such a military-type program in a civilian industry be? Nuclear skeptics have suggested dire consequences.[38] Without necessarily agreeing that plutonium equals a garrison state, we must note that such consequences for political liberties are potentially troublesome and must be thought out in planning any future breeder economy.

Assuming a plutonium economy, the risks that new security measures are designed to discourage have been roughly estimated to be one or two bombing incidents every fifty years.[39] If such incidents were to occur during a game in the Los Angeles Coliseum or during business hours in the Chicago Loop, casualties per incident might reach 100,000; the average spread-out risks per USW, though, would then be less than 3,000 casual-

---

[34] See Ramsay, "Coal and Nuclear," chap. 3 and 4.

[35] See, for example, *Nucleonics Week* (31 March 1977) p. 7.

[36] For a nuclear industry generating, say, 500 billion kWh per year, extra safeguards could cost $500 million, according to some government estimates. See Ramsay, "Coal and Nuclear," append. G.

[37] See MITRE Corporation, *The Threat to Licensed Nuclear Facilities*, MTR-7022, MITRE Technical Report, prepared for the National Research Council (McLean, Va., MITRE Corporation, September 1975) p. 102.

[38] See Lovins, *Soft Energy Paths*, p. 156.

[39] *Nucleonics Week* (26 June 1975) p. 5.

ties.[40] The dangers could be greater, of course, but they could easily be much less. Furthermore, the unknown risks from other terrorist weapons used instead of nuclear weapons should ideally be subtracted out in our analysis. Unfortunately, it is not clear how much increases in guards and locked doors can affect nuclear terrorism risks, but discouraging reprocessing and cheap enrichment could probably make them very small.

Finally, however, these risks are in the hands of persons—like the Baader-Meinhof German revolutionary group—operating outside of the usual rational balancing of alternatives; terrorism is theater and the script is not available to us. Irrational actions could also act on irrational or exaggerated fears in the mind of the public. Furthermore, we do not know what the effects of sustained terrorist campaigns on society could be.[41] So the consequences of nuclear terrorism could be grave, both to the public health and to the national morale.

Conclusion

The proliferation of nuclear weapons capabilities among nations is a critical and complex aspect of the nuclear power issue. The connection between nuclear power, weapons-grade material, nuclear weapons, and nuclear war is exceedingly complicated and, therefore, controversial. But if a significant connection does exist, the U.S. policy to discourage a world plutonium economy—if followed by other nations—could have some effect in preventing or delaying the process of proliferation. Under similar assumptions, a moratorium or phasing out of all civilian nuclear power could also further discourage proliferation and, possibly, the likelihood of nuclear war. The practicality and effectiveness of technological and institutional means of mitigation have not yet been established.

The likelihood of diversion of nuclear fuel material into bombs by criminal or revolutionary groups is difficult to assess, but if there were no reprocessing and no cheap enrichment, the dangers are probably relatively small. Terrorism, however, is unpredictable, and nuclear terrorism could have distinct psychological—as well as physical—impacts.

[40] The rate for 400 reactors (about 1.3 USW, perhaps an average number within the next fifty years), at one chance in twenty-five years, for about 4,000 expected casualties (see Ramsay, "Coal and Nuclear," append. G). Compare National Advisory Committee on Criminal Justice Standards and Goals, *Disorders and Terrorism: Report of the Task Force on Disorders and Terrorism* (Washington, 1976) p. 447.

[41] Ibid., p. 450.

Appendix: Proliferation Risks

The complex chain of reasoning connecting nuclear generation of electricity to future nuclear wars can be divided into several key links:

1. Nuclear weapons use and catastrophic wars. An initial use of nuclear weapons may or may not lead to a catastrophic major war. Obviously, the result could depend on whether the weapon is used by Uganda or the USSR, for example. Even then, the use of a weapon by a small state could well lead to a consequent widening of the war into a major nuclear catastrophe. Although one can only guess at the probability of such a linkage, it is evident from the diplomatic history of the past few decades that major powers fear that such a detonator effect is not improbable.

2. Proliferation and nuclear weapons use. The probability of the use of nuclear weapons is affected by how many different nations own how many weapons of what type. Students of the problem have especially emphasized the instabilities that might be produced if many nations obtained the bomb (the "N-th nation problem").[42] We can only guess at the level of probability associated with this link in the chain by noting the evident high level of international concern on this issue.

3. Nuclear materials availability and weapons proliferation. Nuclear materials must be available to make weapons, but the acquisition of weapons also depends on political and economic factors. A nation can acquire nuclear weapons in order to carry out its own foreign policy initiatives, or in response to nuclear threats from a neighbor. Internal or external ideological conflicts may be important. Analogies with other weapons might be enlightening, but is the correct analogy to be made with the machine gun or with poison gas?

4. Nuclear fuel and nuclear materials. Nuclear power fuels add to the store of nuclear materials from other sources. Plutonium and highly enriched uranium fuels are especially desirable for weapons use. As has been discussed in the text, the ready and unplanned availability of weapons materials from fuels may make them an important factor in proliferation.[43]

---

[42] See Herman Kahn, *On Thermonuclear War* (2 ed., New York, Free Press, 1969) p. 493.

[43] Ted Greenwood, "Discouraging Proliferation in the Next Decade and Beyond," in Greenwood, Feiveson, and Taylor, eds., *Nuclear Proliferation*, pp. 23–122. On

5. U.S. nuclear policy and nuclear fuels. U.S. nuclear policy can affect the world nuclear power economy both through the force of example and through U.S. foreign policy initiatives. As has been suggested, this connection is one of the most controversial of all. Nevertheless, the Carter administration has justified the delay or cancellation of a breeder economy in the United States on the basis of this link.

The Size of the Problem

If we were able to make sensible estimates of the probabilities of each link in the chain described above, it would enable us to estimate the dangers from proliferation. Such estimates seem difficult to make, but we also should note that: (1) the current level of international concern about proliferation indicates that there is great fear that the annual probability of catastrophic wars, as a result of the first two or three links in the chain, is not small, say, not less than once in a hundred years; and (2) the consequences of a catastrophic nuclear war are very great, probably not adequately measured by the 100 million casualties or so commonly posited in postwar discussions of the problem.[44] Consequently, even though a reasonable case can be made that the last links in the chain— from U.S. nuclear policy to a proliferation of weapons capabilities—are very weak, even a weak link (say, involving one chance in one million or less) might not have negligible consequences from the point of view of health effects associated with U.S. use of nuclear energy. Nevertheless, we cannot exclude the opposite possibility, that these last links in the chain might be *so* weak that proliferation dangers tied to energy use are indeed negligible.

Whatever the case, it is easy to imagine that the expected consequences could be of the same magnitude—or rather more than—those associated with other health impacts.

---

p. 111, Greenwood lists it as one of four factors: (1) the positive feedback system between one state's actions and another's; (2) whether or not nuclear weapons have actually been used; (3) the way in which the government's internal decision-making processes act; and (4) the diffusion speed of civilian nuclear power.

[44] See Kahn, *On Thermonuclear War*, p. 113.

7   *Changes in Climate*

Are we courting disaster by fouling the atmosphere with elements that could cause climatological catastrophes?

Is climate the ultimate argument against coal?

The Greenhouse Effect

The carbon in coal and other fossil fuels comes ultimately from carbon dioxide that was absorbed by plants during past geologic times and converted by photosynthesis into plant tissue. The burning of fossil fuels— just as the decay of plants—forces the carbon to return to carbon dioxide in the air. It is both interesting and alarming to find that the burning of coal, oil, and other fossil fuels seems to have measurably increased the concentration of carbon dioxide in the air throughout the world.[1] It is known that carbon dioxide acts as a kind of insulator, holding in the atmosphere a part of the sun's heat re-emitted by the earth which would otherwise be radiated again into space. It seems possible that a 100 percent increase in the amount of carbon dioxide in the world's atmosphere—a level that might be reached by the increased burning of coal and other fossil fuels by the year 2050—might also raise the temperature of the world several degrees Celsius.[2] While the world has undergone similar changes in past eons, civilization, as we know it, might not react favorably to the possible results—changes in rainfall and wind patterns, with severe consequences for agriculture and, perhaps, even a widespread melting of ice caps and consequent flooding of coastal areas everywhere.

[1] See William Ramsay, "Coal and Nuclear: Health and Environmental Costs" (Washington, Resources for the Future, August 1978) pp. 5-19–5-24, for a review of the weather-modification problem.

[2] See Friedrich Niehaus, *A Nonlinear Eight-Level Tandem Model to Calculate the Future CO_2 and C-14 Burden to the Atmosphere*, RM-76-35 (Laxenburg, Austria, International Institute for Applied Systems Analysis, May 1976) p. 5. One degree Celsius is equal to 1.8 degrees Farenheit.

Actual numerical prediction of effects is exceedingly speculative. But it has been suggested that it requires the emission of perhaps 1.2 trillion metric tons of carbon dioxide (1 metric ton is equal to 1.1 short ton) to raise the temperature of the earth as much as one degree Celsius.[3] This could mean that the amount of carbon dioxide emitted per USW (2 trillion kWh)—an amount about one thousand times less, or 1.6 billion metric tons per year—corresponds to a rise in temperature of somewhat more than one-thousandth of a degree Celsius.[4]

The problem is especially vexing because there are so many unknowns. It is not even entirely certain that the increases in carbon dioxide that are seen are due principally to the burning of coal, oil, and gas. The clearing of forests and modifications in agricultural patterns may also have increased carbon dioxide levels through changes in patterns of uptake and release by plants. The net carbon dioxide emitted from the biosphere and the burning of fuels does not necessarily remain in the atmosphere, either. Excess carbon dioxide has apparently been absorbed in the past by the deep layers of the oceans, although it is not certain that the oceans will absorb relatively as much in the future as they presently do. It could also be that a greater input of carbon dioxide would stimulate the growth of plant life so as to lead to lower than expected levels of atmospheric carbon dioxide.

Nevertheless, the fact that observed levels have been growing is a legitimate cause for concern. Climate modification might even be desirable: a consideration of the favorable climates existing tens of thousands of years ago in such present-day arid areas as Iraq suggests that modification toward higher temperatures might be worthwhile. Such an artificial warming might be especially beneficial if the present short-term general trend toward worldwide cooling—from a variety of causes—persists.[5] But the situation might be analogous to that of genetic mutations: a given human

---

[3] See Wolf Haefele, and Wolfgang Sassin, *Energy Strategies,* Research Report RR-76-8 (Laxenburg, Austria, International Institute for Applied Systems Analysis, March 1976) tab. 7; and ibid., which extrapolate the doubling of carbon dioxide producing a change of 2.4 degrees Celsius to lower inputs.

[4] See National Research Council, National Academy of Sciences, "Energy and Climate: Studies in Geophysics" (1977) p. 61, for coal parameters, with each plant emitting 5.25 million metric tons of carbon dioxide per year. The balance between carbon dioxide in the various sources and sinks is complex and may not resemble this simplified extrapolation (see ibid., p. 273). Also, note that the temperature predictions are based on simplified models (see Niehaus, *A Nonlinear Eight-Level Tandem Model*).

[5] See, for example, the testimony of Stephen H. Schneider in Hearings on H. 78 before the House Subcommittee on the Environment and the Atmosphere of the Committee on Science and Technology, *The National Climate Program Act,* 94 Cong. 2 sess. (May 1976) pp. 37ff., for a brief discussion of factors and uncertainties.

mutation might be favorable (most are not), but it might be better to live with what one has than to risk producing a monster. It would be rash to assume that we know enough about the situation to assume that all is well: climate modification by carbon dioxide presents a formidable and important challenge.

As a curious sidelight, we have to realize that through our choice of a nuclear power policy we could influence the amount of carbon dioxide emitted by other nations that affects the world climate. As has been discussed, the United States may have an effect on the ability and desire of other nations to either go nuclear or go breeder. But if so, we might also be indirectly encouraging them to burn more coal and other fossil fuels, thus creating more carbon dioxide pollution. Hypothetically, if every phased-out U.S. reactor induced the phasing out of several foreign reactors, the influence of a U.S. policy to replace nuclear with coal would effectively multiply the contribution of carbon dioxide released by U.S. coal-fired plants. Naturally, all the "ifs" add up to a very speculative connection indeed.

The problem is complicated by the presence of soot and other particles put into the air by burning fossil fuels. On balance, it is not certain whether these particles tend to absorb heat or to scatter it away from the earth, so that it is unclear whether the net effect of these particles is to cool or to heat. Recent evidence from long-term radiation balance experiments in Arizona, however, suggests that the heating effect predominates.[6] Nitrogen oxides and other compounds produced from burning fuels may also contribute to greater worldwide heating rates.[7]

Nonetheless, it is possible to clean up the carbon dioxide. Under high pressure it could be kept in a liquid state underground or beneath the sea.[8] But the practical problem appears formidable because the emissions of carbon dioxide are enormous. A single 1,000-MW plant can emit about 5.2 million metric tons a year.[9] Yet it has been suggested that emergency tree- or plant-growing programs, coupled perhaps with a peat formation

[6] See Sherwood B. Idso and Anthony J. Brazel, "Planetary Radiation Balance as a Function of Atmospheric Dust: Climatological Consequences," *Science* vol. 198, no. 4318 (18 November 1977) pp. 731–733.

[7] See Ford Foundation, *Nuclear Power Issues and Choices,* report of the Nuclear Energy Policy Study Group, administered by the MITRE Corporation (Cambridge, Mass., Ballinger, 1977) p. 203.

[8] See Cesare Marchetti, "On Geoengineering and the CO_2 Problem," Rm-76-17 (Laxenburg, Austria, International Institute for Applied Systems Analysis, March 1976), where a cost penalty of 20 percent of fuel costs is estimated for a 90 percent efficiency in carbon dioxide removal.

[9] See National Research Council, "Energy and Climate," p. 61.

effort, could provide a stopgap solution:[10] the carbon dioxide would be converted into plant tissue, and the plant tissue would then be preserved from decomposition in the favorable chemical environment of a peat bog.

The Ultimate Pollutants: Heat and Water

Power plants inevitably turn out a certain amount of waste heat. Even modern coal plants reach only 40 percent efficiency, meaning that some 60 percent of the heat energy is not turned into electricity but escapes into the atmosphere. Nuclear efficiencies are somewhat lower, so that two-thirds or more of the heat energy is not turned into useful energy. This excess heat will tend to raise the temperature of the air in the vicinity of the power plant. Furthermore, to obtain this energy in useful form, steam must be created and then condensed. The condensing is usually done by using an outside source of cooling water that is subsequently cooled to a great extent by evaporating water into the atmosphere. Thus it could have an effect on the local weather. We have reason to believe that measurable local climatic effects will indeed occur. It is already known that cities change the climates around them, by the emission of heat from burning fuels, by the changes that asphalt and concrete make on the reflecting qualities of the earth's surface, and by differences in moisture levels brought about by replacing porous ground with hard surfaces. And the heat changes that power plants bring about can be locally comparable in magnitude to those seen in cities: a planned system of three nuclear stations in central Illinois would create a heat flux (flow) half that emanating from the District of Columbia.[11] These electricity "heat islands" can be presumed to cause local and, perhaps, more far-reaching weather effects.[12]

The effects of the moisture could be done away with by the use of dry cooling towers—working on a principle similar to that of an automobile radiator—at some cost in extra equipment and in a loss of power output from the plant. But the heat problem itself is very difficult to deal with. True, large local heat fluctuations—that could conceivably contribute to the formation of severe storms—could be eliminated by dissipating the

[10] See Freeman J. Dyson, "Can We Control the Carbon Dioxide in the Atmosphere?" *Energy—The International Journal* vol. 2 (1977) pp. 287–291.

[11] Ralph Rotty and Robert Rapp, private communication, 1974.

[12] See R. T. Jaske, *Solving the Problems of Thermal Effects and Outputs,* BN-SA-221 (Richland, Wash., Battelle Pacific Northwest Laboratories, October 1973).

heat into large bodies of water. But the total quantity of heat energy constitutes another problem entirely. There have been many schemes for using waste heat in the industrial or agricultural sectors, for example, and the conclusion is plain: waste heat can perform many useful functions, and performing these functions may lower the temperature of the final heat output, but it is very difficult to eliminate a large dumping of heat at some (noticeably) excess temperature. If the expansion of the electric power industry ultimately leads to the creation of heat in so great an amount that there is a large-scale climatic effect, we could conceivably be faced with a fundamental environmental crisis. But at present, such a crisis seems a century or more away, while the carbon dioxide–particulate is of more immediate concern.[13]

Thunderstorms and Krypton 85

Most of the climatic effects come from coal alone or equally from coal or nuclear, but there is one particular effect that could result solely from the nuclear fuel cycle. If the rest of the world, or the United States alone, decides to reprocess fuel in order to recover plutonium, the radioactive element krypton 85, a noble (that is, chemically inactive) gas, would be released from the fuel. It is a calculated risk that within the next century this gas could reach levels at which its radioactivity could have a profound effect on the ionization level of the air. This change in the electrical character of the atmosphere would affect in turn the way rain forms, particularly rain in thunderstorms. Since thunderstorms are a major element in the exchange of heat between layers of the atmosphere, such an increase in krypton-85 levels could possibly have a harmful climatic effect.

If there is no plutonium recycling so that the spent fuel rods are not opened, only small leakages of krypton 85 would escape into the atmosphere. Even if plutonium were used as fuel, it would still be possible

---

[13] See Ralph M. Rotty and Alvin M. Weinberg, *How Long is Coal's Future?* IAEA Research Memorandum IAEA (M) 76-1 (Oak Ridge, Tenn., Oak Ridge Associated Universities, Institute for Energy Analysis, February 1976); J. V. Ramsdell, B. C. Scott, M. M. Orgill, D. S. Renne, J. E. Hubbard, and K. A. McGinnis, *Postulated Weather Modification Effects of Large Energy Releases,* Battelle Pacific Northwest Laboratories for U.S. Nuclear Regulatory Commission, BNWL-2162 (Richland, Wash., Battelle Northwest Laboratories, February 1977). The National Research Council ("Energy and Climate," p. 195) suggests that energy fluxes would have to be fifty times greater than they are at present.

to install special equipment to trap the krypton at the reprocessing plants.[14] Clean-up costs would probably not be very high—or not high when compared to the dangers prevented—if theories of atmospheric ion modification prove to be correct.

Conclusion

It is suspected that products of energy generation could eventually cause a significant change in the world's climate. Carbon dioxide—and possibly particulates—from all uses of coal and other fossil fuels could be expected to change average world temperatures within the next one hundred years. U.S. coal-fired power plants now contribute each year enough carbon dioxide to raise the temperature of the earth by little more than one-thousandth of a degree. Nevertheless, the contribution could mount over time, and it is not necessarily negligible as part of a total picture. Furthermore, U.S. nuclear policies could affect foreign use of coal for utilities.

Heat and moisture from either nuclear or coal will likely change local weather and over a long period could cause climatologic changes. Krypton 85, a radioactive gas released as part of the plutonium economy, could have a similar climatic impact.

Cleanup may be expensive or impossible for the worst climate-modification problems. On the other hand, all the dire predictions are subject to many uncertainties, both in data and analysis.[15] So it is too early to decide, for example, that the use of coal is climatically unacceptable, even though the situation demands careful watching.

---

[14] Note that krypton 85 may also have radiation impacts worthy of mention (see chap. 3). Cleanup for both climate and health reasons may be desirable by cryogenic entrapment or any other means suitable for noble gases.

[15] Problems in predicting climate changes are briefly reviewed in the International Council of Scientific Unions (ICSU), Scientific Committee on Problems of the Environment (SCOPE), *Environmental Issues 1976,* Report to ICSU General Assembly, October 1976 (Paris, ICSU, August 1976) pp. 81–86.

8 Impacts on Water, Land, and Society

Do the impacts on our land and water resources or on our natural and human environment make any difference?

Is the impact of strip mining on land use a trenchant argument against the use of coal?

Water

Thermal Pollution

Modern power plants need large volumes of water for cooling and condensing the steam that drives the generator turbines. Quantities of lukewarm water result, and if this water were dumped directly into neighboring streams or lakes, it obviously could have an effect on the fish and other animals and plants in the water. The word *effect* is used advisedly here, because it is conceivable that in some cases the warm water (typically, about 40°C) could have a positive health effect on fish life. Unfortunately, the effect on local fish could be bad, especially when the plant fails to operate for some reason, as for example, when it is shut down for its regular refueling, and the water turns suddenly colder.[1]

The quantity of water needed is large by any standard. Using 1,600 cubic feet (ft³) of water per second, a modern nuclear plant can turn out enough warm water in ten seconds to fill a two-bedroom, 2,000 ft² home from basement to attic.[2] Whether this is to be considered a large amount

---

[1] Water impacts are reviewed in William Ramsay, "Coal and Nuclear: Health and Environmental Costs" (Washington, Resources for the Future, August 1978) chap. 5.

[2] This assumes 16,000 ft³ in the house and 1,600 ft³ per second used by the plant. See U.S. Atomic Commission (AEC), *Nuclear Power Facility Performance Characteristics for Making Environmental Impact Assessments*, WASH-1355 (Washington, AEC, 1974) tab. 6; and ibid., pp. 5-2 and 5-4. Note the 2,500-MW capacity that is assumed in the AEC reference.

of water as far as the local fish are concerned depends upon the size of the body of water and on the temperature levels prescribed by local regulations. For a cooling water supply, the FitzPatrick nuclear plant near Oswego, New York, uses Lake Ontario, which has an inflow of 200,000 ft^3 of water per second. Even so, meeting New York State temperature standards for discharges of water presented some problems.[3] In practice, under recent laws, the Environmental Protection Agency (EPA) has ruled that when the disturbance of the local body of water is too great, the water must be cooled off in a special cooling tower or pond and then recirculated once again to the steam condenser. Consequently, only small amounts of water are taken out and discharged into nearby bodies of water in order to prevent the buildup of salts in the cooling system.

In theory, therefore, the thermal problem can be dealt with, although this sometimes creates other problems. We have seen that the local emissions of moisture and heat could cause changes in the local weather conditions. And closed-cycle cooling systems, such as cooling towers or ponds, also cause large amounts of local water loss from evaporation. Furthermore, cooling ponds are often large lakes that prevent substantial areas of land from being used for other purposes.

Water Supply Problems

Much of the cooling of water from the power plants takes place through evaporation. If the water simply passes in and out of the plant, a process termed *once-through cooling,* then most of the evaporation takes place downstream. If the cooling towers or cooling ponds are used, evaporation is a more local affair and could more obviously use up a sizable portion of local water resources. The amount of evaporated water (30 ft^3 of water per second) from a standard plant using a typical cooling tower would fill the two-bedroom house mentioned before in less than ten minutes.[4] The quantity of water need not be necessarily large as compared with that used by others in typical streams. However, power plants can sometimes be locally dominant: during drought conditions, the Wolf Creek nuclear station near Burlington, Kansas, would require over one-half the flow

---

[3] See U.S. Atomic Energy Commission (AEC), "Final Environmental Statement Related to Operation of James A. FitzPatrick Nuclear Plant," Docket No. 50-33 (Washington, AEC, March 1973) pp. 2-11 and 3-29.

[4] See fn. 2.

from a local reservoir with a 2.7 billion ft³ capacity.⁵ If we look at the total energy needs for the year 2000, it is quite possible that power plants might come into conflict with other users in special areas, where planned needs are already great, such as the Colorado River and the Delaware River basins.⁶ Coal plants use some 40 percent less water than do comparable nuclear plants, primarily because of heat loss through smokestack gases, and this difference could be important in some water-short regions.

There are other sources of possible water problems in the energy picture. Coal mining requires water for operations and, nowadays, for reclamation of surface-mined areas, perhaps 0.2–3 ft³ of water per second per plant.⁷ Coal-slurry pipelines also use large amounts of water. True, most of the water is not consumed (it would take two hours to fill up the two-bedroom house with the 2.2 ft³ per second water loss from a slurry pipeline supplying a typical plant),⁸ but the movement of water can involve bringing large amounts from arid or semiarid regions, such as Montana, into more humid areas, such as Arkansas—certainly a perverse result from the point of view of water resources.

Water is a valuable resource, yet it costs very little in some areas but is either expensive or impossible to get elsewhere. Therefore, it is difficult to generalize about water costs and hence about the effects of energy water needs on national water resources, especially since energy competes with so many other uses—many of them established by law years ago. But the problem of energy and water resources is one that bears watching, and could take on special importance if large "energy centers" should become common.⁹

---

⁵ See U.S. Nuclear Regulatory Commission (NRC), "Final Environmental Statement Related to Construction of Wolf Creek Generating Station Unit 1," Docket No. STN 50-482, NUREG 75/096 (Washington, NRC, October 1975) p. 5-1.

⁶ See Ramsay, "Coal and Nuclear," append. M.

⁷ From estimates of 0.5 to 4 acre-feet per acre per year [U.S. General Accounting Office (GAO), Comptroller General of the United States, *U.S. Coal Development— Promises, Uncertainties*, EMD-77-43 (Washington, GAO, 22 September 1977) p. 6.43], and land use given in the text.

⁸ Testimony of John J. Sloan in *Greater Coal Utilization*, Hearings before the U.S. Congress, Senate, Joint Committee on Interior and Insular Affairs and Committee on Public Works, 94 Cong. 1 sess. (June 1975) Ser. 94-18, pt. 1-3; see also Council on Environmental Quality (CEQ), *Environmental Quality: The Seventh Annual Report of the Council on Environmental Quality* (Washington, GPO, September 1976) p. 81.

⁹ See U.S. Nuclear Regulatory Commission, *Nuclear Energy Center Site Survey— 1975*, NUREG-0001 (NECSS-75) (Washington, NRC, January 1976) p. 7-1, where water constraints on multiple siting of reactors are discussed.

Effects of Mechanisms and Chemicals

Within the past decades, biological scientists have been concerned about the effects on local fish life of chemicals, such as chlorine put in the cooling water at both nuclear and coal power plants in order to kill algae. It is hoped that new EPA regulations restricting discharges of toxic chemicals will help to alleviate this problem. The new regulations may also reduce the killing of small fish and microscopic aquatic animals that are drawn into the power plant's condenser system. Adequate sieves and screens, while expensive, can probably reduce damage to manageable levels. Nevertheless, the ill-understood nature of the behavior of biological systems means that some uncertainties will probably remain for the foreseeable future.[10]

In the past water quality in the coal industry has been less regulated than it has been for nuclear energy. Unquestionably, coal presents more of a hazard so far as chemical pollution of the water is concerned. Wastes at coal-fired power plants could pollute local water bodies; these wastes are now closely regulated, however. Both surface and underground coal mines can, however, produce sedimentation problems in local streams. Such impacts, especially from coal-spoil banks, can be mitigated by the use of dams and control structures.[11] Even more serious is the problem of chemicals—especially sulfur—that are dissolved during the mining process and carried from coal mines into local watersheds.[12] Locally, this has been a severe problem, leading to the deposit of sulfur compounds in stream beds. In 1974, for example, nearly 6,000 miles of streams in eight Appalachian states were reported to be continuously polluted by acid mine drainage.[13] Other sulfur compounds can leak out while the coal is being processed to remove impurities. Fortunately, there are methods by which the acidic mine waters can be neutralized and by which acidity

[10] See AEC, "Final Environmental Statement . . . FitzPatrick," for a sample set of calculations and discussions of problems.

[11] See J. Bhutani, A. Brice, J. Elliott, D. Ellis, W. Jacobsen, J. Just, E. Krajeski, and J. Savadelis, *An Analysis of Constraints on Increased Coal Production,* MTR-6830 (McLean, Va., MITRE Corporation, January 1975) tab. 9-3.

[12] See Ramsay, "Coal and Nuclear," pp. 5-11–5-13; and U.S. Congress, House, Committee on Interior and Insular Affairs, *Surface Mining Control and Reclamation Act of 1977.* Report Together with Additional Concurring, Separate and Dissenting Views to Accompany H. R. 2 (Including the Congressional Budget Office Cost Estimate), H. Rept. 95-278, 95 Cong. 1 sess. (April 1977) p. 127.

[13] See U.S. Congress, House, Committee on Interior and Insular Affairs, *Surface Mining Control and Reclamation Act of 1974: Report to Accompany H.R. 11500,* H. Rept. 93-1072, 93 Cong. 2 sess. (1974) p. 109.

possibly can be removed in operating mines.[14] Currently, the major acidity problem occurs, however, in abandoned mines. For future retirements of mines that lie above the water table, abatement measures could be expensive, or even impractical. Therefore, it is difficult to say to what extent acid mine drainage can be reduced in the years to come.

Options for Mitigation

Total in- and outflows and consequent ecological impacts on water bodies can be and are being significantly reduced through closed-cycle cooling systems. Additionally, dry cooling towers could be used to eliminate evaporative loss, but at some extra cost, say, an additional $2 to $3 on the average "monthly electric bill."[15] Wet–dry towers that change over from one method to the other, depending on weather conditions, offer a compromise solution, one that is less expensive than a completely dry system. However, all these systems still have some effect on the environment.

Chemical treatment of water and other water management techniques in the coal-mining industry can alleviate, if not solve, acidity and sedimentation problems.

Land Use

Energy Use of Land

The amounts of land taken up by power plants vary.[16] Coal-powered facilities, for example, need room enough for the generating plants, sites for slag and ash disposal, and additional space for coal delivery and storage and removal of ashes. It is probably necessary to set aside, say, 100 acres or more for a standard plant.[17] Additional land will, of course, be needed for permanent disposal of the 1,000 tons, or more, of ash that are generated each day. Nuclear plants must have an "exclusion zone" for partial

[14] See Bhutani and coauthors, *An Analysis*, pp. 9-8–9-11.

[15] See R. W. Beck Associates, *Cost Comparison of Dry-Type and Conventional Cooling Systems for Representative Nuclear Generating Plants,* U.S. Atomic Energy Commission, TID-26007 (Washington, AEC, March 1972) p. 86, which gives estimates of about 1 mill per kilowatt-hour.

[16] See Ramsay, "Coal and Nuclear," pp. 5-26–5-33, for a discussion.

[17] See Engineering Science, Inc., *Preliminary Investigations of a Potential Power Plant Site in Cecil County, Maryland: The Bainbridge Naval Training Center Site, Summary,* vol. 1, prepared for the Maryland Power Plant Siting Program, State of Maryland (McLean, Va., Engineering-Science, Inc., February 1974) tab. IV-1, noting some necessary corrections, especially fuel storage requirements for a standard 1,000 MW plant.

protection of the public against possible radiation accidents. Therefore, nuclear stations tend to be somewhat larger than coal-powered plants. Although actual sites vary greatly, they average over 1,000 acres (130 acres for the station area alone).[18] This figure does not count transmission lines. The total amount of land used for a transmission grid may be very large. It has been estimated that every new plant requires 1,800 acres in order for it to reach the neighboring power grid.[19] As mentioned before, cooling ponds can be quite large as well: the 2,500 acres or more proposed for the Wolf Creek, Kansas, station are not untypical.[20]

This land used for power generation is not all used up in the same way. It is important to know what uses are being replaced, and what future uses are being prevented. The immediate vicinity of a coal plant, with ash and slag heaps, may turn out to be unpromising for future use. But such land may be infinitely more reusable than are the few acres of a nuclear plant site that have been committed to a concrete and metal structure that will remain radioactive for hundreds, or even thousands of years. In contrast, the vacant land surrounding a nuclear station as an exclusion zone may serve as one means of preserving a greenbelt area in the midst of urban expansion. This land is often maintained in its natural state, since it serves as a buffer against radioactivity from possible accidents. Formal nature preserves can be and have been established in these areas; for example, the Turkey Point nuclear station near Homestead, Florida, has made some amends for its conversion of natural areas to a vast system of cooling canals by preserving one area of mangrove swamp from possible future subdivision.[21]

Transmission lines can involve a fairly major cutting operation in forestland and some disturbance in farm and grasslands, but newer techniques have kept disruption at a minimum, and transmission corridors can often be easily converted back into other uses. Cooling ponds are a different story. They are generally large, and the withdrawal of this land from the local economy can sometimes have a significant impact. If desirable farmland is used for the lake, the question remains whether the farmland will still be usable when the plant finally shuts down after years of operation. This question can probably be answered affirmatively, but one

[18] See U.S. Atomic Energy Commission, *Nuclear Power Facility Performance,* pp. 4-94 and 4-96, where the requirements are apparently not normalized to generation capacity, but are averaged over all existing stations of all sizes.
[19] Ibid., p. 4-99.
[20] The U.S. Nuclear Regulatory Commission, "Final Environmental Statement . . . Wolf Creek," p. iii; and ibid., p. 4-97, quotes 2.1 acres per megawatt (electric).
[21] See William Ramsay and Phillip R. Reed, *Land Use and Nuclear Power Plants —Case Studies of Siting Problems,* WASH-1319, UC-11 (Washington, AEC, Directorate of Regulatory Standards, 1974).

cannot be quite sure. A related question is whether all farmland should be preferentially preserved; this is a question for general national policy, and not just an energy question. The amount of cropland available in the United States is, however, very large as compared with many other types of land.[22] But this reassuring thought may fail to comfort local groups; for example, a large cooling lake for a nuclear plant sited on prime farmland near Ottawa, Illinois, has been criticized for its effect on agricultural resources.[23]

The electricity-related land use change that is most in the news, however, is the surface mining of coal. Certainly, strip mining changes the face of the land. New legislation promises to require reclamation of the land.[24] Reclamation can certainly be effective, as is demonstrated by the conversion of 125 acres of strip-mined land into a recreational park in Lackawanna County, Pennsylvania.[25] But in drier regions, it is not certain that vegetation can be made to grow again in strip-mined areas. Besides, distinctive natural features—such as the mesas of New Mexico—will presumably not be restored under new laws specifying that land be reclaimed to "approximate original contour."[26] The recharge of groundwater supplies can also be affected, especially in certain valleys, and will, in fact, be regulated under new laws.[27]

The amount of land used for mining is fairly large. The amount varies with the characteristics of the coal seam and the mining method. But a reasonable range, averaged over surface and underground mining, is 350 to 600 acres per plant (yearly), or 100,000 to 200,000 acres per USW.[28] Thus mining impact from coal-fired plants could be greater than that of

[22] See Dwight Lee and William Ramsay, *Assessment of the Use of Farmland for Nuclear Power Station Sites* (Washington, NRC, Office of Standards Development, May 1976).

[23] See Ramsay and Reed, *Land Use.*

[24] See U.S. Congress, *Surface Mining Control and Reclamation Act of 1977,* Public Law 95-87. See also U.S. Congress, House, Committee on Interior and Insular Affairs, *Surface Mining Control and Reclamation Act of 1977,* pp. 173–175, for environmental protection performance standards.

[25] See Frank C. Andreuzzi, *Reclaiming Strip-Mined Land for Recreational Use in Lackawanna County, Pa.: A Demonstration Project,* U.S. Bureau of Mines Information Circular 8718 (Washington, GPO, 1976).

[26] See U.S. Congress, House Committee on Interior and Insular Affairs, *Surface Mining,* p. 46.

[27] Ibid., p. 118.

[28] Thomas W. Hunter, *Effects of Air Quality Requirements on Coal Supply,* U.S. Department of the Interior, Bureau of Mines, supplement to Bituminous Coal and Lignite Distribution Reports (Washington, U.S. Bureau of Mines, May 1976). Hunter gives values for tons per acre and coal usage by region. The result is about 350 to 580 acres per plant-year, where the uncertainty is in regional contributions.

most power plant cooling lakes—prorated over a thirty-year plant life-time—and the disturbance of the land is, though different, also radical in nature. If slurry pipelines for bringing coal to power plants became popular, the acreage impacts for pipeline construction might also become significant, even though underground pipelines should have relatively little long-term land use effect.

Uranium mining, while not as land-hungry as coal mining at present, is not negligible, and could become more important if mining were carried out for lower-grade ores in the future. As it is, areas of 20,000 acres or so are involved yearly per USW. Uranium mills have a special land use importance. As has been mentioned, piles of wastes or tailings contain amounts of radioactive elements that will not decay away much for tens of thousands of years. This kind of land commitment involves 232 acres for the Shirley Basin mill in Carbon County, Wyoming;[29] and for 1 USW, about 2,500 acres of tailings are projected.[30] Also, this land use looks rather permanent, since access must be restricted indefinitely, and revegetation may not be possible.[31] Obviously, the recycling of plutonium, especially in breeders, could, to a certain extent, decrease all these impacts.

Underground mining of coal can also produce problems, such as subsidence or cave-ins over mine tunnels. These effects can be diminished, but at added expense, by taking more care in mining. In the past, the loss from such accidents has often been great, but the present trend is to regulate mining so as to control subsidence.[32]

Using scrubbers to remove sulfur from coal smokestack gases could create vast amounts of a limestone-based sludge that resists solidification, requiring special disposal efforts, especially if the leaching out of environ-

[29] See U.S. Atomic Energy Commission (AEC), Directorate of Licensing, "Final Environmental Statement Related to Operation of the Shirley Basin Uranium Mill," Docket No. 40-6622 (Washington, AEC, December 1974) p. IX-3.

[30] See U.S. Nuclear Regulatory Commission (NRC), *Final Generic Environmental Statement on the Use of Recycle Plutonium in Mixed Oxide Fuel in Light Water Cooled Reactors: Health, Safety and Environment*, NUREG-0002 (Washington, NRC, August 1976) pp. IV F-16 and IV F-22; and Robert O. Pohl, "Land Use for Nuclear and for Solar Energy," *Environmental Conservation* (Spring 1977) pp. 7–8, who report that 334,000 acres are "disturbed" to produce 4,036 GW-years, and about 40 tons of uranium concentrate (U_3O_8) are produced for each acre of tailings and about 0.09 GW-years of energy.

[31] See AEC, "Final Environmental Statement . . . Shirley Basin," pp. IV-21 and IV-22. The planning horizon taken is fifty years, "an adequate time period for the tailings problem to be fully studied and resolved."

[32] See U.S. Congress, House Committee on Interior and Insular Affairs, *Surface Mining*, p. 126.

mentally degrading substances is to be prevented.[33] The type of land use involved is sufficiently noxious as to spur engineers to develop solutions. Solid waste volumes may run as high as 600 acre-feet per year (0.8 ft³ per second) per plant,[34] which could imply large land needs for temporary storage, depending on the height of the sludge piles, and perhaps a final disposal strategy based on other solid waste techniques. It is also hoped that regenerable scrubbers—those that reuse the scrubbing material instead of dumping it—can be developed.

All this does not tell much about how energy uses of land can change patterns of plant and animal life. Certainly, the general progress of civilization has been the important factor in destroying or modifying habitat and, therefore, in eliminating species.[35] Plant life in strip-mined areas may be permanently changed; research on this problem is now under way. If new types of vegetation are purposely introduced, as in experiments in Colstrip, Montana, the change may be beneficial, at least to animal life, by creating improved grazing.[36] Plant life on uranium tailings may be out of the question, unless the tailings are successfully covered or are disposed of by some other way. Even then, tailings piles in arid areas could pose insurmountable problems for permanent stands of new vegetation.

Figure 8-1 displays the magnitude in acres disturbed of a few critical uses of land. The pattern of reclamation requirements is now in a state of flux. However, it is difficult to speculate on the hypothetical monetary equivalent of the environmental damages associated with the land use changes that will remain as *unpaid* costs: for coal, guesses have been made of some $150 million per USW.[37] These would not be out of line with estimates made of coal mine reclamation costs of some $600 million per USW that actually are to be paid under proposed legislation.[38]

[33] See U.S. Congress, Senate, Committee on Interior and Insular Affairs and Committee on Public Works, *Greater Coal Utilization,* pp. 632–633.

[34] See D. W. Locklin, H. R. Hazard, S. G. Bloom, and H. Nack, *Power Plant Utilization of Coal—A Battelle Energy Program Report* (Columbus, Ohio, Battelle, September 1974) p. 79.

[35] See *Science* vol. 184 (1974) pp. 646–647; and William Ramsay, "Priorities in Species Preservation," *Environmental Affairs* vol. 5, no. 4 (1977) pp. 595–616.

[36] See Edward J. DePuit, Waite H. Willmuth, and Joe G. Coenenburg, *Plant Response and Forage Quality for Controlled Grazing in Coal Mine Spoils Pastures: 1976 Progress Report,* Research Report 115 (Bozeman, Montana, Agricultural Experiment Station, Montana State University, August 1977) pp. viii and 56–57.

[37] See Ramsay, "Coal and Nuclear," p. 5-30.

[38] See U.S. Congress, House Committee on Interior and Insular Affairs, *Surface Mining,* p. 147, where 85 cents per ton is the estimated cost. Also, see U.S. Department of the Interior, Bureau of Mines, "Reclamation Costs Estimated for Western Strip Mines" (news release, Washington, 26 July 1977), for an estimate of 7 cents to 60 cents per ton, or $1,000 to $5,000 per acre.

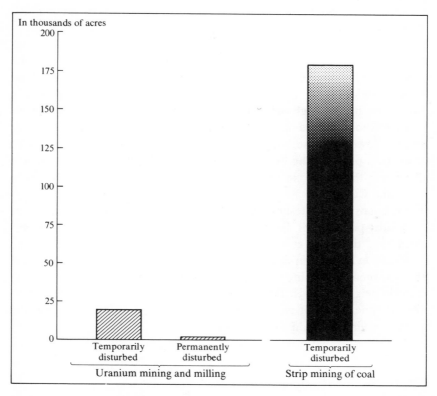

Figure 8-1. Land converted to electricity uses, per USW. Model uranium values are taken from U.S. Nuclear Regulatory Commission, "Final Generic Environmental Statement," IV F-22, tab. S(A)-1.

Indirect Effects of Land Use

Power plants and mines have effects on neighboring lands, too; recall, for example, the effect of acid mine drainage. Erosion from strip-mined areas and consequent sedimentation can also affect nearby valleys. When vegetation is removed to put up transmission lines, the water runoff of an area can be affected. In each case, though, the problem of greatest public concern is one that is hard to measure, that is, the effect on the surrounding landscape.[39] Even transmission towers can strike a disturbing note in an

[39] See William Ramsay, "Siting Power Plants," *Environmental Science and Technology* vol. 11, no. 3 (March 1977) pp. 238–243.

otherwise esthetically satisfying rural scene.[40] The horrors of unreclaimed strip-mined land as a landscape phenomenon have been talked about so much that they hardly need characterizing. But even energy facilities themselves can be a nuisance in some landscapes, and the plumes (the clouds of condensed moisture from cooling towers) can be disagreeable to some onlookers or can produce fogs that could conceivably present a hazard on nearby highways. And although power plants are not necessarily the noisiest kind of neighbor, it has happened that mechanical-draft cooling towers (those with large fans) were rejected in the proposed Dickerson plant on the Potomac River in Maryland, in order to prevent disturbing the public, in particular visitors to the adjoining Chesapeake and Ohio Canal.[41]

An unanswered question concerns the effect of nuclear power plants on nearby populations. Before the power plant is licensed, it must be certified that the population is low enough so that everybody could be promptly evacuated in case of a nuclear accident. As things stand now, though, there is nothing to keep more people from moving into existing nuclear neighborhoods. Perhaps the problem needs greater attention.[42] On the other hand, it is a comment on technology and society that the people moving in would choose to do so.

Options for Mitigation

Reclamation of surface-mined land is now becoming standard practice, but much remains to be done. Stabilization and restoration of land contours deals with known engineering techniques. But it is another problem entirely to recreate vegetation that has been destroyed, especially in an unfavorable (for example, an arid) climate.[43] The unpaid costs in this area—that is, the differences between mediocre and good reclamation—

[40] See William Ramsay, *Transmission Line Externalities and Property Values* (Washington, AEC, Directorate of Regulatory Standards, 1973).

[41] Myron Miller, Maryland Power Plant Siting Commission, private communication, 1976. See also Johns Hopkins University, *Dickerson Site: Power Plant Site Evaluation Report.* Addendum to JHU PPSE 3-1, January 1974, prepared for the Maryland Power Plant Siting Program (Annapolis, State of Maryland, January 1974) sect. 6.

[42] See Dwight R. Lee and Thomas G. Langley, "Designating Power Plant Sites: Methods of Advance Land Acquisition," report submitted to U.S. Nuclear Regulatory Commission, Office of Standards Development (1976).

[43] See DePuit, Willmuth, and Coenenburg, *Plant Response.*

will probably not be apparent for some time, and could well run into hundreds of millions of dollars per USW.[44]

Social Impacts

Local Impacts

Analyzing the effects of new electricity facilities on society in general is one thing; it is quite another, however, when a nuclear power plant comes to town or strip miners move into the next valley. In addition to all the general environmental and health problems that might be associated with a power plant or mine, there is also the quite human problem of the special impacts on local society. The impact of various coal and nuclear facilities may differ in detail,[45] but they resemble each other and other large projects in terms of the great changes that they may inflict on communities.

An influx of construction workers or miners can change the societal structure of the community and by sheer weight of numbers place great burdens on community facilities. Schools, hospitals, housing, roads, and law enforcement may all be put under stress. It may be a real problem for community leaders to get the money, time, and organizational ability to adapt to the changes involved. On the other hand, new facilities like power plants can often produce a financial windfall for a community. In two areas—Plymouth, Massachusetts, and Waterford, Connecticut—a new nuclear power plant has essentially doubled the tax base of the community.[46] This welcome help with taxes, however, can involve two serious drawbacks:

1. The extra community services needed to cope with the social impacts of the plant may be needed before the services become available.
2. If the tax base is widened and tax rates are therefore lowered, an influx of new residents not connected with the project may be attracted into the community. These new residents in turn may create a community growth crisis.

[44] See Ramsay, "Coal and Nuclear," pp. 5-30–5-32.
[45] See Ramsay, "Coal and Nuclear," pp. 5-37–5-39, for a brief review.
[46] See Elizabeth Peelle, Oak Ridge National Laboratory, "Socioeconomic Effects of Operating Reactors on Two Host Communities: A Case Study of Pilgrim and Millstone." Paper presented at Symposium on State of the Art of Socioeconomic Impact Assessment sponsored by Atomic Industrial Forum, St. Louis, Mo., 17 January 1977.

The resulting mix of societal changes and net financing needs and opportunities can make it difficult to characterize the changes as good or bad. One's judgment of the net social impact is generally controversial, since it comes down to a question of community values. Nevertheless, some practical steps can be taken to alleviate the timing problems. Communities in Skagit County, Washington, and in several other states have arranged with electric utilities or other energy suppliers to provide extra financing, either in the form of direct grants to the community or as prepaid taxes.[47] Since communities can compete as sites for energy facilities to some limited extent, it is possible to bargain over such arrangements. This type of negotiation could perhaps lead to a more efficient spreading of the social costs of the energy facilities between those who benefit and those who lose. At the very least, such new cost arrangements can alleviate some of the worst problems that can happen.

General Social Effects

Every economic activity and, therefore, every technology has far-reaching general effects on society, effects usually difficult to trace. Lately, the view has been popularized that systems of large electric grids supplied by giant coal and nuclear plants, such as the ones we have been considering here, have in themselves harmful effects upon the social fabric—effects in addition to the specific health and environmental impacts we have considered up to now.[48] A centralized grid could of course encourage such general social processes as urbanization, although it seems likely that other services (such as sewers) affect living patterns more. More important, the use of electricity generated by complex, large-scale ("hard") technologies such as coal and nuclear has been said to lead to an increase in "interventionist central control" of society, characterized by an elitist technocracy, a complex bureaucracy, and even a paramilitary class to deal

[47] See Skagit County (Washington) Board of County Commissioners, *Resolution No. 6279* (Skagit County, Washington, 26 March 1974); and Elizabeth Peelle, Oak Ridge National Laboratory, "Internalizing Social Costs in Power Plant Siting: Some Examples for Coal and Nuclear Plants in the United States." Paper presented at the International Meeting of the American Nuclear Society, Washington, D.C., 17 November 1976.

[48] See Amory B. Lovins, *Soft Energy Paths: Toward a Durable Peace* (Cambridge, Mass., Friends of the Earth/Ballinger, 1977) pp. 147–157.

with nuclear dangers. New proposals to put nuclear power plants in energy centers, for reasons of safety and safeguards, could be expected, in this view, to increase these tendencies even more.

The point of these arguments is that large electricity technologies require an emphasis on big organizations, such as large corporations and government agencies, great sums of money and great risks, and a general or national interest that allegedly steamrollers protests against energy facilities that may be locally undesirable. Such hard technologies could also be coercive ipso facto, in that, for example, no one in the United States can completely opt out of risks from nuclear power plants. It might also be that the mere existence of these supply technologies turns out to *determine* the demand for electricity and for related products because end uses that are not compatible with a centralized electric system are discouraged and so become uneconomic. In principle, consumption patterns that are lacking in utility to the citizen could then result—along with a general feeling of alienation and discontent on the part of the average member of society.

The validity of these arguments is not self-evident. Society certainly acts coercively on individuals in many ways, but we put up with police power, for example, feeling it provides us with sufficient benefits to outweigh the necessary costs of coercion. It is thus possible that nuclear power could still be socially justified, even if "coercive." Even more relevant to the soft-paths arguments is the question of how coercive the soft technologies themselves are: small-scale localized systems have their own ways of infringing on the individual, at least on the basis of such literary evidence as *Main Street*. And certainly a less electrified world could exert some bias against end uses that favor electricity; whether such a bias would contribute significantly to the denial of free consumer choice, and hence alienation, is difficult to say.

At any rate, this book is mainly a comparative work, and one of the key facts is that both coal and nuclear fall into the same category of large centralized technology. They are both hard. However, because of the official precautions taken to ensure nuclear safety and to provide safeguards against the diversion of nuclear material, the nuclear option probably plays a larger role in producing interventionism and centralized social control. That is, whether hard technology is on balance a bad thing, depending on both the viability and the social drawbacks of the opposing soft (mainly solar) technologies, nuclear appears to be harder than coal-fired generation.

Miscellaneous Impacts

We have mentioned all kinds of health impacts on the public from new electricity facilities. In addition to air pollution from power plants and radiation dangers from nuclear plants, some other by-products from energy generation cause trouble. Erosion and acid mine drainage from coal mines into the water supplies of nearby towns could cause health problems. Drainage from piles of uranium mill tailings can cause not only high concentrations of radium in local water but, as has sometimes been the case, can introduce toxic concentrations of the metal selenium and other impurities from the uranium ore into local streams and wells. High-voltage transmission lines—especially the larger sizes planned for the future—could conceivably have some effect on human health as the result of the strong electric fields surrounding them. Some European evidence of nausea and other illness has been reported for workers in electrical switchyards, but evidence for any serious impact from transmission lines is lacking.[49]

Oddly enough, the coal industry is implicated in one special danger: railway-crossing accidents between automobiles and trains carrying coal. It is difficult to determine which reported accidents involve collisions with coal trains, but some estimates are surprisingly large in comparison with some other health impacts. Exact figures for coal trains alone are not readily available, but 200 to 500 such deaths, as well as other railroad-related fatalities may be attributed per USW.[50] But a set of crossing gates only costs about $25,000 and presumably their use would reduce, though not eliminate, accidents. So as health costs go, it may be reasonably cheap

[49] See David E. Janes, Jr., "Background Information on High Voltage Fields," *Environmental Health Perspectives* vol. 20 (October 1977) pp. 141–147; and also, Battelle Pacific Northwest Laboratories, *Effects of Electric Fields on Large Animals,* EPRI EA-331, Project 799-1, interim report (Palo Alto, Calif., EPRI, December 1976), for experiments on pigs.

[50] See Argonne National Laboratory, "Health and Ecological Effects of Coal Utilization," draft report, U.S. Nuclear Regulatory Commission (December 1976) table 9.1, which gives a range of estimates for various model plants of 0.1 to 1.5 per plant per year; 1.5 seems a possible upper bound. But the lowest estimates for model case appear too small to represent the observed percentages of rail traffic [20 percent, according to U.S. Environmental Protection Agency (EPA), *Accidents and Unscheduled Events Associated with Non-Nuclear Energy Resources and Technology,* Inter-Agency Energy-Environment Research and Development Program Report, EPA-600/7-77-016 (Washington, EPA, February 1977)] attributable to 150 (1-GW equivalent) coal power plants and the approximately 1,000 total fatalities that occur every year [U.S. Department of Transportation, Federal Railroad Administration, *Rail-Highway Grade-Crossing Accidents/Incidents Bulletin: For the Year Ended December 31, 1975* (Washington, DOT, 1976); and *Summary of Na-*

to reduce this transportation safety problem by installing or improving crossing gates on isolated roads, assuming there are not an unreasonable number of crossing gates and that each line carries many millions of tons of coal a year. If coal is moved more by barge or by slurry pipeline, or power plants are placed at the mine mouth, this problem would also of course be much lessened.

Conclusion

In the future, thermal and chemical pollution of water will probably be well controlled as compared with other impacts. Water consumption for energy is difficult to evaluate, at least if it is divorced from other water needs, but, if necessary, we have methods of controlling the needs of power plants.

Land use changes due to surface mining are going to be partially controlled through enforced reclamation. Whether the degree of reclamation will be satisfactory to the public remains an open question, and it is an important factor in assessment of the use of coal. A much smaller amount of land contaminated by radioactive residues will tend to be a permanent land commitment to nuclear energy purposes.

Energy facilities—like other industrial projects—can produce unfair impacts on local communities. It is possible, however, to prevent unfair burdens from being placed on the resources of a community.

If alienation and societal distortion are important consequences of hard technologies, as is argued by some, nuclear appears to be a harder technology than coal. Some indirect impacts from the energy industry, such as transportation accidents, are important enough that mitigation efforts are worthwhile.

---

tional Transportation Statistics Annual Report, Report No. DOT-TSC-OST-76-11 (Washington, DOT, June 1976)]; 0.5, as noted elsewhere [U.S. Atomic Energy Commission (AEC), *Comparative Risk-Cost-Benefit Study of Alternative Sources of Electrical Energy,* WASH-1224 (Washington, AEC, December 1974)], is a believable lower bound.

9 Health Risks to Workers in the Coal and Nuclear Industries

How important are worker illnesses and deaths?

How should we consider the "voluntary" aspect of occupational illnesses and accidents?

Occupational Diseases

Workers in the electrical industry and in the activities supplying coal and nuclear fuel suffer occupational diseases. For both coal and nuclear, the major portion of both fatal and nonfatal diseases occurs in mining. The primary sites of severe occupational disease are the lungs and the bronchial tract.

The most serious disease associated with coal mining is black lung, or more specifically, coal workers' pneumoconiosis (CWP). Severe forms of the disease involve massive fibrosis of the lung; on X rays large areas of the lung appear as dense opacities. There seems to be little doubt that advanced forms of CWP are associated with coal mining and, therefore, contact with coal dust. In its worst forms the disease results in high mortality rates.[1] Less severe accumulations of coal dust in the lungs are less closely connected with fatalities: in a twenty-year follow-up study of a group of British miners, those with simple CWP showed only normal mortality patterns.[2] A variety of other respiratory ailments are also classified as black lung disease when they occur among coal miners. Such diseases—emphysema, for example—may or may not be associated with

[1] See Carl E. Ortmeyer, Joseph Costello, William K. C. Morgan, Steve Swecker, and Martin Peterson, "The Mortality of Appalachian Coal Miners, 1963 to 1971," *Archives of Environmental Health* vol. 29 (August 1974) pp. 67–72.

[2] See A. L. Cochrane, "Relation Between Radiographic Categories of Coal-workers' Pneumoconiosis and Expectation of Life," *British Medical Journal* vol. 2 (2 June 1973) pp. 532–534.

working in the mines, but miners apparently do suffer from a general excess of respiratory disease symptoms and impairments.[3]

All the costs of black lung disease are not exactly unpaid, since a special federal program was set up in 1969 to compensate miners disabled in the past by these diseases.[4] In a recent 3½-year period, $30 million in benefits were paid to victims by the U.S. Department of Labor,[5] and a 25 cent to 30 cent per ton tax on coal is now being paid by coal producers.[6] Figure 9-1 shows as many as 1,000 deaths might occur from CWP disease per USW.[7] Nonetheless, as we will see, the *future* number of fatal illnesses could be very small.

The key nuclear occupational disease appears in the form of high rates of pulmonary malignancies among uranium miners and mill workers, first reported in Europe.[8] Elusive radon gas, which is continuously emitted by uranium ores, decays into dangerously radioactive "radon daughters."[9] If inhaled into the miners' lungs, these daughters can cause cancer. Cancer deaths among miners occur in a somewhat different context from the cancer deaths we discussed before. The doses received in the mines—at least

---

[3] See Joe Pichirallo, "Black Lung: Dispute About Diagnosis of Miners' Ailment," *Science* vol. 174 (8 October 1971) pp. 132–134.

[4] The benefit program has had its problems, especially since lung X rays and the extent of breathing impairment often do not jibe. See Pichirallo, "Black Lung"; and Committee on Mineral Resources and the Environment, National Research Council, National Academy of Sciences (NAS), *Mineral Resources and the Environment,* Supplementary Report: *Coal Workers' Pneumoconiosis—Medical Considerations, Some Social Implications* (Washington, NAS, 1976).

[5] See U.S. Department of Labor, Employment Standards Administration, *Black Lung Benefits Act of 1972: Annual Report on Administration of the Act During Calendar Year 1976,* submitted to U.S. Congress (Washington, GPO, August 1977) p. 1.

[6] *Coal Outlook* (10 April 1978).

[7] Brookhaven National Laboratory, Biomedical and Environmental Assessment Group, "The Effect of Air Pollution from Coal and Oil Power Plants on Public Health," BEAG-HE 11/74 (Upton, N.Y., Brookhaven National Laboratory, 17 May 1974), pp. 53, 61, and 72, for this standard model estimate for the upper bound, based on an unpublished dissertation by D. J. Eaton. This value is based on the assumption that about 50 percent of mining is carried out underground. Also note that a recent study [Howard E. Rockette, "Cause Specific Mortality of Coal Miners," *Journal of Occupational Medicine* vol. 19, no. 12 (December 1977) pp. 795–801] of 23,128 miners showed that 188 deaths from pneumoconiosis occurred over the period 1959–73, with CWP mentioned as a contributory cause in 396 additional cases. If these figures are taken to suggest an individual yearly risk associated with CWP of about 1×10^{-3}, and a corresponding risk of about 0.5 per million worker-hours, from table 9-1 one could estimate for conditions prior to 1971, 0.3 per 1 million tons and 200 per USW.

[8] See Victor E. Archer, Joseph K. Wagoner, and Frank E. Lundin, Jr., "Cancer Mortality Among Uranium Mill Workers," *Journal of Occupational Medicine* vol. 15, no. 1 (1973) pp. 11–14.

[9] See previous discussion of long-lived isotopes in chap. 3, p. 36.

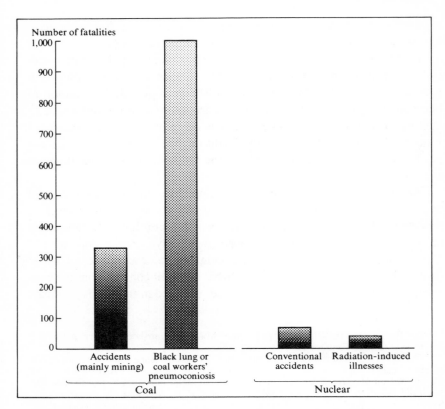

Figure 9-1. Estimates of workers' occupational deaths, per USW.

in the past—were rather large (see table 9-1),[10] and there were definite correlations between the calculated amount of exposure and the increased mortality rates.

Workers in uranium mills are also exposed to radon; and lately it has been speculated that the inhalation by mill workers of both dust from uranium and from one of its decay products, thorium 230, might lead to cancers of the lymphatic system.[11] Workers in other nuclear facilities—especially in mills and reactors—are exposed to radiation as part of their

[10] See Frank E. Lundin, Joseph K. Wagoner, and Victor E. Archer, *Radon Daughter Exposure and Respiratory Cancer: Quantitative and Temporal Aspects,* National Institute for Occupational Safety and Health and the National Institute of Environmental Health Sciences, Joint Monograph No. 1 (Washington, U.S. Department of Health, Education, and Welfare, 1971) tab. 4, where the working-level months can be thought of as approximately 5 rem.
[11] See Archer, Wagoner, and Lundin, "Cancer Mortality."

Table 9.1. Two Sample Occupational Risks

Year	Coal (bituminous) mining accidents			
	Fatal		Disabling	
	Per million worker-hours	Per million tons	Per million worker-hours	Per million tons[a]
January–April 1977	0.33	0.18	33.99	20.57
1976	0.35	0.21	36.16	21.31
1975	0.39	0.24	30.78	17.80
1974	0.42	0.22	28.95	14.88

Uranium miners: respiratory cancer deaths, 1950–68		
Estimated lifetime radiation dose given as ratio to maximum allowed under present regulations (assuming 30 years maximum time in mines)	Deaths expected	Deaths observed (all excesses significant at 1 percent level)
Less than 1	1.81	1
1–3	2.57	12
3–7	2.95	14
7–15	2.52	12
15–30	1.43	21
Over 30	0.42	10

Source: For mining accidents in bituminous coal industry, see U.S. Department of the Interior, Mining Enforcement and Safety Administration, "MESA Safety Reviews: Coal-Mining Industry Fatalities in 1974" (Arlington, Va., January 1975); and "MESA Safety Reviews: Coal-Mine Fatalities in December 1976" (Denver, Colo., February 1977) for fatalities; and "MESA Safety Reviews: Coal-Mine Injuries and Worktime Annual Summary 1974" (Denver, Colo., February 1975); MESA Safety Reviews: Coal-Mine Injuries and Worktime Annual Summary 1976" (Denver, Colo., February 1977); and "MESA Safety Reviews: Coal-Mine Injuries and Worktime, April 1977" (Denver, Colo., June 1977) for disabling illnesses. For respiratory cancer deaths among uranium miners, see Lundin, Wagoner, and Archer, *Radon Daughter Exposure,* tab. 4. The unit used is 120 WLM ("working level month," a unit of dose), or at 5 rem per WLM, 600 rem.

[a] A standard 1-GW plant would use between 2.3 and 3.2 million tons a year, depending on plant efficiency and coal quality.

jobs. These total exposures are relatively lower than those for miners and mill workers but do contribute to the predicted number of deaths from radium-induced latent cancers. Figure 9-1 estimates that twenty to forty excess deaths per USW can be expected for miners and all other nuclear power industry workers.[12]

[12] See U.S. Nuclear Regulatory Commission (NRC), *Final Generic Environmental Statement on the Use of Recycle Plutonium in Mixed Oxide Fuel in Light Water Cooled Reactors: Health, Safety and Environment,* NUREG-0002 (Washington, NRC, August 1976) tab. IV J(E)-9. For mining and milling, the exposure data developed by Dr. Stephen McGuire of the U.S. Nuclear Regulatory Commission (private communication, August 1977) have been used, together with a lung dose-

It is curious that no estimates exist on the radiation disease fatalities to be expected among workers in the case of a nuclear reactor accident—it is apparently presumed that workers could be evacuated in time.[13] Therefore, the values shown in figure 9-1 do not include the possible exposure of reactor personnel during accidents.

Outlook and Mitigation Possibilities

The fatality projections for black lung are quite uncertain, because the upper limit is based on very fragmentary and indirect data and also because there have been major changes in the regulations applied to the levels of coal dust within the mines during the past ten years. The standards now in force should decrease coal dust concentrations to levels similar to those reported as having greatly reduced the incidence of serious cases of CWP among miners in the United Kingdom.[14] Mining conditions in the United States—including the nature of the coal deposits—differ, however, and we will have to see whether laws regulating the amount of coal dust in the air can actually be achieved in the mines over the long run. At any rate, since black lung disease generally takes years to develop to the serious stage, it is still too soon to tell what the outlook is. Naturally, the dangers would be alleviated by a shift from underground mining to more surface mining.[15]

---

response relationship of 0.63 to 1.6×10^{-6} fatalities per rem [National Research Council, National Academy of Sciences, Advisory Committee on the Biological Effects of Ionizing Radiation, "The Effects on Populations of Exposure to Low Levels of Ionizing Radiation" (Washington, November 1972)], and twenty years' assumed time in the mines.

The rem is a unit of dose corresponding to the deposit of 100 ergs of energy by X rays in 1 gm of human tissue.

[13] But this omission has been criticized; see, for example, H.-P. Balfanz and P. Kafka, *Kritischer Bericht zur Reactorsicherheitsstudie, WASH 1400* (Critical Report on the Reactor Safety Study), IRS-I-87, MRR-I-65 (Cologne, Institut für Reaktorsicherheit der TUV E.V., Laboratorium für Reaktorregelung und Anlagensicherung, April 1976) p. 7.

[14] Argonne National Laboratory, "Health and Ecological Effects of Coal Utilization," draft report, U.S. Nuclear Regulatory Commission (December 1976) sect. 7.312.

[15] The estimates shown assume current relative levels of surface and underground mining. Compare with Cyril L. Comar and Leonard A. Sagan, "Health Effects of Energy Production and Conversion," *Annual Review of Energy* vol. 1 (Palo Alto, Calif., Annual Reviews, Inc., 1976) pp. 581–600; and Brookhaven National Laboratory, "The Effect of Air Pollution," pp. 53 and 60 (note 2).

For uranium miners, much stricter standards have been adopted in recent years to decrease drastically the risk from cancer (shown in table 9-1). Since there is probably little more that can be done to prevent the inhalation of radon daughters, the main possibility for lessening the disease incidence is to reduce still further the hours worked by each miner or to resort to expensive closed-cycle breathing systems. It is evident, from table 9-1, that for such low doses we would have to make mitigation decisions on the basis of inferred impacts rather than on the basis of definite data.

Radiation risks in mills can often be reduced by increasing the amount of ventilation. In reactors and other facilities, the calculated doses to most workers tend to be much lower than those in mills or mines.[16] On the other hand, the question of the size of the dose is much more difficult to pin down, since unexpected breakdowns in plant operations may lead to much higher than normal dose rates. At any rate, workers are generally limited to a certain lifetime dose—that is, some kind of compromise between the high doses at which cancer has resulted and the very low doses that we insist on as limits to the general public.

Accidents

Workers in energy industries are subject to the same kinds of industrial accidents as are other workers and, in particular, the special hazards associated with mining such as explosions and cave-ins. Consequently, for the coal industry, the majority of the accidents occur in mining. The minimum levels of projected accidental deaths form an important part of the minimum risks from coal-fired power plants. Not only are the levels significant, but deaths from coal-mining accidents are well-documented statistics, not merely theoretical predictions or inferences from other data (see table 9-1). The expected number of deaths ranges between one hundred and three hundred, from coal mining and other coal-related accidents (see figure 9-1), with nonfatal injuries and illnesses occurring in the tens of thousands (see figure 9-2 and appendix to this chapter).

Most industrial accidents to nuclear workers happen in mining and milling operations. The amount of uranium needed to generate 1 USW is

---

[16] Certain specialized trades among reactor occupations, such as pipefitters and millwrights, tend to accumulate relatively large doses.

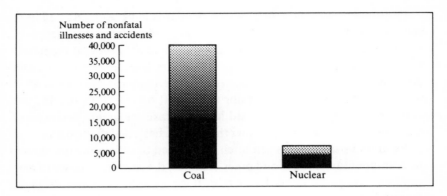

Figure 9-2. Workers' occupational nonfatal accidents and illnesses, per USW.

considerably less than the tonnage of coal required. Therefore, we expect fewer accidental deaths in the uranium industry. However, the patterns of uranium mining—that is, the scale of operations and grade of deposit— have been changing over the past quarter-century, and it is not as easy as one might imagine to estimate the number to be expected in the future. Nevertheless, figure 9-1 estimates fatal accidents of 20 to 70 per USW, while the estimate for nonfatal accidents and illnesses (see figure 9-2) is somewhat less than 10,000 (see appendix to this chapter).

Outlook and Mitigation Possibilities

The future statistics for coal accidents will depend on the pattern of mining, underground or strip—strip mining being inevitably safer. It may also depend on the results of the coal legislation passed within the last decade. Safety measures—for instance, those that guard against explosions in mines—can save lives. Perversely enough, though, they can also lower productivity, so that more worker-hours are required to supply the coal needed for a given amount of electricity generation. An increase in the number of worker-hours needed to produce each ton of coal would tend to raise accident rates per unit of electricity produced (see table 9-1). Also, if workers are less well trained, they are apt to have more accidents; therefore accident rates should depend on the uncertain levels of training and capability of new workers in both coal and uranium mines. Naturally, moves to automation in mining would tend to change occupational accident—as well as disease—patterns.

Health Risks, Compensation, and Costs

Should damage to the health of workers be considered on the same level as damage to the health of the general public?[17] A worker voluntarily agrees to undergo the risks in his trade. It may be that his salary includes an extra premium for those risks. Coal workers can even collect black lung disability benefits as partial compensation for work-related disease. Should the worker be entitled to the same level of consideration as a member of the general public who has no choice as to whether a coal- or nuclear-fired plant is located next door? In other words, should voluntary and involuntary risks be considered differently?

The main difficulty in trying to make this distinction is that the theoretical "voluntary" and "involuntary" aspects may not make much difference in practice. We get certain benefits from the voluntary activity, such as swimming—at the risk of drowning—and from services produced by facilities outside our voluntary control, like electricity—at the risk of cancer or bronchitis. It is not clear that these are really different in kind. Furthermore, it is not clear that the general public has no say in matters of public risks. Members of the general public are always free to move away from a hazardous locality, and can persuade their political representatives to introduce legislation banning unwanted power plants or strip mines. On the other hand, a coal miner may not have other skills, or the psychological or economic freedom to move from his established home in West Virginia. Also, premium pay for workers in many dangerous industries is negligible, if it exists at all.[18]

Comparing the risk level to workers with that to the general public is, therefore, a difficult task. Obviously, it is complicated by socioeconomic considerations. However, there seems no clear evidence to justify our placing relatively smaller emphasis on the workers' risks in making energy policy decisions.

---

[17] See William Ramsay, "Coal and Nuclear: Health and Environmental Costs" (Washington, Resources for the Future, August 1978) p. 6-24, and append. H.

[18] See Bureau of National Affairs, "Section 93: Wages," in *Collective Bargaining Negotiations and Contracts* vol. II (Washington, Bureau of National Affairs, 21 August 1969) pp. 601–606. See also rates such as time-and-a-half for working on towers higher than 60 feet or for fighting fires, and 25 cents per hour extra for work on outside scaffolds.

Conclusion

The incidence of disease and conventional accidents to workers in the coal and nuclear industries is large relative to other routine risks—except for the special case of coal-transportation accidents and possibly when compared with the uncertain health risks from air pollution. Statistics on deaths and disabilities are more certain, too, because they are observed rather than inferred. The impacts on workers in the coal-mining industry are greater than those for workers in the nuclear industry. It is not self-evident that these impacts are to be neglected or downgraded merely because a worker exercises some freedom in choosing an occupation.

Appendix: Accidents to Workers

Coal Workers

Total basic accident rates for surface and underground mining (four times the surface rate) have been estimated at about 0.2 per million tons for the current mix of about 45 percent underground and 55 percent surface mining.[19] Assuming that in future 40 to 70 percent of coal will be surface-mined—or alternately, a somewhat lower rate of future underground accidents—one can obtain (assuming that coal quality ranges from 21 million to 24 million Btu, or 10^9 joule, per ton), a mining accident rate of 0.30 to 1.0 per plant-year. Processing accident rates of 0.02 to 0.04 per plant-year have been estimated.[20] These are consistent with U.S. Department of the Interior data.[21] Also to be included are plant construction accidents and other conversion fatalities, at $1–2 \times 10^{-4}$ per worker-year (following the nuclear rate derived below), or for an average of 4,000 total worker-years,[22] 0.01–0.03 fatalities per plant-year. This gives a total occupational accident rate for coal workers of 0.34 to 1.1 per plant-year, or about 100 to 300 accidents per USW. Injury statistics from a standard source have been corrected to a 50 per plant mini-

---

[19] U.S. Department of the Interior, "MESA Safety Reviews: Coal Mine Fatalities in December 1976," tab. 4.

[20] Comar and Sagan, "Health Effects," p. 588.

[21] U.S. Department of the Interior, "MESA Safety Reviews: Coal Mine Fatalities in December 1976," tab. 4.

[22] Maryland Power Plant Siting Program, *Power Plant Cumulative Environmental Impact Report*, PPSP-CEIR-1 (Annapolis, Maryland Department of Natural Resources, September 1975).

mum,[23] as reflected in accident reports,[24] and 1,000 to 2,000 nonfatal construction accident injuries have been added, again on the nuclear model, giving a total of about 20,000 to 40,000 (mainly disabling) accidents and illnesses.

Transport accidents to railroad workers have been reported as 5 to 10 percent or so of the rate given for the general public (see chapter 8).[25] However, they are not disaggregated from that total here.

Nuclear Workers

Nuclear accident values are derived from a standard source,[26] with corrections reflecting recent data.[27] As pointed out in a recent study, construction accidents for reactors could contribute measurably to the total occupational impact.[28] One estimate, for one year, of reactor-related fatalities is two fatalities out of 20,365 workers in one year or about 1×10^{-4} fatalities per worker-year.[29] Combining SIC codes 15, 16, and 17, for the construction categories that might be involved in a nuclear power plant,[30] gives 750 fatalities out of 3,457,000 workers,[31] or about 2×10^{-4} per worker-year. Taking 7.62×10^3 worker-years,[32] one gets a rate per reactor of 0.75 to 1.5, or over a thirty-year reactor life, 0.025 to 0.05 fatalities per plant-year, or 8 to 15 fatalities per USW. Taking construction injuries at a rate of 5.5 per 100 full-time employees per year,[33] one would

[23] Comar and Sagan, "Health Effects," p. 588.

[24] U.S. Department of the Interior, "MESA Safety Reviews: Coal Mine Injuries and Worktime, Annual Summary 1976."

[25] U.S. Department of Transportation, Federal Railroad Administration, *Rail-Highway Grade-Crossing Accidents/Incidents Bulletin: For the Year Ended December 31, 1975* (Washington, 1976) p. 31.

[26] Comar and Sagan, "Health Effects," pp. 588–589.

[27] K. Thirmalai, U.S. Department of the Interior, private communication to E. Salmon, 18 November 1976.

[28] Ford Foundation, *Nuclear Power Issues and Choices,* report of the Nuclear Energy Policy Study Group, administered by MITRE Corporation (Cambridge, Mass., Ballinger, 1977) p. 176.

[29] Leonard A. Sagan, "Human Costs of Nuclear Power," *Science* vol. 177 (11 August 1972) pp. 487–493.

[30] U.S. Bureau of Labor Statistics, "Number of Occupational Injury and Illness Fatalities, Private Sector, by Industry, United States, 1976" (table) (1978).

[31] U.S. Bureau of Labor Statistics, *Occupational Injuries and Illnesses in the United States by Industry, 1975,* Bulletin 1981 (Washington, GPO, 1978) tab. 1.

[32] U.S. Atomic Energy Commission (AEC), *Nuclear Power Facility Performance Characteristics for Making Environmental Impact Assessments,* WASH-1355 (Washington, AEC, 1974).

[33] U.S. Bureau of Labor Statistics, *Occupational Injuries,* tab. 1.

similarly get 419 or, on a thirty-year basis, 14 per plant-year. Sagan shows that about 16 work days are lost per 100 full-time employees,[34] compared to approximately 101 shown in national statistics.[35] This could conceivably represent an actual rate smaller than industry averages. Therefore, we adopt a compromise range for total injuries of 7 to 14 per plant-year, or 2,100 to 4,300 per USW.

The nuclear total adopted here is therefore 6.4–23 × 10^{-2} per plant-year (fatalities) and 12 to 24 injuries, or 20 to 70 fatalities and 4,000 to 7,000 lost-day injuries per USW.

[34] Sagan, "Human Costs of Nuclear Power."
[35] U.S. Bureau of Labor Statistics, *Occupational Injuries.*

10 An Overall Look at Coal and Nuclear Energy

How do the overall impacts of coal and nuclear energy, considered separately, shape up?

Which are the key impacts that would probably most influence decisions?

Are the uncertainties impossibly great?

The impacts that we have looked at are of such varied natures and degrees that it is exceedingly difficult to make any sensible overall comparison. Why is this so? Is electricity generation so unusual that exceedingly complicated decisions must be made on the basis of insufficient evidence? The answer is no. The electrical energy problem is just one of many that have become complicated by the fact that the world is becoming a small place: we can no longer throw out our rubbish without considering whether it will land on our neighbor's doorstep. And our system of economics is not set up so that we can easily bargain back and forth to determine who is to get the rubbish. Health and environmental problems are a part of this crisis; industries can pollute such public resources as the air, water, and land without paying the full cost in illness or degraded ecosystems.[1] But, as members of the public, we all pay for these damages. It is essential that we assess these costs in order to set our system of social accounts straight, so that the so-called economic technologies—like coal and nuclear—do not turn out to be costly in human lives and lost environmental values.

The health and environmental effects of coal and nuclear, therefore, are not generally bargained for; that is, they are not usually included in the cost of electricity generation. Since engineers and accountants do not account for them in their budgeting decisions, there is no agreed upon mon-

[1] See, for example, William Ramsay and Claude Anderson, *Managing the Environment: An Economic Primer* (New York, Basic Books, 1972).

etary value for these effects, making it difficult to tell what their relative values should be. How do we equate coal miners' deaths with acres of uranium tailings, for example? Many answers are possible, depending on who is asked. Indeed, it becomes evident that the structure of values or ethics that each of us possesses must affect the way we look at the question.

Here we will summarize what the most important effects of coal and nuclear on health and the environment appear to be. However, any *overall* comparison must be held off until chapter 12, where the question of values is considered in more detail. There, we will see that some impacts of each technology appear to be dominant from the point of view of certain value "orientations," such as an orientation toward resource preservation.

The impacts of coal and nuclear energy are many and varied, and in general, all imaginable health and environmental effects must be taken into account. Some impacts, though, have exercised more influence in past policy decisions, or else they promise to play important roles in the future. Therefore, without implying that all other impacts can be neglected, here we will stress a few that can be labeled *key impacts*.

Coal—Summary of Key Impacts

Air Pollution- and Mining-induced Deaths and Illnesses

Even though our predictions of fatalities and illnesses stemming from power plant air pollution are very imprecise, there is still understandable concern that the emission by each coal-fired plant of so many known irritants and toxic elements into the atmosphere may cause a fair amount of disease and, possibly, a number of deaths in particularly susceptible populations. We take the sulfur-particulate estimates (see figure 2-1) as an indication of possible total illnesses and deaths from coal-fired plant emissions.[2]

A much more certain impact—but one which may change, depending on safety laws and on worker training—is based on the number of accidents from coal mining and other parts of the coal industry and, to a more

---

[2] The air pollution models to which we refer took sulfur-particulate parameters as identifying the level of impact, so that the rough estimates here also use them as a surrogate measure.

Note that errors could be introduced when considering impacts from sizable fractions of 1 USW because of interactions of emissions with ambient levels (see chap. 11, fn. 11).

uncertain extent, the problem of black lung (severe coal workers pneumoconiosis or CWP) from breathing coal dust. These two impacts are shown in figure 10-1; here, we detail the total number of fatalities expected if U.S. electrical requirements for 1975 had been supplied by coal alone (1 USW); ranging from 200 to 9,000 fatalities, they reflect especially the uncertainties in air pollution effects. Nonfatal illnesses and accidents from occupational causes (20,000 to 40,000 per USW) can be compared with the pollution illnesses shown in figure 2-1: 100,000 to 10 million asthma attacks; 600,000 to 60 million person-days of aggravated heart-lung symptoms in the elderly; 60,000 to 6 million cases of chronic respiratory disease in adults; and 10,000 to 1 million cases of lower respiratory-tract disease in children.

Climate Modification

Even though scientific evidence is inconclusive, the dreadful possibilities of destructive climatic changes from carbon dioxide and particulate emissions from coal-fired power plants must also be considered a critical impact. About 1.6 billion metric tons of carbon dioxide are emitted every year per USW (see chapter 7) and a small temperature change (perhaps $1 \times 10^{-3}°C$) might be associated with this increase in carbon dioxide. This contribution could be multiplied several times if other nations used more coal as a result of U.S. nuclear policy decisions.

Land Disturbance

Strip mining of coal causes, on the average, a sizable disturbance of land. Even though reclamation seems to be the order of the day, unanswered questions about the efficacy—or acceptability—of reclamation in some areas force us to consider this as a key impact. The amount of land involved is about 100,000 to 200,000 acres.

Other Impacts

A sizable amount of property damage—to paint and metals and agricultural products—is attributed to air pollution. Acid rain from power plant emissions could also be the source of a potential ecological catastrophe, but the scientific assessment of the question is still far from complete. Such problems may be of critical importance—probably even more so

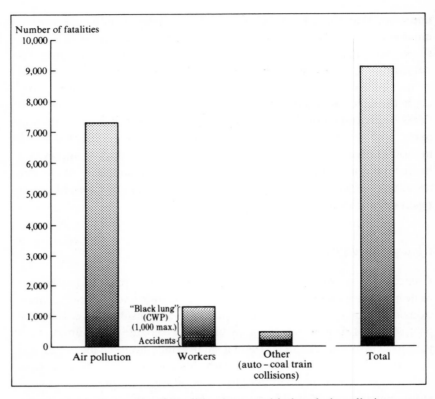

Figure 10-1. Summary of fatalities from coal-induced air pollution, occupational diseases, accidents, and transportation, per USW. For data, see figures
2-1 and 9-1 in this volume.

in the future—but the solutions to them will quite likely be based on attitudes toward the effect that sulfur oxides and nitrogen oxides have on
health and environment. Thus the social treatment of these miscellaneous
problems will likely come about as a consequence of our concern about
other aspects of air pollution. The esthetic effects of air pollution are
probably important in local land use impacts—even if the implied losses
in property values are not always recognized.

Acid mine drainage, when it occurs, is a serious problem, although it is
difficult to predict the extent of the problem in new mines because of
changing water quality regulations and related mining practices.

Another special impact is the problem of automobile collisions with
trains carrying coal and other coal-related railroad accidents. Even though
the number of fatalities attributed to this is surprisingly large, it is likely
that policymakers would consider this in the context of a motor vehicle

problem that might—incidentally—be significantly mitigated at fairly reasonable cost. At any rate, the hefty contributions from this impact (see page 106) are included in the total coal fatalities of about 200 to 9,000 per USW, as shown in figure 10-1.

Nuclear—Summary of Key Impacts

Proliferation and Diversion

A recent study has called the proliferation problem the chief obstacle to the use of nuclear power as an energy source.[3] In a plutonium economy, the possibility of diversion of nuclear fuel and related materials by terrorist groups must also be a critical factor. The connection between the nuclear industry and proliferation is very speculative, and is not included in the totals given in figure 10-2.[4]

Nuclear Safety

Even though the calculated average impact of nuclear reactor accidents has been judged small by the only definitive study existing, the peculiar yes-or-no quality of the problem, typical of potential disasters, makes it remain one of special concern.

In figure 10-2 the expected deaths from nuclear accidents (see chapter 4) are given. The almost 50,000 expected deaths for the worst accident considered are also shown, in order to demonstrate why a relatively small "average" impact could deserve separate treatment as a possible catastrophic event. Twenty to 200 cases of nonfatal thyroid illness (not shown) would also be expected.

Nuclear Waste

The impact from high-level waste storage cannot be determined yet—we must await new government decisions and the results of pilot operations.

---

[3] See Ford Foundation, *Nuclear Power Issues and Choices,* report of the Nuclear Energy Policy Study Group, administered by MITRE Corporation (Cambridge, Mass., Ballinger, 1977).

[4] See chap. 6 in this volume. Diversion dangers also depend on foreign production of plutonium, so that risk estimates are subject to complex reasoning on foreign policy, as is the proliferation problem.

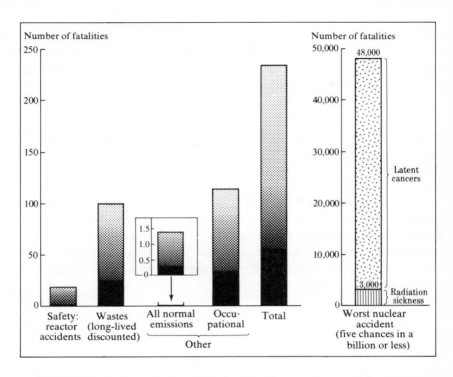

Figure 10-2. Summary of nuclear fatalities from reactor accidents, wastes, and other sources, per USW, and a worst-accident case of low probability. For data, see figures 3-1, 3-2, 4-1, and 9-1.

On the other hand, when compared with the effects of other nuclear impacts, those from long-lived radioisotopes in *existing* waste gases—while small on a yearly basis relative to many other impacts—are persistent, having a cumulative effect over time. The number of fatalities we attribute to it depends on our attitude toward the future; that is, on the discount rate we choose. The size of these impacts per USW (see chapter 3) vary considerably as a function of discount rate: the effects are still modest at most finite discount rates (60 to 400 fatalities at 1 percent), but as the discount rate approaches zero, the total of deaths becomes relatively large (30,000 to 200,000). The impacts (20 to 100 fatalities per USW) at one particular discount rate (5 percent) are included in the nuclear total shown in figure 10-2.[5]

---

[5] The value adopted for the long-lived isotopes is 5 percent, an approximate deflated rate for returns to assets in the American utilities industry. See Stephen A. McGuire and Jose G. Martin, "A Monetary Correction Model of Economic Analyses

Other Impacts

Nuclear energy can also produce a climate modification, but only in a plutonium economy where a good deal of krypton 85 is released. This is of concern for the future if we or others institute a breeder regime. In that case, the release of krypton would need further attention.

Nuclear generation also has its own land use impacts (20,000 acres per USW), primarily resulting from the surface mining of uranium (see figure 8-1). Presently we require a permanent conversion of a relatively small amount of land (2,000 acres per USW) for the storage of wastes from uranium mills—at least for the next few tens of millennia. In addition, other land must be devoted to decommissioned reactor sites.

The use of nuclear energy results in occupational illnesses and routine accidents. Uranium mining, especially, involves many accidents to workers, but so far our experience with uranium mines indicates that the number of accidents is relatively small compared with those occurring in the coal industry, perhaps because many fewer tons of nuclear ·fuel per gigawatt-hour are needed. On the other hand, nuclear use results in fatalities from exposure to radiation in mines and in reactors. These occupational impacts (30 to 100 fatalities per USW) are included in the summary shown in figure 10-2, together with the small impacts from routine releases from reactors (0.3 to 1 per USW). Some 4,000 to 7,000 cases of nonfatal occupational accidents and illnesses also have to be considered. Figure 10-2 shows the total nuclear fatalities to be in a range of about 60 to 200 per USW.

Impacts Common to Both Coal and Nuclear

In chapter 8 it was shown that there are environmental impacts common to both coal and nuclear. Effects of moisture and heat on local weather conditions are apt to occur both for coal and nuclear, although to a somewhat lesser degree for coal. The impacts of water use, of transmission lines

Applied to Nuclear Power Costs," *Nuclear Technology* vol. 18 (June 1973) pp. 257–266; and Edison Electric Institute, *Statistical Year Book of the Electric Utility Industry for 1975*, no. 43, EEI Publication No. 76-51 (New York, EEI, October 1976), and previous annual editions, for comparisons of equity returns and debt per equity ratio.

on the countryside, and the general social impacts of coal mines or nuclear reactors on the surrounding communities, are all important in specific local and regional contexts. Although now heavily regulated, the problem of thermal pollution may still remain a question of *local* concern.

All these impacts—while they may be large—are probably of lesser importance in the comparison of coal and nuclear electricity because the impacts are so similar for either fuel. But this does not mean that in examining the nation's total energy picture they do not play an important role. In particular, the needs of energy facilities and competing industrial, agricultural, and residential water needs is a complex subject that goes beyond the scope of this book, as do issues that have been raised concerning the general social consequences of a dependence on central station electricity.

Analytic Uncertainties

The uncertainties in all this analysis have been emphasized. It should be evident that by any strict standards of scientific investigation, we have very little firm information about many of the electricity problems. In that sense, many "health risks" are actually uncertain in many different aspects: (1) Who suffers the effect; (2) Will the effect occur at all (especially in the case of catastrophes); (3) How much physical impact occurs; and (4) How much health damage will that impact do? We have seen that problem from the first, for instance, in the discussion of air pollution from coal-fired power plants. Deficiencies in data and theory exist in many fields—physics, engineering, meteorology, and medicine. For all the impacts, we are often faced with three basic questions and very imperfect understanding of the answers: What is happening? Why? How serious is it? And, of course, the question is not just for coal. Even though a great deal of research has gone into nuclear radiation, very little is known about the effects of low-level radiation on the human body.

It might be thought that the situation is easier when we are talking about explicit deaths inflicted on real people, such as fatal accidents to coal miners. But we must remember that we are projecting over the future. The proportion of strip mining to underground mining can change, the level of coal workers' training may vary, new laws and regulations may make mines safer—or will they? The same question comes up, of course, regarding damages to the environment. The amount of land needed for strip-mining coal obviously depends on the thickness of the coal seams, if nothing else. Acid rain, presumably from pollutant compounds dissolved in local rainfall, may be very injurious to plants. On the other hand, there is some chance that the effect is either not of critical environmental importance or even that power plants are not the major culprit.

The uncertainty extends to clean-up measures. It is all very well to talk about systems such as stack gas scrubbers that remove a certain amount of the sulfur naturally present in the coal, but until these systems are adequately tested, it is not clear exactly how much sulfur can be removed on a daily basis, what the reliability of the scrubbers is, and, therefore, what their real cost is. Again, we can only sketch some of the possibilities for clean-up (or abatement) of various pollutants or other impacts that could cause health or environmental problems.

All of this, of course, is not a counsel of despair. Policymakers must constantly make decisions based on inadequate data. We may be of necessity less than satisfied with our knowledge about many of the effects we have considered, but we have kept these uncertainties in mind in describing the impacts in the previous chapters. Therefore, the partial descriptions made there of each impact should already reflect the various ranges of possibilities in each field. But we want to point out here certain general differences in what we know about each of these areas.

First, the estimates of the effects from air pollution have a very wide range. Recent reviews have emphasized the deficiencies of the studies supporting even the very rough estimates that have been quoted.[6] On the basis of such criticisms questioning whether statistically valid relationships do in fact exist,[7] one might want to give the lower part of this range more credence than the higher.[8]

Second, on the other hand, the estimates of the impacts from nuclear radiation may be more reasonably bounded. Some argue they are prob-

---

[6] See Ford Foundation, *Nuclear Power*, p. 195. See also chap. 2, append. A, of this volume.

[7] See Greenfield, Attaway, and Tyler, Inc., *Sulfur Oxides: Current Status of Knowledge*, EPRI EA-316, Project 681-1 (Palo Alto, Calif., EPRI, December 1976) p. 2-35.

[8] One problem with cases of illness resulting from air pollution is that the illness can range from a bad cold to crippling cardiac symptoms. The large number of illnesses associated with coal are, of course, predicted from models based on epidemiological studies, that is, on studies of health statistics made during periods of air pollution. Measurements are, of course, very indirect and therefore somewhat suspect, even forgetting the different nature of the various illnesses.

Even so, the illness figures are possibly more correct than those shown for deaths, since it is quite plausible that low levels of air pollution could cause lung irritation, while it is less likely that a significant number of fatalities result. The fatalities that do occur may be premature by only a day or so, judging from some indications (ibid.).

ably too low; and others, that they are likely too high (see chapter 3, appendix B). Although further research is needed, the middle range of the estimates may therefore be a plausible compromise for routine radiation, and especially for short-range radiation from waste gases. [Note chapter 3, appendix B, and that radon involves high linear energy transfer (LET) radiation.] However, the situation could be different for nuclear catastrophes. The likelihood of a nuclear reactor accident could be either understated or overstated, just on the basis of the many unknowns involved and the relative youth of the nuclear industry. The probabilities of nuclear warfare or explosions through proliferation or terrorism are, of course, highly speculative.

Third, the climatic effects have the virtue of involving the volume of emissions of carbon dioxide, a well understood physical process. But so little is known about all the other mechanisms of climate and weather that one must be very cautious. The temperature changes that have been quoted are based on incompletely validated models of complex physical processes.

Fourth, the biggest and most identifiable ecological impacts are probably in degradation of land by strip mining and, in a more complex context, water consumption. The sizes of the impacts are relatively certain here, but the question of how the impacts are to be valued by society is another story.

Finally, coal occupational health effects are in a way a relatively simple question. The upper end of the range of effects could be too high, but enough latitude has been allowed in the estimate adopted that it is difficult to persuade oneself that the lower limits for coal can be much reduced by changes in technology or safety procedures in the near future, unless mining automation increases at a very rapid pace. Nuclear occupational estimates for radiation effects depend on inferred doses, and any value within the range given seems as good as any other.

The unavoidable uncertainties in the unpaid costs of electricity have some implications for the directions future policy might take. If we are ignorant about phenomena that might be very costly to us—such as air pollution from power plants—then research into the question might be relatively cheap, on the average. And, in addition, the nation might want to hedge its bets, in the sense that we might want to keep both the coal- and nuclear-generating alternatives alive until we find out more about the effects of each one of them. We will return to these questions in the last chapter.

Conclusion

Coal and nuclear impacts vary both in kind and in degree. Listing them side by side does not yet solve our problem. But the following have been identified as key impacts and totals of a sort have been made for each:

Coal	Nuclear
Air pollution and mining: deaths and illnesses	Proliferation and diversion
Climate modification	Reactor safety
Land use disturbance	Nuclear waste, including waste gases

Other problems, however, exist and cannot be neglected in any total analysis: for example, nuclear occupational fatalities, acid rain, and property damage from air pollution.

The existence of unavoidable uncertainties in the problem may have policy implications in itself.

11 Consequences of National Energy Policies

What impact will proposed national energy policies have on the health and environmental costs of electricity?

What can we say about electricity-generation choices on the basis of the impacts we have seen so far? We have made detailed estimates of health and environmental impacts where possible. But many of the unpaid costs that have been examined are exceedingly vague and indefinite, and the fact that value judgments may conflict complicates the matter. Nevertheless, the problem is so important that the most reasonable judgment must be made on the basis of what information and analytic capabilities are in our possession.

It may be, however, that other forces and events will shape actual national energy directions. So before we are able to discuss the general virtues and defects of coal and nuclear power, it is first necessary to look at what the future U.S. energy picture is apt to look like on the basis of present policy trends, and what pattern of unpaid costs is likely to emerge. Incidentally, it also might be wise to determine whether the whole is greater than the sum of the parts; that is, what are the cumulative effects, if any, on health and the environment?

Recently the Carter administration has proposed a National Energy Plan (NEP) that suggests policies for reaching certain energy goals by 1985. We can try to see what health and environmental impacts this or similar energy supply and demand projections have. It may also be possible to infer something about how the policies of the present U.S. administration are related to various human values involved in the electricity-generation question.

Fixed Features of the U.S. Electricity Economy

Future plans must take into account the present system of central station power plants, having a generating capacity of over a half-billion kilowatts.[1] This system serves more than 70 million residential customers plus millions of industrial and commercial users. At present, less than 10 percent of the electricity generated by this system is derived from nuclear plants and about 45 percent is from coal-fired plants, with the rest being produced by oil, natural gas, and hydropower. This system is supported by a transmission and distribution system that includes over 420,000 miles of high-voltage transmission lines. We also have a world in which oil and gas are apparently running out, long-term supplies of low-cost uranium are unsure, and new sources of hydroelectric power are scarce.

But there are also flexibilities in the system. Gas- or oil-fired stations can be converted from one to the other with relative ease, but to convert them to coal would be much more difficult and expensive—for example, often storage space for coal and ash is lacking. Other fuels can sometimes be substituted for electricity. Indeed, one important feature of the plan proposed by the Carter administration was that although electricity would grow in importance up through 1985, it would not become the dominant factor in the total energy picture. This could mean that producible coal may have to be used elsewhere, rather than for the generation of electricity.

Another difficulty is that everything takes time, and the expansion of energy industries to meet new needs may require time, money, and other important resources, such as skilled labor. Constructing a power plant takes a number of years, and, in the case of nuclear plants, preparing environmental impact statements and passing safety reviews, for example, also take a considerable length of time. Some critics believe that the 50 percent expansion of coal production from now to 1985 envisaged in the Carter plan is unrealistic.[2] Others believe that it could be done.[3] At any

[1] Edison Electric Institute, *Statistical Year Book of the Electric Utility Industry, for 1975*, no. 43, EEI Publication No. 76-51 (New York, EEI, October 1976).

[2] Hans H. Landsberg, "Balancing the 1985 Energy Accounts," *Washington Post* (16 May 1977); David E. Gushee, "The Carter Coal Conversion Plan for Industry: A Critique" (Washington, Library of Congress, Congressional Research Service, 10 June 1977) mimeo.

[3] J. Bhutani, A. Brice, J. Elliott, D. Ellis, W. Jacobsen, J. Just, E. Krajeski, and J. Savadelis, *An Analysis of Constraints on Increased Coal Production*, MTR-6830 (McLean, Va., MITRE Corporation, January 1975); Carl E. Bagge, letter of 23 May 1977, to Rep. John D. Dingell, Chairman, Subcommittee on Energy and Power of the House Committee on Interstate and Foreign Commerce, with "Background Information and Responses to Questions Relating to Section F of H.R. 6831 on Coal Conversion" (mimeo).

rate, our available choices in the use of coal and nuclear that could take effect by 1985 (or even by the year 2000) would probably be restricted.

The U.S. Energy Future—Environmental and Health Aspects

Planners feel that the near-term future for U.S. electricity will not be subject to much change. The effect of government policies on electricity—such as those proposed in the NEP—would be to reinforce those changes in fuel use that are already coming about because of higher oil and natural gas prices and the lessened availability of the latter. For example, figure 11-1 estimates the amount of electric power (in terms of "quads" of input[4]) that would be generated in 1985, with and without the NEP, and compares it with the 1976 input.[5] Electricity use is expected to increase by more than 50 percent, but the effect of the plan itself on the level and composition of electricity output appears relatively minor. Therefore, it is perhaps safe to take the NEP world as a good example of what the year 1985 might become. At any rate, the difference between 1976 and either world in 1985 is dramatic. Hydropower would be relatively less important for baseload generation, oil use would be reduced radically under the plan, and gas would be greatly deemphasized. To take up the slack, the proportional contribution from coal would increase, and the nuclear contribution would rise dramatically. The difference between the 1985 with-NEP and the without-NEP scenarios would be some slight increases in nuclear and coal power, a redirection of natural gas to residential and commercial uses, and a reduction in oil imports. A little less electricity would be produced but residential and commercial electricity users would presumably avoid shortages by conservation.

The greatest consequences of the NEP proposals might not result from direct environmental and public health or safety measures, such as strip-

---

[4] In this chapter, the commonly used energy unit, the quad, is utilized. This is a unit corresponding to 10^{15} (quadrillion) British thermal units (Btu). One Btu of electrical energy will light a 100-watt bulb for 10.5 seconds, but it takes over 75 quadrillion of them to run the United States. Per capita, this amounts to about 12,000 watts per person. Kenneth Boulding, in a private communication, has pointed out that one can visualize U.S. per capita energy use by imagining oneself surrounded by the blinding light from 120 100-watt light bulbs.

[5] Executive Office of the President, Energy Policy and Planning, *The National Energy Plan* (Washington, GPO, 29 April 1977) p. 95. The without-NEP case is also a Carter administration projection.

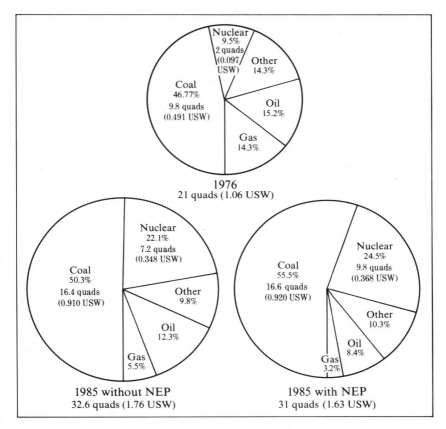

Figure 11-1. Electricity generated in 1985 with and without the NEP, in percentages, quads (10^{15} Btu) input, and USW ($=2 \times 10^{12}$ kWh) output. This has been adapted from the NEP figure IX-1, where 1 million barrels of oil equivalent per day have been taken as equal to 2 quads (10^{15} Btu). Output in the 750-MW year (plant-year) units of Ramsay, "Coal and Nuclear" is 29, 106, and 112 (nuclear); 149, 277, and 280 (coal), for 1976, 1985, and 1985-NEP, respectively. (Conversion for 1976 for coal and "other" is at efficiencies of 35 percent; for 1985 at 38 percent; nuclear efficiency is 33 percent.)

mining legislation, but from the indirect influence of the energy objectives themselves. Every encouragement of energy conservation, from home insulation to utility rate reform, every new government-sponsored solar demonstration project would decrease to some extent the amount of electricity needed from coal and nuclear power plants, thus decreasing indirectly their environmental effects. Even though this book deals solely with a comparison of the coal and nuclear choices, such potential *indirect* effects cannot be entirely overlooked. The NEP and similar initiatives would also indirectly discourage the growth of residential electricity use by increasing industrial coal use so that oil and gas supplies previously needed by industry could be utilized for household energy needs.[6] But the most important indirect effect of general energy policy on electricity could stem from initiatives that are the main thrust of the Carter program—the conservation of oil and gas by tax schemes and other regulations. Every barrel of oil or cubic foot of gas that is not burned by utilities has to be replaced, mainly by coal or nuclear energy. Gas is relatively clean, while oil has its own, but comparatively fewer, environmental problems. Decisions on fluid fuel conservation, then, ultimately have environmental consequences, although they may not have that appearance.

Other features of current U.S. policy affect the balance between nuclear and coal in a less subtle manner. In the long run, the administration decision against the breeder reactor would encourage more health effects from coal-fired generation, assuming, as many do, that uranium supplies are relatively limited. Related policies could also discourage our nuclear industry; for example, efforts to promote nonproliferation abroad could affect U.S. sales of nuclear facilities and fuel to other countries. On the other hand, the NEP does encourage uranium enrichment in the United States as an incentive to other nations to give up plutonium. The NEP also advocates better estimates of uranium and thorium resources and the investigation of new types of nuclear fuel cycles from which it might be more difficult to obtain weapons material.

The NEP also takes explicit positions on nuclear health and environmental control measures. The plan recommends nuclear safety improvements and more remote siting of nuclear power plants.[7] On the other hand, the NEP statements about nuclear wastes contribute nothing new to what was probably going to be done anyway, and the NEP ignores some of the more interesting problems involving gaseous wastes.

The plan also treats some very direct health and environmental decisions on the coal question; for example, it favors going to the Best Available Control Technology (BACT) for power plant emissions. This prin-

[6] It is necessary to remember that oil and gas sent to households could replace coal-generated electricity there, but it may also mean more coal-burning in the industrial sector.

[7] Executive Office of the President, *National Energy Plan,* p. 72. If the Executive branch were—as is implied—to encourage the Nuclear Regulatory Commission to locate nuclear power plants farther from population centers, there could be some safety improvements; but such modest improvements may not produce radical changes in citizens' apprehensions regarding possible nuclear catastrophes.

ciple has since been included in recent clean air legislation,[8] perhaps a sensible recommendation for resource and administrative reasons since it is relatively simple to enforce, and it makes all grades of coal equally useful. But we must recognize that a uniform control technology would affect drastically the clean up of coal-induced health effects. It would make the environment cleaner because the total amount of sulfur emitted could be considerably less, especially where low- or medium-sulfur coals are burned, than present EPA standards. On the other hand, a blanket abatement method could, at least for a time, lock the country into one particular kind of technology (presumably scrubbers), indirectly discouraging further research and investment in other technologies such as low-Btu gasification, fluidized-bed combustion, and solvent refining of coal—even though the NEP gives at least some pro forma encouragement to those processes also.

Other ideas expressed in the NEP are also endorsements of long-standing legislative initiatives (since passed) in the environmental field. The new "nondeterioration" provisions of clean air legislation could mean even more severe environmental constraints on coal use in the near-term future. Even coal plants with scrubbers might not be good enough in some areas with certified "very clean" air, or—oddly enough—in others with "very dirty" air. That is, changes in the air quality in an especially clean area such as a national park, would—under the new laws—be very restricted,[9] but also no new sources of emissions would be allowed in an industrialized area that already exceeded national air quality standards.

New federal strip-mining legislation that makes reclamation obligatory will be a step toward mitigating the environmental impact on the landscape. But of course it will not prevent all such impacts; for example, in the arid West, adequate reclamation might be difficult.[10] We have too little experience with strip-mining reclamation, however, to be able to sort out the net results. In fact, neither the full future effects of the Clean Air Act and its related regulations nor those of enforced land reclamation can be easily foreseen at this time. Nevertheless, at this point it is necessary to project the consequences of these decisions for the years 1985 and 2000 (see also chapter 12).

[8] U.S. Congress, Senate, Subcommittee on Environmental Pollution, Committee on Environment and Public Works, *Clean Air Act Amendments of 1977: Hearings on S. 251, S. 252, and S. 253,* bills to amend the Clean Air Act, as amended, 95 Cong. 1 sess., ser. no. 95-H7, pt. 1 (Washington, 1977).

[9] Ibid., pp. 381–389.

[10] Genevieve Atwood, "The Strip-Mining of Western Coal," *Scientific American* vol. 233, no. 6 (December 1975) pp. 23–29.

Key Impacts for 1985

Whether any particular government policies are adopted, the Carter administration predicts that economic forces will produce a pattern of electricity generation similar to that proposed in the NEP for 1985. Presumably, environmental and health constraints—and resource limitations—would not prohibit the levels of electricity generation shown in figure 11-1.

From figure 11-1 a simple pattern for key health and environmental impacts can be inferred. One applies the amounts of electricity energy inputs predicted in the NEP—0.920 USW for coal, and 0.368 USW for nuclear—to the impacts per USW (see chapter 10) to find the results for the United States in 1985. Figure 11-2 shows the fatal health effects for the whole nation under the levels projected. Looked at on the basis of an actual coal–nuclear mix serving the entire country, the predicted number of fatalities is still sobering. Even for the smaller nuclear contribution to electricity generation, one could predict from twenty to ninety fatalities per year. The coal impacts are larger and dominate the coal–nuclear total for the nation. The national total is somewhat under 300 to somewhat less than 8,000 fatalities per year. One can see that the maximum fatalities associated with air pollution are somewhat less than would have been predicted from chapter 10.[11] The difference is due to the probable introduction of new pollution controls for new plants in the interim.[12]

Even with BACT, air pollution still accounts for 10,000 to 1 million cases of lower respiratory-tract infections among children and 100,000 to 10 million asthma attacks, plus corresponding totals for other diseases.

---

[11] The air pollution impacts adopted, as suggested by studies on incremental changes in capacity, are applied here to the total U.S. generating capacity. Errors could be made by neglecting the differences between increasing pollution above and below thresholds. Errors also could be made in assessing old generating capacity at parameters relating to new capacity, although retrofit would tend to eliminate this distinction. It also neglects the separate fact that ambient levels from other sources will decrease (or increase) as the result of new policies. In view of the opposing or unknown tendencies of these errors, and the very approximate nature and wide range of the impact estimate, such possible sources of error are not taken into account here.

[12] Here it is assumed that the BACT will remove 90 percent of the sulfur in coal, thus reducing emissions to about one-third the value shown in the New Source Performance Standards (based on the existing sulfur percentages, averaging 2.2 percent, as given in Thomas W. Hunter, *Effects of Air Quality Requirements on Coal Supply*, U.S. Department of the Interior, Bureau of Mines, supplement to Bituminous Coal and Lignite Distribution Reports (Washington, U.S. Bureau of Mines, May 1976) p. 11; and 0.72 percent sulfur-equivalent for NSPS). Nineteen percent of all plants operating in 1985 are assumed to have BACT, assuming the growth rates shown in figure 11-1 and taking 1983 as the first year of new plants, giving an 87 percent correction to be applied in 1985 to figure 10-1 impacts per USW.

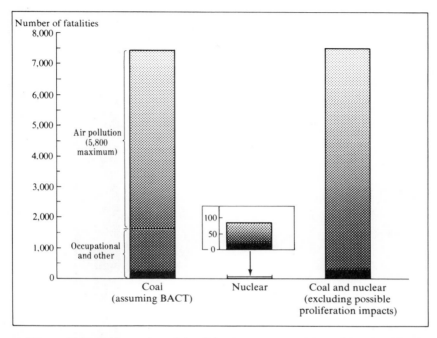

Figure 11-2. Estimated total fatalities from power plants under the NEP in 1985. "Nuclear" does not include proliferation and diversion, but does include radon and other persistent isotopes, discounted at 5 percent. Air pollution effects are included, as predicted under proposed NEP controls (see text). Data are based on figures 10-1, 10-2, and 11-1, taking into account the BACT outlook (see footnote 12).

Combined property and crop damage from air pollution (compare with figure 2-2) under the same assumption could range from $200 million to $2 billion in 1985.

Long-lived isotopes from certain gaseous nuclear wastes, as projected by the nuclear energy estimates, are a special kind of problem. Only 0.1 to 0.8 fatality can be expected to occur in 1985 from radon.[13,14] On the

---

[13] The situation is even more complex, since the deaths "caused" in 1985 may actually occur from ten to thirty years later, depending on the latency period. These questions are discussed in U.S. Nuclear Regulatory Commission, *Reactor Safety Study: An Assessment of Accident Risks in U.S. Commercial Nuclear Power Plants,* WASH-1400, NUREG-74/014 (Washington, NRC, October 1975); and William Ramsay and Milton Russell, "Time-adjusted Impacts from Energy Generation," *Public Policy* vol. 26, no. 3 (Summer 1978). Also, the discrepancy between the time when the mill tailings are produced and when the power is generated (which involves a time lead instead of lag) is neglected here.

[14] This is true if we look only at the radon produced in 1985. But since the radon

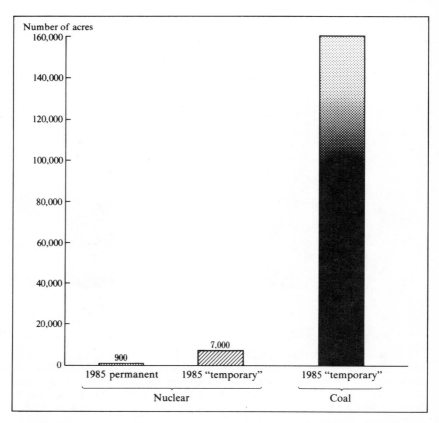

Figure 11-3. Land use impacts under the NEP. Data are based on figures 8-1 and 11-1.

other hand, unless properly disposed of, the "grandparent" isotopes that emit radon will continue to do so and could cause fatalities for tens of thousands of years into the future. No way of looking at the long-lived gaseous waste problem is completely satisfactory, as has been discussed before, but one compromise figure for radon combined with carbon 14

grandparents keep accumulating over the period between 1976 and 1985, the total number of fatalities conceivably caused within these nine years by radon emitted within those nine years is disproportionately larger (that is, 2 to 10 fatalities). Indeed, the total number of fatalities occurring between 1986 and the year 2000 from the radon grandparents exposed to the atmosphere in the course of producing power between 1977 and 1985 is over four times greater, or from 8 to 60 fatalities. Naturally, we must remember that this number of deaths is a cost that is balanced by the benefit of all the nuclear-generated electricity used within periods ranging from nine to fifteen years.

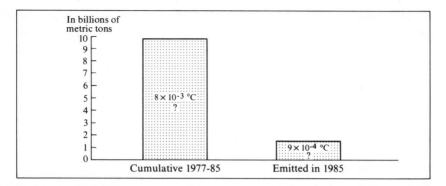

Figure 11-4. Effects of carbon dioxide emissions from coal-fired power plants on climate, under the NEP, 1985. Data are taken from chapter 7 and figure 11-1.

still represents 8 to 40 fatalities, almost half of the maximum value of all predicted nuclear fatalities (see figure 11-2).[15]

The impacts on climate and on land are also of concern. Figure 11-3 shows some of the land use changes brought about as a result of coal and for comparison, nuclear operations, even though the latter were not identified previously as a key impact. Coal will utilize probably over 100,000 acres in 1985 and nuclear much less, by a factor of 10. The land devoted to uranium mill tailings (less than 1,000 acres), however, is probably permanently lost to other uses, unless a much better clean-up job is done in the future.

The coal-fired plants will also produce carbon dioxide, which could affect the climate. The amounts of carbon dioxide emitted by U.S. coal-fired power plants in 1985 is also shown in figure 11-4. Projected effects on the temperature are probably small from this source alone; perhaps close to one-thousandth of a degree Celsius,[16] or even on a cumulative basis (1977–85), less than one-hundredth of a degree.

Since electricity generation will be encouraged by market forces and public policy to move away from oil and gas, it is likely that the NEP may reflect only the fact that there may well be little freedom of choice for 1985. Nuclear plants could be added faster, but only if site approval and

[15] Discounted at 5 percent, a weighted utility discount rate. See chap. 10, fn. 5.
[16] See R. Niehaus, J. J. Cohen, and H. J. Otway, *The Cost-Effectiveness of Remote Nuclear Reactor Siting,* RM-76-34 (Laxenburg, Austria, International Institute for Applied Systems Analysis, April 1976) p. 5, where the model results are extrapolated in the present text to very small changes.

other factors regarding nuclear construction are speeded up. Some also
think that even current hopes for 1985 coal consumption—1 billion tons
per year—may be difficult to attain. Looking into the more distant future,
to the year 2000, there should be a great deal more choice in how we
apply coal and nuclear to the production of electricity.

Key Impacts for the Year 2000

What will be the result of present national policies on the longer-range
picture, at least as far in the future as the year 2000? We can guess at
some of the directions that reasonable policies would take. While it would
be rash to assume that either the present or succeeding administrations
would follow the detailed NEP proposals, the general principles expressed
in the Carter plan may still exert a strong influence over the next quarter-
century. It is clear, for one thing, that many of the NEP goals are also
those of the Nixon–Ford Project Independence;[17] in particular, the principle of minimizing the use of imported oil has long been a bipartisan,
although not uncriticized, national goal. More controversial is the stand
taken by the Carter plan against the development of a nuclear energy
economy based on plutonium. On the other hand, the well-publicized nuclear "last resort" nevertheless received grudging but fairly definite support in the NEP. The plan projections may have then represented some
kind of compromise between all-out nuclear development and a rejection
of nuclear power altogether. At any rate, any reasonable projections for
future nuclear use probably requires also an important role for coal in
the year 2000.

If we take the NEP's 1985 projections as reasonable estimates of energy
use, at least for electricity, independent of a wide range of governmental
policy decisions, and also accept a 4 percent growth rate as a credible figure, then the predicted amount of electricity energy inputs required in the
year 2000 would be about 55.8 quads.[18] In order to determine the electricity supply picture we would need, first of all, to determine the amount
of electricity that would be generated by natural gas and oil. The NEP's
prediction that virtually no utilities would be burning gas by 1990 fits

[17] See especially U.S. Federal Energy Administration (FEA), *Energy Supply and
Environmental Coordination Act of 1974, Coal Conversion Program, Environmental Statement*, sect. 2, FES 75-1 (Washington, FEA, April 1975).
[18] This corresponds roughly to the projections given in James Schlesinger, Testimony before the Subcommittee on Fossil and Nuclear Energy, Research Development and Demonstration of the House Committee on Science and Technology (7
June 1977).

roughly with probable market trends in this increasingly scarce resource anyway,[19] so that we can probably assume only a negligible contribution from gas in the year 2000. Utilities will, of course, be discouraged from burning oil, if not by governmental action, then by high oil prices. The conversion of existing oil plants has been predicted by the NEP, but it seems likely that in many cases Clean Air Act regulations would prevent coal from being used, either to prevent a "significant deterioration" of local atmosphere or to satisfy national pollution standards. At any rate, most of what conversion does take place would undoubtedly occur by 1985. Therefore, we can possibly assume half as much oil-fired capacity in the year 2000 as in the year 1985. This is based on the assumption that on the average any additional plants—perhaps allowed under NEP exceptions for economic and environmental reasons—would be balanced by the number of old plants converted, and that half the old plants would become obsolete within the fifteen-year period.[20]

How much electricity from other sources would be available in the year 2000? Other sources include the established hydropower technology, plus solar, shale oil, nuclear fusion, and so on, depending on speculative assumptions about future developments. We will use a value, 5.9 quads, that is a compromise with some other projections.[21]

This leaves coal and nuclear to fill out the rest of the electricity fuel needs in the year 2000. In predicting the amount of nuclear, it would be interesting to know what the Carter prescription for nuclear as a "last resort" source of power would mean in this context. If last resort meant—as it now appears to do—a necessary expansion of nuclear to fill demand, then the recent administration proposals would correspond to a more or less laissez-faire outcome for nuclear in the year 2000. At any rate, the recent estimate by an administration official of 380 GW nuclear capacity by the year 2000 could be taken as a reasonable base case estimate.[22] The amount left over, in this case 28.7 quads, must be supplied by coal.[23] This

---

[19] See Executive Office of the President, *National Energy Plan*, p. xix. Perhaps this will not be true everywhere, such as in regions where air quality constraints are critical.

[20] This value for oil-fired generation is not too different from the scenarios used in Ronald G. Ridker and William Watson, Jr., project report by Resources for the Future for the National Institutes of Health (1977).

[21] This is Ridker's two scenarios (ibid.), averaged with the IEA projections (Oak Ridge Associated Universities, Institute for Energy Analysis (IEA), *Economic and Environmental Implications of a U.S. Nuclear Moratorium, 1985–2010*, vol. I, ORAU/IEA-76-4 (Oak Ridge, Tenn., Oak Ridge Associated Universities, September 1976).

[22] Schlesinger, Testimony before the Subcommittee on Fossil and Nuclear Energy.

[23] This translation assumes 33 percent efficiency and a 58 percent plant factor for nuclear.

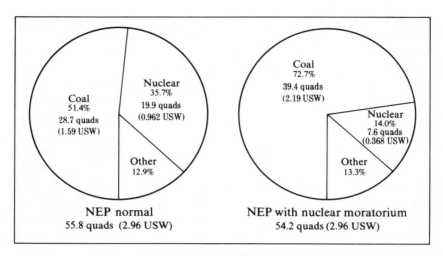

Figure 11-5. Electricity use in the year 2000, carried to that year from the NEP projection at 4-percent electricity growth. These two versions of the nuclear–coal balance show equal electricity outputs; because of differences in efficiencies, the nuclear moratorium case requires only 47.0 quads input (7.6 quads nuclear and 39.4 quads coal) as compared with 48.6 quads input (19.9 quads nuclear and 28.7 quads coal) for the regular case. The electricity generated from coal plus nuclear is the same: for nuclear, 293 plant-years and for coal, 485 in the normal case, and 112 and 666 for the nuclear moratorium case.

case is labeled *NEP normal* in figure 11-5. Of course, we must recognize that the amount of nuclear capacity in the year 2000 could be much larger or even nonexistent, and this possibility is considered briefly on page 150.

Another interpretation of the last-resort philosophy would be that the present (or succeeding) administrations would want to discourage nuclear growth in the future, once the shorter-term goals of the NEP have been attained. A perhaps not too extreme example of this would be a nuclear moratorium or phaseout (termed *NEP with nuclear moratorium* in figure 11-5), so that the number of nuclear plants in the year 2000 would be exactly the same as that for the year 1985. Regardless of present policy trends, it is certainly conceivable that antinuclear sentiment or new safety considerations could lead to such a situation. This would mean having the same 7.6 quads input to nuclear capacity in the year 2000 as in 1985, with 39.4 quads of coal to take up the slack.[24] Incidentally, the 39.4 quads

[24] Coal burning is more efficient than nuclear power, so that the total input needed is less for the generation of the same amount of electricity.

means over 1.7 billion tons of coal for electric utilities alone, perhaps a formidable goal.

Figure 11-5 shows the electrical energy fuel sources according to the two versions of electrical energy projections that are consistent in some sense with the 1985 NEP projections. From these figures—1.59 USW for coal and 0.962 USW for nuclear (normal) versus 2.19 USW for coal and 0.368 USW for nuclear (nuclear moratorium)—we can calculate some key impacts for the year 2000.

Figure 11-6 compares the number of fatalities attributed to the two projections for the year 2000. If we neglect proliferation and diversion dangers, the nuclear moratorium case would increase the number of predicted coal fatalities over the NEP normal development of the nuclear option by a range of from 200 to more than 2,000. The same nuclear moratorium scenario would involve a decrease in nuclear fatalities by a range of from 30 to more than 100. So the amount of the *net* reduction attributable to the so-called normal case depends on which end of each fatality estimate range is correct; the answer could be either less than one hundred or several thousand fatalities.[25]

The ambiguity is especially bothersome because of our very uncertain data based on air pollution-related deaths and the real problems of evaluating the future in relation to long-lived radioisotopes. Whatever the health impact from air pollution, the effect of BACT on emissions will be large.[26] Therefore, the maximum number of air pollution fatalities predicted would have been 12,000 instead of the approximately 4,000 shown for the normal case without BACT regulations. In the nuclear moratorium, the maximum would have been 16,000 instead of the 5,000 under BACT. And, even if we accept a 5 percent discount rate for future fatalities, the annual quota of fatalities from radon and carbon 14 would decrease in the nuclear moratorium case by a range of from 10 to 60.

Illnesses related to air pollution from power plants are shown in table 11-1. Air pollution-related illnesses appear to have an impressively large impact. The upper estimate of the differences between the two projec-

[25] Note that the uncertain ranges of values for nuclear and coal can each be directly compared as a sum of national effects. However, in subtracting two options, we must recognize that the low coal estimates and the high nuclear estimates could well be correct (or vice versa).

[26] Ninety-four percent of coal-fired power plants are assumed under BACT in the normal case and 96 percent for the moratorium, both under growth rates assumed in the projections in figure 11-5. These new plants achieve 70 percent reduction, for an overall correction factor of 34 and 33 percent for the year 2000 of the values per USW shown in figure 10-1.

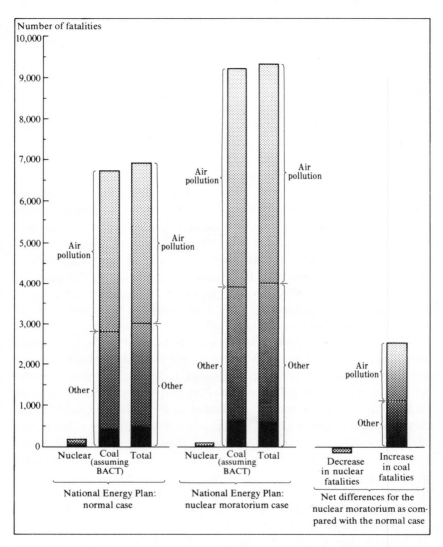

Figure 11-6. Fatalities for the year 2000 from coal-fired and nuclear plants, based on the NEP's 1985 prediction and two alternate projections given in figure 11-5. Data are based on figures 10-1, 10-2, and 11-5, modified per footnote 12.

Table 11-1. Diseases Related to Air Pollution from Coal-fired Plants in the Year 2000

Disease	NEP-normal	NEP-nuclear moratorium
Children's lower respiratory-tract disease	8,000–800,000 cases	10,000–1 million cases
Chronic respiratory disease in adults	30,000–3 million cases	40,000–4 million cases
Asthma	60,000–6 million attacks	90,000–9 million attacks
Heart-lung symptoms in the elderly	300,000–30 million person-days	400,000–40 million person-days

tions—for example, 3 million related asthma cases—may seem incredibly large for a U.S. population of, say, 275 million in the year 2000, especially considering that coal-fired power plants are only a part of the total emissions problem. But if the lower limits are correct, the predicted difference between the normal and nuclear moratorium projections for estimated illnesses is still in the tens or hundreds of thousands.[27]

Figure 11-7 shows the impacts on land use. For land use, we again may have to ask the questions, How much? and What kind? What is the relative significance of the several hundreds of thousands of acres of strip-mined land a year versus several thousand acres or so of land irretrievably committed yearly to uranium mill tailings? A great deal could depend on how effective reclamation is, and how effective is "effective" could well start an argument. And the land use impact depends on geography since some western lands might turn out to be unreclaimable,[28] while elsewhere reclamation, according to European models,[29] could prove very successful. The impact of scrubber wastes on land use is also an open question. The location of the uranium mill tailings makes a difference too—many but not all are now in very isolated areas,[30] but that also could change.

Figure 11-8 indicates that there is a difference of 1 billion metric tons of carbon dioxide emitted between the two electricity projections for the

[27] A "case" may be hard to define. Often it is only an aggravation of an existing disease. See U.S. Congress, Senate, Committee on Public Works, *Air Quality and Stationary Source Emission Control,* Report prepared by the Commission on Natural Resources of the National Academy of Sciences/National Academy of Engineering, of the National Research Council, 94 Cong. 1 sess., ser. no. 94-4 (March 1975) chap. 2.

[28] Atwood, "The Strip-mining."

[29] A. Nephew, "Healing Wounds," *Environment* vol. 14, no. 1 (January–February 1972) pp. 12–21.

[30] U.S. Atomic Energy Commission (AEC), Directorate of Licensing, "Final Environmental Statement Related to Operation of the Shirley Basin Uranium Mill," Docket No. 40-6622 (Washington, AEC, December 1974).

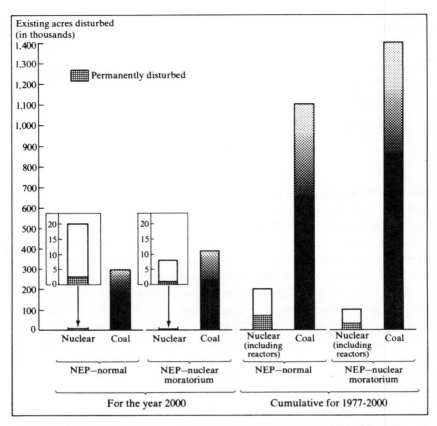

Figure 11-7. Land use impacts in the year 2000 and cumulative land use impacts (assuming certain cycles of reclamation) for 1977–2000, based on two alternative NEP projections (see text page 149). Data are based on values given in figure 8-1, also including a prorated 100-acre reactor contribution for each nuclear plant (see page 149). See also Ramsay, "Coal and Nuclear," and AEC, "Final Environmental Statement."

year 2000. As we discussed in chapter 7, this kind of difference is probably very small. In terms of temperature changes, this increase in the amount of carbon dioxide emissions could correspond to, perhaps, a difference in temperature of only about 0.0008 degrees Celsius. Of course, we are looking only at the narrow U.S. electricity problem here. There are many other sources of carbon dioxide in the world, all of which would have to be counted in calculating total temperature changes. And the possible effects of U.S. energy policy in discouraging foreign nuclearization

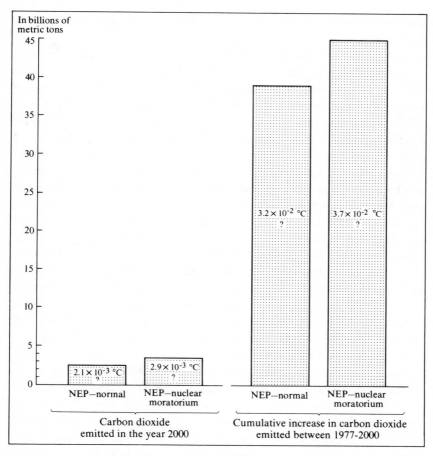

Figure 11-8. Carbon dioxide emissions and related climate impacts, for the year 2000 and the cumulative total for 1977–2000, for two alternative NEP projections. Data are taken from chapter 7 and figure 11-5.

and, therefore, encouraging foreign coal use should be included in looking at this problem.

Cumulative Effects

What is the significance of such impact comparisons in the year 2000? We have assumed that the relative amounts involved are proportional to the number of power plants that go on line, so that we should not expect any fundamental surprises. But we should first investigate possible *cumulative* effects that might come into the national picture.

Nuclear proliferation and diversion are—if not exactly cumulative—to a large extent on/off phenomena. While the ease with which criminals might steal plutonium depends on the amount of plutonium that is around, the existence of a breeder or plutonium recycle economy is in itself the most important factor in the diversion danger. As far as proliferation is concerned, it is very difficult to imagine any connection between the exact size of the U.S. nuclear economy and any ecouragement of the spread of nuclear weapons. It is, however, possible to imagine a connection between the nature and health of the U.S. nuclear economy and the world nuclear situation. One breeder reactor more or less does not matter, but whether the United States has a breeder economy may well be important. One light water reactor (LWR) more or less may not matter, but the difference between a normal nuclear growth and a nuclear moratorium or phaseout may make a difference. Therefore, we can expect that the NEP-normal projection could well involve greater proliferation dangers than the NEP-nuclear moratorium version. Whether such an effect does occur depends on how we assess the arguments given in chapter 6. But if the pessimistic arguments given there are correct, it is easy to see that a yearly quota involving thousands of casualties is not an incredible figure to attach as an extra health-risk penalty to the NEP-normal scenario.

One of our fundamental environmental examples—land use—is in an area where cumulative effects might indeed be important. First, this is because our attitudes could well be colored by the total amount of land available. The existing supply of various land categories now seems to be very large,[31] but in the future, certain categories might derive a high scarcity value. For example, within the past decades, "worthless swamps" have come into their own. Therefore, land scarcity might make us increasingly concerned about each acre lost. We can see that the amount of land used annually for coal seems "large" in relation to that utilized by nuclear plants—if not in relation to total land masses of the country. The difference between coal and nuclear—leaving aside future possible increases in average land disturbed in mining lower grades of uranium ore—depends again on our opinions of the kinds and consequences of the land use. For example, most of the land disturbed by uranium open-pit mining and coal surface mining is slated to be reclaimed under state and new federal

---

[31] See William Ramsay, "Coal and Nuclear: Health and Environmental Costs" (Washington, Resources for the Future, August 1978) append. M.

laws. The cumulative land use effect would therefore depend on the length of the reclamation cycle. According to present regulations and plans, it is assumed that a typical cycle could last ten years for uranium[32] and four years for coal.[33]

Finally, in the year 2000 we will be faced with the problem of old-line reactors. Thus it will be necessary to determine what amount of land must be set aside for reactor sites in addition to that used for the other impacts we have considered so far. Presumably, 100 acres or more per plant will be permanently withdrawn from other uses.

Considering all these effects, the coal impact remains still significantly larger. But it is interesting to see the lower range, at least, of the land use estimates for coal now move significantly closer to the uranium estimates (see figure 11-7). In any event, land use impacts for coal and nuclear might become more commensurate as time goes on if there were no development of the breeder so that lower grades of uranium would be mined. At any rate, the calculations are rough and must be seen as such.

As far as climate is concerned, small calculated changes in temperature might be meaningless, but what about larger changes? Figure 11-8 shows that even the difference between the cumulative effects for coal burned in power plants in the United States for 1977–2000 under the two projections can be estimated to be small (about 0.005 degrees Celsius), at least in relation to natural fluctuations in temperature. If there is a threshold for the temperature effects, then this smallness *could* mean that the unpaid climate costs are low or nonexistent. But still that would not necessarily mean that in the long run the coal-fired power plants in the United States would be a negligible part of the possible world problem. And the effects of small changes are *not* known to be negligible.

Other Impacts

Other lesser impacts have been neglected here, both for 1985 and for the year 2000 nuclear moratorium and normal scenarios, except for the nuclear land use question, which has been included in the discussion on

[32] See, for example, the uranium mining operation described in AEC, "Final Environmental Statement . . . Shirley Basin."

[33] According to the state regulations reviewed in *Coal Surface Mining and Reclamation—An Environmental and Economic Assessment of Alternatives*, Committee Print 93-8, Senate Committee on Interior and Insular Affairs, 93 Cong. 1 sess. (March 1973) chap. 2, three years seems to be the maximum period allowed after the expiration of one-year strip-mining permits.

coal. It should be evident, however, that we could expect proportional decreases in nuclear occupational deaths under a nuclear moratorium, but would see perhaps $50 million to $500 million more in air pollution property damage and unassessable increases in the probability of acid rain, plus more transportation accidents involving coal. Water and societal impacts—because they are connected with both technologies—would show less change.

Noncompromise Alternatives

A coal–nuclear mix such as that which the NEP envisages has a lot to be said for it. In the first place, it is inevitable since there is not much else that can be done during the short time between now and 1985. There are also many arguments for having such a mix in the year 2000: economics, caution or bet-hedging, lack of knowledge, or merely an indifference to any distinctions between the health and environmental effects of coal and nuclear or, at least, between their patterns of economic and noneconomic costs. Chapter 12 will evaluate some of the features of a coal–nuclear mix from the health and environmental points of view.

But such an energy mix is not necessarily desirable. For example, if all of the 2.96 USW output supplied by both nuclear and coal for the normal version of the NEP, as extended to the year 2000, were supplied by one fuel source alone, we could entirely eliminate a number of deleterious impacts. The question then would be whether eliminating health and environmental effects from either coal or nuclear would be better for the nation than would using the mixture of coal and nuclear.

A Nuclear World

A completely nuclearized United States would feature a dramatic decrease in the health risks that would otherwise result from coal. The coal impacts shown for the normal case, shown in figure 11-6, would be eliminated:[34] 400 to 3,000 fatalities from coal mining and coal transportation would be eliminated, as would the possible impacts from coal-fired power plant emissions. It might result in a decrease of thousands of deaths—or in few

---

[34] This discussion ignores the questionable economics or even feasibility of using nuclear plants for "intermediate" generation loads, that is, intermittent plant operation.

or none. Perhaps hundreds of thousands, or indeed millions, of cases of respiratory disease, including asthma and other illnesses, would be eliminated, especially aggravations of existing illnesses. The coal surface-mining impacts would be eliminated (see figure 11-7). The contributions to the world overload of carbon dioxide, also shown in figure 11-8, would be eliminated. Acid rain and atmospheric haze should also decrease.

On the other hand, if we were to adopt such a supernuclear economy we would, as best as we can tell, increase the level of nuclear fatalities shown for the normal case in figure 11-6 by 165 percent, to 100 to 600 deaths yearly. We would also be increasing to 6,000 acres the amount of land going yearly into permanent storage of mill tailings and, of course, the amount of land disturbed annually by surface uranium mining would increase to over 50,000 acres. Some special effects not mentioned before might become more prominent: carbon-14 impacts would be strengthened as less normal, nonradioactive carbon dioxide was emptied into the atmosphere, and less dilution of the radioactive atoms took place.

There are two special caveats associated with the all-nuclear world that arise from problems that are outside our scope here. First, many have doubts that there is enough uranium ore for any reasonable period of operation. We do not deal with that question here, which has been treated elsewhere, although not conclusively.[35] Naturally, the problem would be much alleviated if the breeder option were chosen. The other warning is that just the replacement of electricity generation in the year 2000 by nuclear power does not replace the rest of the gas, oil, and coal used in the U.S. economy. As far as we know, that does not matter, for any decrease in coal impacts is good. However, it is conceivable that even a sizable reduction in coal impacts would not have enough impact to satisfy public desires for better land use or cleaner air. The solution to such problems of public taste—how much environmental quality is required—has yet to be reached.

The All-Coal World

If all electricity-generation sources were replaced by coal, nuclear power could be done away with entirely. Naturally, we do not know whether coal could be made available that fast to carry out such a program, even

[35] Ford Foundation, *Nuclear Power Issues and Choices,* report of the Nuclear Energy Policy Study Group, administered by MITRE Corporation (Cambridge, Mass., Ballinger, 1977) chap. 2.

if it would be thought desirable on both economic and social grounds and in the total fuels context. But the effect, as we can infer from figures 11-5, 11-6, and 11-7, would be to eliminate the nuclear impacts shown, and also lead to a 60 percent increase (or a total of 600 to 10,000 fatalities) in the impacts from coal, including the health risks from air pollution and occupational accidents, transportation accidents inflicted on the general public, and so on. The yearly contribution of the U.S. electric power industry to the total world inventory of carbon dioxide would also increase to 4 billion metric tons, as would the special contributions to acid rain. Strip-mined acreage would increase to 300,000 to 500,000 acres.

In return, we might get some indirect economic and political effects that would reduce the tendency toward nuclear proliferation. As we have stressed, the connection of this patently political problem with the social and economic context of power generation is very hard to trace. But the effects of a completely nonnuclear United States on the rest of the world—through political influence, the effects on U.S. suppliers of nuclear goods, and the moral influence on foreign nuclear protests—could be great. But we would have to be ready to concede some awkward facts: First, that we are not acting alone in the world, and that, for example, diversion of nuclear material from a foreign plutonium economy could blow up buildings in the United States as easily as could U.S.-controlled plutonium.

The situation is somewhat different for nuclear accidents. A unilateral antinuclear decision on the part of the United States would eliminate the reportedly small but ever present possibility of disastrous accidents. The troublesome commercial radioactive wastes of all kinds would cease increasing, presumably making future generations more content with their environmental legacy from existing nuclear wastes.

A Comparison Between Coal and Nuclear

It should be clear that the choice between nuclear and coal in this hypothetical commitment to only one fuel for electricity generation is not a question of obvious preference, but a question of differing values that should be decided by public decision making. Either option would, of course, be subject to the proviso that it is possible to produce the needed amount of coal or nuclear power. And, of course, we do not consider here the possibility of *neither* coal- *nor* nuclear-generated electricity—if such an option is indeed possible. One proposed way of thus avoiding the electricity problem would be to replace inefficient uses of electricity, such as providing low-temperature space heating, with other energy sources. Technical fixes and conservation strategies, such as reducing commercial overlighting, would also help. It is then conceivable that the 15 percent of U.S. energy use now supplied by electricity could be reduced to 5 percent.[36] On the other hand, such a nonelectric option could turn out to be impractical or overly expensive. But in any case, the impact portrait we have painted could be applied as a standard of comparison in order to make judgments about component technologies of other energy supply-and-demand patterns.

Conclusion

The total health and environmental impacts of electricity for the years 1985 and 2000 can be estimated roughly by examining general energy scenarios. The total impacts can also be usefully compared in terms of the effects we have labeled as *key impacts*.

A projection for the years 1985 and 2000 can be made which is consistent with that proposed in the recent NEP and with many other projections. The consequences for the health and environment in these projections are given in terms of the key impacts listed in chapter 10.

Key Impacts for Coal in 1985

Deaths and illnesses from air pollution and mining. Estimates of air pollution-related deaths range from near zero to 6,000. Occupational fatalities, especially mining, range from about 100 to over 1,000. Predictions of respiratory disease are typified by figures for children's nonfatal lower respiratory-tract illnesses, which range from 10,000 to 1 million, while the estimated occupational nonfatal diseases and accidents range from 10,000 to 40,000.

Climate modification. The amount of carbon dioxide emitted in one year would produce a world temperature rise of less than one-thousandth of a degree, according to speculative estimates based on existing climate models.

Land disturbance. The estimated amount of strip-mined land ranges from 100,000 to 200,000 acres.

---

[36] See Amory B. Lovins, *Soft Energy Paths: Toward a Durable Peace* (Cambridge, Mass., Friends of the Earth/Ballinger, 1977), who argues that it is possible.

Other impacts.   Transportation accidents would account for 100 to 500 fatalities. Property and crop damage from air pollution could range from $200 million to $2 billion in monetary losses.

Key Impacts for Nuclear in 1985

Proliferation and diversion.   The expansion of the nuclear industry could lead to some extra proliferation dangers. The exact impact is immeasurable, but the existence of the U.S. nuclear industry could conceivably be associated with thousands of expected (averaged-out) war fatalities per year. The antibreeder decision, if it holds, should greatly reduce diversion dangers within the United States, even though estimates are hard to come by.

Reactor safety.   Unless radical changes take place in reactor safety, one must consider that an expected averaged-out total of up to eight fatalities will be attributed to nuclear reactor accidents. The annual chance of any 50,000-fatality accident in the United States could be as much as 500 in 1 billion.

Nuclear wastes.   At a 5 percent rate of discount, the present and future fatalities expected from radon and carbon 14 would range between 10 and 40.

Other impacts.   The amount of land permanently dedicated annually to nuclear milling wastes would be about 1,000 acres. Nuclear occupational fatalities are predicted to range from 10 to 40.

There are at least two kinds of projections that appear roughly and reasonably consistent with the principles and assumptions outlined in the NEP. An NEP-nuclear moratorium case can be compared with the NEP–normal case chosen here that presupposes some kind of normal development of nuclear energy. Consider that the normal case is the base case. Projected increases in impacts for the year 2000 for the nuclear moratorium case *over* the normal case are as follows.

Key Impacts for Coal in the Year 2000

Deaths and illnesses from air pollution and mining.   A nuclear moratorium would imply an increase of between 60 and 800 mining and other coal occupational fatalities, and possibly an increase of 1,000 fatalities or somewhat more in air pollution-related deaths and illnesses. For children's lower respiratory-tract disease, for example, between 3,000 to 300,000 extra cases might be expected.

Climate modification.   The increased use of coal in the United States could cause a small increase in average world temperature, on the order of one-thousandth of a degree Celsius, or perhaps five-thousandths of a degree, based on the difference between *cumulative* 1977–2000 emissions.

Land disturbance.   A total of from 60,000 to 100,000 extra acres would be disturbed by strip mining. Existing inventories of unreclaimed land would be increased by several hundred thousand acres.

Other impacts.   Fatalities from transportation accidents would be increased by from 90 to 300.

Key Impacts for Nuclear in the Year 2000

Proliferation and diversion.   If the nuclear moratorium case involved a phasing out, more or less, of most of the nuclear industry, it might reduce the risk of proliferation, perhaps by as much as the equivalent of several thousand extra (averaged-out) casualties per year.

Reactor safety.   On the average, it is predicted that the nuclear moratorium case would result in a reduction of up to 10 fatalities from a possible nuclear accident (or accidents). The chance of a major, 50,000-fatality accident would be decreased from over 1,000 down to 500 chances in 1 billion.

Nuclear wastes.   The predicted (discounted) fatalities from waste gases would be decreased by from 10 to 60.

Other impacts.   The land permanently devoted to radioactive mill tailings plus reactor sites for the 1977–2000 period would decrease by about 30,000 acres. Nuclear occupational fatalities would decrease, however, by 20 to 70.

Noncompromise Alternatives

Noncompromise alternative solutions to the NEP projections exist—provided that they are economically feasible. The all-coal or all-nuclear world could eliminate, or at least greatly reduce, some key impacts but only at the cost of increasing impacts from the other technology.

12 *The Cautious Society*

How do coal and nuclear power compare?

What implications are there for a national energy strategy?

Noncomparability of Impacts

We have examined individually the key impacts of coal and nuclear, plus some others of lesser importance. We have also considered the collection of impacts that might take place as a result of alternative national energy policies that might be followed within the next quarter-century. What we have not faced, however, is the problem of how to add up all of the different impacts so as to answer the question, Would we be better off in an all-coal or all-nuclear world—as far as electricity generation is concerned—or is a mix of the two a better energy strategy? Leaving economics aside, this is equivalent to asking, Are the environmental and health effects of coal worse than those of nuclear, or vice versa?

In the last few chapters we have seen a formidable variety of different effects—fatalities, illnesses, land use changes, and climate modification. Not only do these impacts differ because various things are affected, but there is also another difference in that some risks are routine while others are catastrophic or disastrous. Some classes of fatalities, such as those in coal mining, occur regularly year after year, while others may never occur; for example, there may never be a serious nuclear meltdown accident.

There is, of course, a standard way of attacking the problem of different kinds of costs—through monetization. A monetary value can be put on each of the health risks, on the impact of strip mining on a piece of land, and even on the effect of a temperature change on the world economy. This monetization philosophy seems to be a good idea in principle, but in practice it is often difficult to carry out.[1] It is not followed here because a sensible common denominator is lacking.

If we admit that it is difficult or impossible to attach some agreed-upon monetary value or any other common denominator to all impacts, then we must necessarily consider the various impacts within a less all-inclusive context. Such a context is provided by certain human values to which different individuals attach greater or lesser importance. Let us turn now to these values as a means of developing a systematic comparison of impacts.

Value Orientations

Individuals possess different attitudes toward values that are relevant to the electricity technology question. These so-called value orientations affect personal choices—given the means to express them—of policy alternatives. Let us categorize certain important value orientations and see how the impacts relate to them.

Four overall value orientations—involving (1) routine health risks, (2) the environment in general, (3) special attitudes toward disastrous risks, and (4) problems involving fairness or equity—are helpful in analyzing the electricity problem.

Preservation of Health

The preservation of health is a value that would influence one to choose electricity technologies that minimize fatalities, illnesses, and nonfatal accidents. Individuals may have differing outlooks on the importance of health versus other values, and they may differ on specific values within the health orientation. For example, the relative weight given to deaths as

---

[1] Various attempts have been made to get agreed-upon values for such economic but nonmarket goods as health and environmental values [see William Ramsay, "Siting Power Plants," *Environmental Science and Technology* vol. 11, no. 3 (March 1977) pp. 238–243]. These attempts may be useful for decisions regarding the siting of power plants, where certain values may dominate and where one is comparing alternatives so that some of the inaccuracies may cancel one another out. However, for national policy purposes, chances for error appear to be disturbingly large. Nevertheless, see William Ramsay, "Coal and Nuclear: Health and Environmental Costs" (Washington, Resources for the Future, August 1978) append. O, for an illustration of monetization in the present context.

compared with illnesses is a matter of opinion. Many will also consider routine illnesses, that is, those that are familiar and self-limiting, as different phenomena than the "averaged-out" radiation sicknesses stemming from hypothetical nuclear accidents (see the section entitled "Avoidance of Catastrophes"). Various types of illnesses, such as emphysema and lung cancer, may be viewed differently. Finally, even the way in which an illness occurs can, in some instances, be valued differently; for instance, some persons fear nuclear carcinogenic risks more than other cancer risks.[2]

Protection of the Environment and Resources

The word *environment* encompasses a wide range of phenomena. Here we treat it as having to do with the core aspect of the environment, that is, concerning plants, animals, and the general structure of lands and waters. For example, the preservation of a diversity of animal species would fall under this heading,[3] as would also the conservation of land in current use, particularly land presently in a natural state. It is evident that various states of nature, or deviations from them, can be valued differently by individuals: for example, are grasslands or mountains more important from an environmental point of view? Others place special emphasis on the conservation of land, minerals, and other resources in order to minimize usage that is considered excessive or wasteful.

Avoidance of Catastrophes

The avoidance of catastrophes to public health or to the environment could be valued solely on the basis of the averaged-out impact, which would depend on the consequences of each incident and on how often we expect catastrophes with such consequences to occur. Such an averaged-out value, however, would properly be included under the preservation of health or protection of the environment and resources. But often there

---

[2] See Philip D. Pahner, *A Psychological Perspective of the Nuclear Energy Controversy*, RM-76-67 (Laxenburg, Austria, International Institute for Applied Systems Analysis, August 1976); and R. Maderthaner, P. Pahner, G. Guttman, and H. J. Otway, *Perception of Technological Risks: The Effect of Confrontation*, Research Memorandum RM-76-53 (Laxenburg, Austria, International Institute for Applied Systems Analysis, June 1976).

[3] See, for example, William Ramsay, "Priorities in Species Preservation," *Environmental Affairs* vol. 5, no. 4 (1977) pp. 595–616.

is an *extra* value attached by some persons to the avoidance of a catas-trophe over and above its average consequences. For example, an indi-vidual might give relatively little weight to the few predicted yearly fatalities, averaged out over all years, of all hypothetical nuclear melt-down accidents. But he might choose to put considerable weight on avoid-ing the 50,000-fatality worst-case accident for each reactor that has a probability of occurrence of 5 chances in 1 billion.

Also, it is necessary to consider the total impact of events where we have little idea of what the average impact is; for example, any increased likelihood of nuclear war attributed to the civilian nuclear industry or any climatic changes attributed to carbon dioxide.

Equity Values

Impacts may not be spread evenly among the members of society. There-fore, decisions that can work for the greatest good of all might be grossly unfair to certain segments of the population. Individuals will naturally oppose impacts that affect them inequitably, even though society as a whole may benefit from a specific technology choice. For example, a vaca-tioner may be injured by the strip mining of a favorite recreation area, even though the general effect on electricity generation could provide a net benefit to the national economy.

Several types of equity questions arise. Impacts could affect some in-come levels more than others, or could differentially affect property owners. For example, air pollution from burning coal could especially affect farmers or owners of buildings. Critics have also made the contro-versial contention that complex technologies—especially nuclear—re-quire the existence (and enrichment) of urban technological elites and the neglect of nonelite interests.[4] Regions may be impacted unfairly; for example, inhabitants of regions in the immediate vicinity of a nuclear power plant would be exposed to possible hazards from a nuclear acci-dent. Workers may be affected more or less than the general public. For example, substituting strip mining for underground mining can save miners' lives, because it does away with underground mining accidents, but, on the other hand, it may degrade land use and so affect environ-mental values held by others. Persons of different ages could be affected

---

[4] See Amory B. Lovins, *Soft Energy Paths: Toward a Durable Peace* (Cambridge, Mass., Friends of the Earth/Ballinger, 1977) p. 155.

more by some kinds of diseases than others. In particular, future generations may be affected by long-lived impacts, such as nuclear wastes, while
not receiving the benefits of nuclear-generated power.

It seems apparent that the value orientations described here are viewed
as more or less important by different individuals in our society. It is
therefore difficult for a policymaker to say that one type of orientation is
superior to another. But it is possible that within each value category a
more tractable comparison of impacts and their importance can be made.
Thus, it is useful to classify each key impact into one value category or
another before determining how coal and nuclear fare in terms of particular types of values.

The Effect of Coal and Nuclear Impacts on Values

Instead of taking on the impossible task of evaluating the overall coal and
nuclear impact on health and environment, we can work toward a more
practical goal by using the categories of values mentioned above. That is,
we can see, within each value category, how the coal and nuclear technologies compare.

Preservation of Health

The health impacts are summarized in table 12-1, in terms of 2 trillion
kWh (or 1 USW) of electricity generation. These include coal-related air
pollution and occupational fatalities and illnesses and, of course, coal-
transportation accidents. The nuclear fatalities and illnesses associated
with routine radiation from nuclear facilities, including especially gaseous
wastes, are obviously much less than the routine impacts from coal, even
when combined with the average impact to be expected from nuclear accidents. This is true, even if the uncertain deaths associated with coal emissions are not counted.[5] Not only are the fatalities much more numerous for
coal, but the number of illnesses predicted are strikingly larger—even
though it must be noted that there is a chance that the lowest estimate

---

[5] Even if the discount rate for waste gases were not correct, it would require a
very small discount rate to even up the coal and nuclear impacts. (Radon impacts
are approximately proportional to the inverse of the discount rate, so that a 90 percent reduction in the rate would be needed in order to increase the impact by a
factor of ten.)

Table 12-1. Summary of Fatalities Affecting Main Value Orientations, per USW

Impact	*No. of persons*[a]
Coal fatalities	
Air pollution	
With BACT	0–2,000
Without BACT	0–7,000
Occupational	100–1,000
Other (auto-coal train collisions, etc.)	200–500
Total coal	
With BACT	200–4,000
Without BACT	200–9,000
Nuclear fatalities	
Reactor accidents	1–20
Long-lived wastes (discounted)	20–100
Other	
All normal emissions	0.1–1
Occupational	30–100
Total nuclear	60–200

[a] Totals may not add because figures have been rounded off.

made here of air pollution-related illnesses could be too high. We must also bear in mind that if we were able to average out the probable casualties from any nuclear weapons explosions connected with the U.S. civilian nuclear industry, the average impacts from nuclear proliferation and diversion *could* be large.

Therefore, we can say that the goal of preserving health—expressed in terms of routine health impacts and of the annualized health impacts from disasters that can be calculated—favors the nuclear option.

Protection of the Environment and Resources

Land use changes are probably one of the biggest environmental impacts. Comparing the coal and nuclear land use changes, the expected impacts of disturbed land acreage are much larger for coal (ranging from 100,000 to 200,000 acres) than for nuclear (20,000 acres). On the other hand, the permanent land use changes connected with uranium mine wastes and mill tailings can represent an especially severe impact; however, even that problem can perhaps be mitigated by taking special measures (see chapter 3).

Coal-related air pollution sometimes obscures visibility, and there is the possibility of severe ecological damage from acid rain. The extra water needed for the cooling process in nuclear plants is probably counterbalanced by water problems associated with coal mining.

Therefore, we conclude that for routine—that is, noncatastrophic—environmental concerns, the negative environmental impacts of coal are larger than those of nuclear.

Avoidance of Catastrophes

The primary catastrophic effect from coal is the possibility of a drastic climatic change resulting from the production of carbon dioxide and perhaps particulates. Acid rain could also produce ecological disasters but probably on a smaller scale and on a more reversible basis. As we have seen, however, many questions of scientific fact and theory on the climate-modification problem remain unresolved. Severe health catastrophes from air pollution could occur, but are perhaps less likely to do so under current regulations.

The dangers of nuclear diversion and proliferation (discussed at some length in chapter 6) are exceedingly complex and difficult to analyze, especially in relation to the role of a breeder economy or even of a light water reactor (LWR) economy in the United States. However, the possible consequences of such diversion or proliferation are great. The breeder economy might also produce possible climatic problems due to emissions of krypton 85. On a somewhat more modest scale, at least in this global context, nuclear power plant accidents could produce local health disasters that might be regarded differently from averaged-out impacts.

Since problems with nuclear proliferation, diversion, and accidents are so immediate in nature—particularly when contrasted with the problem of carbon dioxide emissions—nuclear technology is clearly associated with a significantly larger possibility of catastrophes occurring within the next quarter-century.

Equity Considerations

Although it is difficult to reach definite conclusions about the balance of fairness of coal versus nuclear, we can see certain patterns of inequity in either case.

Impacts on income and property.   Air pollution damage to property or crops will impact upon some economic classes more than others; in particular, farmers, businessmen, and property owners affected by the cost of paints, metals, and other items that are prone to damage from air pollution.

Nuclear and coal technologies both require the existence of a special scientific and engineering stratum of society. But it remains to be seen whether significant class inequities can be plausibly blamed on complex, large-scale electricity-generation technologies.

Regional impact.   Coal mining can have an inequitable effect on a coal resource region. Surface mining, in particular, degrades the regional landscape, while underground mining can add an extra health risk to those already present in local occupations. The issue is clouded, however, by compensating mechanisms that come into play; for example, increased employment, higher wages, or coal severance taxes.

Power plants can have a greater effect on the health of the immediate neighborhood than on the general public. Coal plants will produce higher increases in ambient air pollution at closer distances, but the effect of atmospheric processes, which are imperfectly understood, and the existing health uncertainties (see chapters 2 and 10) make it difficult to substantiate the contention that an unfairness exists. Nuclear power plants can best be categorized as inflicting a supposedly slight, but nevertheless definitely inequitable chance of a catastrophic nuclear accident on the population within the site neighborhood—the consequence of which is death or radiation illness.

Impact on workers.   The impact on workers from routine activities is greater in the coal industry than in the nuclear industry. But it is more to the point to determine whether the impacts from one or the other fall proportionately more on workers than on the general public. This question, however, is impossible to answer without more knowledge of the uncertain impacts of air pollution. If air pollution impacts turn out to be very low, effects will fall inequitably on coal workers, at least in relation to the worker–public ratio in the nuclear case.

Impacts on different age brackets.   Nuclear radiation impacts tend to fall differentially on the very young and the middle- aged.[6] Fatalities associated with severe air pollution episodes seem to occur more often in the elderly, while the more uncertain fatalities stemming from low levels of

[6] For a discussion of age-bracket effects, see William Ramsay and Milton Russell, "Time-adjusted Impacts from Energy Generation," *Public Policy* vol. 26, no. 3 (Summer 1978) pp. 387–403.

air pollution seem to occur more in the very young and the very old. Both, of course, affect particularly susceptible populations of all ages.[7] But both the patterns of these impacts and the social attitude toward such age inequities remain obscure.

Impact on future generations. The entire nuclear waste problem is a prime example of *intergenerational equity* problems, or of fairness to future generations. The inequity includes both high-level and long-lived gaseous wastes from nuclear operations. Surface storage of fuel wastes, the problem of uranium mining wastes and mill tailings, and the problem of decommissioned reactors will result in health-related land use problems for the future. This may be the most intractable of the electricity-generation equity issues, if only because the solutions must extend into time frames which are beyond our control.

Therefore coal and nuclear power both involve social equity problems. Nevertheless, it may be significant that many of the coal inequities could be or are now being alleviated by compensation mechanisms; for example, competitive businesses suffering air pollution damage to metals should pass the costs along to customers. Communities or states tax mining industries; coal miners receive black lung compensation, which spreads the cost around without, to be sure, diminishing the total societal impact.

The average scope and effectiveness of such compensation can well be questioned. Nevertheless, the possibility itself throws into sharp focus those sectors where compensation mechanisms are weakest: for particular age brackets and for future generations. Nuclear and, more particularly, nuclear waste impacts seem to offer the greatest danger to these two groups.

Therefore, while each equity value question must be decided on an individual basis, the nuclear option involves inequities of a more intractable sort. For even if we wished to compensate especially injured individuals or groups, it would be difficult—either politically or economically—to actually do so.

Summary of Values and Technologies

Some of the four main value orientations are dominated by coal and some by nuclear impacts. In addition, some values are more *strongly* dominated

---

[7] Private communication from N. Robert Frank, October 19, 1977.

by either coal or nuclear impacts than others. This complication, plus all the uncertainties discussed above, must be kept in mind in the overall comparison.

1. As far as the preservation of health is concerned, the coal technology impact is larger than the nuclear impact, its dominance depending strongly on the effects of air pollution on health.
2. The impact of coal is also greater than that of nuclear in regard to the environment and resources; its dominance depends on how successful the reclamation of strip-mined land is and on the effectiveness of the Clean Air Act.
3. Nuclear impacts have a greater near-term chance of being catastrophic, while global catastrophes associated with coal appear to be a more long-term threat and to have a greater chance of being reversible.
4. Nuclear impacts are greater when it comes to equity considerations—a heterogeneous collection of values involving relative fairness to different parts of society. Their intractability, rather than their dominance, is the key criterion.

The Certain Implications of Uncertainty

We see that each value orientation is dominated by a certain pattern of impacts from either coal or nuclear. But this assessment is still not adequate for making rational energy technology choices. We still do not know (1) which values are more important for society, and by how much; or (2) how dominant the impacts within each value orientation are. Obviously, these considerations cannot be given plausible answers within the framework of what is now known about impacts and values. In other words, it is impossible to add up the unpaid costs of either coal or nuclear energy in any simple, straightforward way. Consequently, it is also not possible to say exactly what the total costs for particular energy strategies would be in the years 1985 or 2000. It is especially impossible to give a sensible answer to the crude—but important—question, Which is better for the public health and environment, coal or nuclear?

We can readily characterize the roots of this dilemma: it is uncertainty that is a pervading factor in the analysis. Uncertainty runs amok in our calculations of fatalities, illnesses, acres of land, nuclear wars, increases in world temperatures, and in our views of human preferences and values.

The uncertainties occur in three different contexts: data and measurements; causes and effects; and value judgments. We have seen many examples of these along the way. No data exist on severe nuclear meltdown accidents because none have ever occurred. If one were to occur in the future, we have only unsure cause-and-effect calculations about resulting deaths, illnesses, and property damage. We do have some real data for the land use effects of surface coal mining, but we are not sure how much coal will be strip-mined as opposed to that mined underground in the future, and we are not sure of the physical results of such mining on the land. If strip mining is the cause of the impact, will the effect be a desert of mine spoils, or will the reclamation be satisfactory to the public? Then, even if the impacts were known, we would still have to use value judgments in comparing them with other types of impacts. Whether reclamation works acceptably or not, how do we value the acreage disturbed against the deaths and illnesses due to our hypothetical nuclear accident? The same problem, of course, comes up in context after context, in questions of smog from coal-fired power plants, in the disposal of high-level nuclear wastes, and in the effects of carbon dioxide emissions on the average world temperature.

This demon of uncertainty must be taken into account when drawing overall conclusions about the unpaid costs of coal and nuclear energy and the implications of these costs for U.S. energy strategy. Putting aside, in this context, any questions of operating economics and the future of electricity, any recommendation for either a coal or nuclear future, or a quantitatively specific mix of both must depend on the arbitrary mixture of value orientations used in judging the problem, and on the uncertain scientific data and estimates that are available. Such a recommendation at the present time would be very shaky indeed and an inexcusably deficient basis for policy decisions.

Even if one were to drop all reservations about the adequacy of the data base, a hard choice between coal and nuclear could be made only if the policymaker gave paramount importance to one (or two) main value orientations. But can the democratic policymaker do that in a justifiable and consistent way? If votes were taken among various groups of individuals in our society on the values to be adopted, most electorates would be unable to choose wisely between the options. It is plausible that most persons—and it is virtually certain that society as a whole—would be unable to decide rationally between coal and nuclear. After all, it is difficult to imagine a concern with routine health risks, which would favor nuclear, without concern about abnormal risks of illness or death from catastrophes such as nuclear accidents or diversion or proliferation of nuclear weapons. Similarly, those especially concerned with obvious environmental impacts, such as land use, may favor a nuclear technology over coal. But a concern with the environment often goes along with an interest in the welfare of future generations, which—considering the problem of nuclear waste—would favor the use of coal. And so it goes.

If a mix of values is more the rule than the exception, it also follows that the degree of dominance—that is, the importance of the net impact—*within* each value orientation will be critical. Does a nuclear technology "dominate" catastrophes more than a coal technology "dominates" health? Such currently unanswerable questions merely compound the already intractable problems of balancing off different value orientations.

Therefore, we are brought to several logical conclusions. First, in a static, never-changing world, the fundamental uncertainty in values and in the effects of the impacts on the values could force us to conclude that no reasonable choice could be made between coal and nuclear technologies on the grounds of health and environment. But the world is *not* static. Our knowledge about impacts and about ways to mitigate them is continually growing, even if sometimes at a snail's pace. And this ability of our society to improve both knowledge and technology is crucial here. Second, we also have to keep in mind that a choice we make today may affect our ability to make new choices in the future. For example, if we were to decide against nuclear power now, we could be foreclosing that energy option permanently, since a nuclear industry implies a vast continuing commitment to a scientific and technical body of expertise, to an existing mining and enrichment industry, and to a whole set of established economic operations. The situation is the same for coal, although the ongoing use of coal other than in electrical utilities means that a hypothetical anticoal decision could be reversed more readily than a hypothetical antinuclear decision. In other words, our knowledge of impacts will be greater in the future than it is now; and if we were to drop one option now, it would be difficult—that is, either very time-consuming or very expensive—for us to change our minds in the future.

Consequently, the conclusion we believe to be inescapable is that—although at the present time no choice could be convincingly defended on health and environmental grounds of a one-technology electricity industry or of a particular mixture of the two—future additions to our knowledge through research and experience could radically change the situation. At some future time a choice for one technology or the other may become more clear-cut, even if a wide range of differing value judgments have to be considered. Or, as time goes on, we may gain more convincing evidence that reinforces our motivation to preserve a mixture of the two. An alternate possibility has to do with newer sources of energy. It could become possible to calculate in a convincing way an "environmental premium" that could be paid for newer, cleaner sources of energy, based on a comparison with improved knowledge of the health and environmental effects of either coal or nuclear, or both. Therefore, our safest bet at present—given the current problems of cost and feasibility of renewable, clean energy sources and the difficulties of recreating a whole technology at some future time—is to maintain and propagate a mixture of coal and nuclear electrical generation capacity.

Energy Strategies

Choosing a coal–nuclear mix because of the importance of uncertainty implies that certain strategies should be followed in energy policy. First of all, since our lack of information is one of the crucial problems, we must give a high priority to research on the impacts of such a policy. Compared with some other policy instruments, research is relatively cheap. But, of course, it does not come free, especially in the use of scientific expertise, so that priorities will still have to be taken into account. We must find out which problems are apt to be the most dangerous to health and environment, and at the same time determine which ones will be most likely to be responsive to research efforts.

The second major element in the strategy of living with a coal–nuclear mix is that of mitigation, such as abatement of air pollution by stack gas scrubbers. Mitigation is more expensive to carry out than research, and, as a consequence, priorities must be even more carefully considered. Ordinarily, we try to decide for or against mitigation by comparing the benefits expected—that is, the unpaid health and environmental costs that can be avoided by the abatement effort—and the cost of the effort itself.

But costs and benefits, at least in the conventional sense, are not the whole story. It would be wise to keep in mind—as background in the present context—that disagreements about mitigation can produce costly delays, price rises in alternate fuels, and other types of obscure but real costs to society.

Therefore, more mitigation should be allowed than might be immediately evident on the basis of health and environmental costs alone. *In other words, extra mitigation can be justified as a premium paid by society to ensure timely and adequate supplies of energy.*

Possible research and mitigation efforts for coal and nuclear technologies are classified below, according to our four value orientations. From our assessment of both the key impacts and lesser ones and their relation to the values, priorities or preferences for the various policies are suggested. These preferences are not recommended because of the relative seriousness of each impact alone, but rather because of both its seriousness and the probable effectiveness of the possibilities of dealing with it.

Preservation of Health

Coal-related pollution. Air pollution from coal-fired power plants is one of the big question marks in health impacts. This suggests that research on air pollution should be a first-priority effort. A great deal of work is already being done, and suggestions have been made for research on the problem of sulfur oxides.[8] These efforts deal with the monitoring, emission, transformation, transport, and fate of sulfur oxides in the atmosphere on the one hand; and the health effects of sulfur oxides on the other. While both of these areas are important, it would seem that the health effects link is the most critical. After all, even the consequences of measured ambient levels are unknown, let alone the fate of emitted pollutants. In particular, given the difficulty of establishing convincing parameters for epidemiological studies with a less than complete biomedical foundation, the design of detailed animal experiments may be a first priority. Studies on the health effects of nitrogen oxides, particulates, and other residuals are undoubtedly deserving of support. There are, in fact, so many possible studies that it is essential for some policymaking body to construct an overall priority list as a guide to future research.

Mitigation of emissions is necessary just because of the strong possibility that the impacts may be very large. The question is, How much mitigation? The mitigation efforts required under the New Source Performance Standards legislation are expensive. Similarly, the efforts that would be required under the proposed Best Available Control Technology (BACT), recommended in the National Energy Plan (NEP), are substantial. If the extra cost of the BACT measures runs to an additional

---

[8] Greenfield, Attaway, and Tyler, Inc., *Sulfur Oxides: Current Status of Knowledge,* EPRI EA-316, Project 681-1 (Palo Alto, Calif., EPRI, December 1976).

charge of $3.50 on the "monthly electric bill" (1.6 mills per kilowatt hour), the total expenditure would be perhaps $3.2 billion per USW.[9] Such an expenditure is so large that extra impetus must be given to research efforts needed to improve estimates of how important the health consequences are that would be avoided by mitigation. Naturally, any data on catastrophic air pollution inversions would also be relevant. Alternately, as we will see below, expensive mitigation could be justified on environmental instead of health grounds. The Clean Air Act is already strongly environmentalist in tone, stressing the preservation of special, very clean airsheds, as opposed to reducing the overall exposure of population to pollutants (see chapter 11). Further mitigation decisions might, in fact, have to come to terms with the problems of protecting pristine as opposed to average-quality airsheds. One option represents a special value on a "pure" environment; the other option would imply a greater importance to preserving the health of the average citizen.

Auto-coal train collisions.   The problem of the relatively large number of deaths resulting from collisions of coal trains with automobiles and trucks could be mitigated by putting in additional crossing gates at a cost of, say, $25,000 each. Since collisions with trains carrying coal to coal-fired power plants are only a fraction of the total number of collisions, the net costs attributable solely to electrical energy could amount to a fraction of the cost of gates. While one would need to investigate for each plant and its transportation network the total number of crossing gates needed and their expected effectiveness, the number of lives saved per USW could run into the hundreds.

Coal-mining accidents and illnesses.   From the size of its impact, coal-mining safety deserves a great deal of attention. What is questionable, however, is the effectiveness of increased safety measures in reducing accidents. The measures taken under the 1969 legislation have been blamed for reductions in output,[10] since often as injuries per worker have dropped so also has output per worker (see chapter 9). From the point of view of society, a persistent high accident level is being spread out over a larger worker population, with the total number of accidents remaining

---

[9] Assume that the extra costs of the BACT (above that of scrubbers needed for existing New Source Performance Standards) are about half the cost of scrubbers on all plants, or $5.00 on the "monthly electric bill" (see chap. 2). If we assume $1.50 (see fig. 2-2) for crop and property damages saved, then the addition to the "monthly electric bill" (see chap. 2, fn. 33) would be $3.50, or about $10 million annually for every plant, or $3.2 billion a year per USW.

[10] See U.S. Congress, *Federal Coal Mine Health and Safety Act of 1969, as amended* (30 U.S.C. 801-960).

large. Therefore, the safety improvement problem is still a very serious one. Even in the face of economic repercussions, an investigation of further requirements for the training of workers or for mine safety equipment could be justified—if they achieved significant decreases in accidents per ton.

As for deaths and illnesses from black lung, it is difficult to separate out the best strategies in the context of ongoing disputes regarding compensation payments and definitions of disease and health. At a minimum, however, research on existing coal-dust levels and their relation to present standards should be supported.

Nuclear wastes: radon and carbon 14. Mitigation of the radon from mining and mill wastes can probably be justified, especially since the costs of a significant amount of mitigation would result in about a one-cent addition to the "monthly electric bill," or $10 million a year per USW.[11] Of course, even these expenditures could be avoided if further research were to show that models of the atmospheric diffusion of radon are incorrect.

At the discount rate adopted in this book, the impacts from radon and carbon 14 are about the same. But if a higher discount rate were chosen, the carbon-14 impacts would become more important. Should carbon 14 then be abated? Carbon 14 could be trapped in the form of carbon-14 dioxide at the reactor site; however, the cost for this could be large. The result also depends on the behavior of carbon 14 in the atmosphere and the oceans, and it could be that information on carbon 14 could be derived from much needed research, required to assess the climate-modification effect of carbon dioxide emissions from coal-fired plants.

Of course, all these effects would be considered negligible, if it could be shown that low-level radiation is relatively harmless, a conclusion that could be drawn from the few data that we have. Standard approaches to effective research on this topic, which could, of course, affect all nuclear impacts, seem to be extraordinarily expensive to carry out.[12] New experimental ideas are needed and should receive support.

---

[11] See William Ramsay, "Radon from Uranium Mill Tailings: A Source of Significant Radiation Hazard?" *Environmental Management* vol. 1, no. 2 (1976) pp. 139–145, where the cost per acre of mill tailings was estimated to range from $8,000 to $20,000. At 0.77 plant-years per acre, this ranges from $10,000 to $26,000 per plant-year, or an addition of 0.3 cent to 0.9 cent on the "monthly electric bill" (or less than .01 mill per kilowatt hour). We assume here that the larger impacts from mines could be alleviated at comparable cost.

[12] If effects only show up in one case in a million, for example, then millions of experimental animals would be needed.

Protection of the Environment and Resources

Reclamation of coal lands.   Research on the effectiveness of reclamation, particularly in arid areas, should have high priority. This land use impact appears to be the key environmental impact of both coal and nuclear, and the success of reclamation is an essential element in mitigation. It is possible that reclamation could produce undesirable changes in vegetation, for example, and the effects on regional ecologies require further study. If existing reclamation efforts would turn out to be unacceptable, the importance of the impact might dictate either a de-emphasis of the coal option, as supplied by surface mining, or the development of newer, more effective reclamation techniques.

Coal-related air pollution.   The value of retaining or recovering a pristine atmospheric environment is difficult to assess, even within a specifically environmental context. However, the successful passage of the Clean Air Act and its recent amendments (see chapter 11) implies that these values have strong legislative support. Therefore, the rather expensive mitigation efforts proposed in the NEP might be justified on the basis of these environmental values. The possible disastrous effects from acid rain might also give us added motivation to clean up coal-fired power plant emissions.

Avoidance of Catastrophes

Nuclear proliferation and diversion.   There is an urgent need for research on new fuel cycles, as has been proposed in the NEP, if we are to keep alive the possibility of breeding nuclear fuel while minimizing proliferation dangers. The molten-salt breeder and the uranium–thorium cycle concepts, together with the idea of proliferation-resistant enrichment methods, are examples deserving of study. Some institutional answers are promising, especially the more radical versions of international or regional schemes that truly keep nuclear weapons-grade materials out of the hands of nation-states by centralizing all "dangerous" nuclear operations. But the political difficulties in implementing such schemes seem formidable. Perhaps the most critical institutional initiative lies in the developing U.S. policy toward international nuclear technology, fuels, facilities, and the spread of weapons-grade materials. Efforts could also be made to stop U.S. support of research that may encourage proliferation, such as research into cheap ways of enriching uranium and the presently widespread use of weapons-grade materials, much of U.S. origin, in research and test reactors all over the world.[13]

Research on nuclear reactor safety. Safety research on LWRs has reached a point of greatly diminished returns. Research efforts might more profitably concentrate on breeders that are both proliferation-resistant and relatively safe to operate.[14] Investigations should be done on truly remote siting, comparing the extra costs of electricity transmission against the consequences of an accident. For example, nuclear energy centers containing many reactors plus fuel cycle facilities could conceivably have pronounced safety advantages if they were sited at remote locations.[15]

The effect of coal burning on carbon dioxide emissions. Modeling efforts on the behavior of pollutants in the atmosphere, particularly carbon dioxide and particulates, are of prime importance and should be supported. It is of great importance to obtain new data on the carbon cycle in order to assess the dangers of a climatologic catastrophe.

Methods of collecting and dispersing carbon dioxide from a power plant have been neglected and deserve special study. Estimates of collection costs and other consequences should be made for both standard cryogenic and liquid disposal systems and for more exotic storage in living or preserved biomass.

Equity Considerations

Equity questions are among the most troubling, because the question is not one of costs and benefits alone, but one of costs and benefits for whom? Nevertheless, there are at least two areas where such action could pay off: the problem of workers versus the general public, and the problem of future generations with respect to nuclear wastes.

Coal workers' accidents. In recognition of occupational safety and

[13] Research reactors need highly enriched fuel to keep cores small and easy to cool. Exports to research reactors are often made in kilogram amounts of 93 percent enriched uranium. Naturally, the value of the research done needs to be considered here. But also it must be borne in mind that essential research can almost always be done in larger reactors using low-enriched fuels.

[14] This hypothesizes that a switch to a considerably safer reactor might only be economically worthwhile if it were part of a move to a new technology, such as the breeder.

[15] See U.S. Nuclear Regulatory Commission, *Nuclear Energy Center Site Survey—1975*, NUREG-001 (NECSS-75) (Washington, NRC, January 1976) p. 3-23, for impacts at nonremote locations.

health problems, existing institutions provide safety regulations and sometimes compensate workers; for example, payments are now made to victims of black lung. Nevertheless, the relatively large number of deaths
and injuries associated with coal mining suggests that a study of risks suf-
fered by coal miners, and the relation of these risks to the general economic structure of coal prices and labor costs, is called for. The degree of
unfairness of this unpaid cost is significant enough to justify giving substantial priority to this problem of risk-acceptability.

Effect of nuclear wastes on future generations. Research and development on nuclear fuel wastes is an existing high-priority item. Pilot operations are now in progress to test geologic storage of high-level or fuel
wastes, and other options are being considered as well (see chapter 5).
A concern for future generations would strongly justify comprehensive
mitigation methods for this facet of the nuclear cycle. The same concern
would dictate that the long-lived gaseous wastes radon and carbon 14
should receive more attention than would be justified on short-term
cost–benefit grounds. Indeed, we have emphasized this point in our consideration of effects stretching into the future. At the very least, then,
this intergenerational equity question should reinforce the relatively in-
expensive mitigation efforts that could be applied to the radon wastes, as
well as the somewhat more expensive means needed to contain high-level
wastes.

L'Envoi

Listing rough preferences for programs within each of the value orientations does not help us with making overall choices among the different
main values. Such decisions would have to be made by policymakers on
other grounds. In any case, the uncertainty in all the parameters is so
great that a continual reevaluation of priorities must be a necessary part
of any rational policy. The suggestions here can be viewed as illustrative
of the kind of actions that might be taken in the context of certain per-
ceptions of impacts and values.

Primarily, what should be emphasized here is the overall strategic purpose that is based on our perception of both the large inherent dangers of
the health and environmental impacts of the coal and nuclear technologies, and the great uncertainties of the extent of the impacts and of our
value judgments on them. This perception follows from the entire complex discussion of the impacts above, the problems of measurement, and
the problems of comparing incomparable concepts.

These salient facts demand the emphasis we have placed here on two aspects of an energy strategy founded on a coal–nuclear mix: research to gain more information so as to reduce the present paralyzing level of uncertainty, and mitigation efforts at a generous level to protect the public health and the environment from the threat of very large coal and nuclear impacts, while permitting the development of necessary supplies of electrical energy.

Index

Library of Congress Cataloging in Publication Data

Ramsay, William, 1930–
  Unpaid costs of electrical energy.

  Report on work performed for the National Energy
Strategies Project.
  Includes index.
  1. Electrical power plants—Environmental analysis—
United States.   I. Resources for the Future.
II. National Energy Strategies Project.   III. Title.
TD195.E4R35   363.6   78-15668
ISBN 0-8018-2172-X
ISBN 0-8018-2230-0 pbk.